The Story Behind Manitoba Names

How Cities, Towns, Villages
and Whistle Stops Got Their Names

Ted Stone

Red Deer PRESS

Published by
Red Deer Press
A Fitzhenry & Whiteside Company
1512, 1800–4 Street S.W.
Calgary, Alberta, Canada T2S 2S5
www.reddeerpress.com

Credits
Copyedited by Mark Giles and Kirstin Morrell
Cover and text design by Erin Woodward
Cover images courtesy the Manitoba Archives
Printed and bound in Canada by Friesens for Red Deer Press

Acknowledgments
Financial support provided by the Canada Council, and the Government of Canada through the Book Publishing Industry Development Program (BPIDP).

Canada

THE CANADA COUNCIL | LE CONSEIL DES ARTS
FOR THE ARTS | DU CANADA
SINCE 1957 | DEPUIS 1957

National Library of Canada Cataloguing in Publication
Stone, Ted, 1947–
The story behind Manitoba names : how cities, towns, villages and whistle stops got their names / Ted Stone.
Includes bibliographical references.
ISBN 0-88995-341-4
1. Names, Geographical--Manitoba. 2. Manitoba--History, Local.
I. Title.
FC3356.S74 2006   917.27   C2006-904651-4

Acknowledgements

Many people have helped with this book, some who have not even given me their names. A few that I would especially like to thank are Gerry Holm, Alan Hadfield, Archie Henry, Vera Thomas, Felix "Rusty" Weisgerber, Jim Crang, Fred McGuinness, Rob Wyton, Gary Olson, Tom and Margaret Woods, Jane Burpee, Kathleen Brown, Esaias Beardy, Eldon Campbell, Norman Wood, Brian Bighetty, Karen McCreary, Sharon Foley, Lee Richels, Robert Garson, Elmer McClelland, Kay Moubrae, Steve Stadnyk, Peter Schroedter, Garry Jackson, Diane Dube, Leah Boulet and Carol Tanner.

Table of Contents

Introduction

I've always loved maps, but my fondness for them probably stems from an even deeper love for stories. Every map suggests potential journeys that are tales waiting to unfold. Unrevealed yarns are already woven into the history of every place on every map. Each place marked on a map has a tale of some kind in its history and every place name holds the possibility of a good story.

Perhaps because of their frontier heritage, the place names of North America are among the richest in the world for the possibilities of the imagination. Names like Deadwood, Truth or Consequences, Whiskey Gap, Moose Jaw, Medicine Hat, Hell, Hidden Point and Point No Point dot the maps of the continent and set us up for a yarn by the simple force of a name. Spanish, French and aboriginal languages give us (no matter what the original meaning of the words) exotic-sounding names like Tallahassee, Arroyo Hondo, Las Cruces, Coeur d'Alene, Terre Haute and Tucumcari. Descriptive names like Red Lake, Great Falls, Water Valley, Little Rock, Poplar Bluff and Yellow Springs abound. Place names in North America recount past events, celebrate pioneers, promote commerce, honor historical and political figures, celebrate our literature, recount local legends and reflect cultural and spiritual values.

Manitoba place names reflect this abundance of imagination. Place names here include Coca Cola Falls, Dumbell Lake, Dead Horse Creek, Smugglers Point, Pancake Lake, Pistol Lake and Pack Horse Creek, potential tales all. Stories must abound behind the names of Manitoba towns with names like Waterhen, Sprucewoods, Snowflake, Sundance, Seven Sisters Falls, Bacon Ridge, Brokenhead and Big Black River.

Not every city, town or whistle stop comes with a name backed by a compelling tale. Some names are more interesting, and more fun, than others. Sometimes, nobody knows for sure how a community came up with the name it has. And too often, early settlers chose a perfectly good name, reflective of the place where they lived, only to have the name changed later by post office bureaucrats or railroad officials.

Descriptive and aboriginal names were all too often replaced by the names of politicians, businessmen, generals or Englishmen with no known connection to the town or even the province. In Manitoba, Badger Creek became Cartwright, Cherry Creek became Boissevain, Oak Ridge became Culross, Scratching River became Morris, and Partridge Crop was renamed Fairford.

Residents even changed impressive names to ordinary ones all by themselves. Postmasters or railroad officials named new communities on whims of their own making, with no community discussion. It's no wonder so many of our place names seem questionable or commonplace.

But the most common and bland-sounding names often turn out to have stories of some kind. This book attempts to gather some of these stories, the plain and the striking, the straightforward and the elaborate.

Sometimes more than one story explains the name of a Manitoba community. People may know a story that supposedly lies behind the name of the town in which they live, but there are often other conflicting reports of how that place was named. In this book I've sometimes included more than one explanation for a name. Other times I've gone with the story that seems, to me, to be the most reasonable.

Even the name Manitoba comes from uncertain origins. The word is probably from the Cree, or the related Ojibwa language, meaning "spirit narrows" or "voice of the Great Spirit." It refers to the Manitou or Great Spirit living at the Narrows on Lake Manitoba. Evidence of the Manitou lingers here because the water makes loud, unusual noises as it passes between the narrow, rocky east and west shorelines. Sometimes in winter the water moves about with so much ferocity ice fails to form. Both the name of the lake and the province, according to this version of the story, derive from this aboriginal name.

Certainly the Cree knew the Lake Manitoba Narrows as *Manitowapaw,* while the Ojibwa called it *Manitou-bah,* but there is still some doubt if those names are responsible for today's name for the lake and province. The Assiniboine, who spoke a Siouxian language, called the lake *Minni-toba,* or "Lake of the Prairies," and that too may be the source of the provincial name.

La Verendrye called the lake *Minni-toba* after meeting and being told of it by Assiniboine people. The lake has been called something akin to that ever since, so who's to say for sure if the origin of today's name goes back to the Cree, Ojibwa or Assiniboine. Each explanation seems satisfactory. Perhaps all three are right, with each partly contributing to the naming of the province. Time clouds the story.

Many of the entries in this book share these fuzzy origins. It's been at least 100 years since the naming of most Manitoba communities and much longer for many towns. A few names go back hundreds of years to their first use by the aboriginal people of the region. We may or may not know what lies behind the names, but we do know that place names that have lasted so long are never completely random. A story always lurks. We might not know it, but it's there. This book is an attempt to recount some of those stories.

The purpose of this book is to shed light on the stories behind some of the communities listed on the Manitoba Official Highway Map. Whether a thriving city or a Manitoba ghost town, if it's on the map it qualifies to be in these pages.

Not every town or village on Manitoba's map makes it to these pages. Someday, I'd like to complete the job, but space considerations and the requisite amount of knowledge prevent that from happening, at least for now. Perhaps readers will know the story behind some of the missing names, and if so, I'd like to hear from them. I'd also like to hear from people who know about stories other than the ones recounted here. Anyone with a new or different story to tell about the origin of a town's name can contact me at tedston@gmail.com.

A list of source materials is in the back of this book, but special note should be made of four of the most important. Robert Douglas's *Place-Names of Manitoba,* compiled in 1933 is the first. It is Douglas's work that provides the beginning for any investigation into the names of Manitoba communities. Likewise, J. B. Rudnyckyj's *Manitoba Mosaic of Place Names* and Penny Ham's *Place Names of Manitoba* were invaluable tools while putting together this collection, as was the catalog of place names, *Geographical Names of Manitoba,* assembled by former provincial toponymist Gerry Holm and published by the Manitoba Conservation Department.

Just as important as the source materials have been the dozens of people who have offered me their help in communities all over Manitoba. To all of them I owe my thanks. Whether their leads were fruitful or only deepened the mysteries, this collection of names is more complete because of their contributions.

Readers will note that the various communities listed in these pages are usually called cities, towns, villages, settlements or rail points. But clearly defining what is a town versus a village in Manitoba is sometimes confusing. In Manitoba, communities on a map may be incorporated as cities, towns, villages or even local urban districts, so using these designations would normally seem appropriate. The problem arises with matters of population and consistency.

Generally speaking cities are larger than towns, towns larger than villages, with local urban districts in Manitoba coming in somewhere in the latter two categories. (Local urban district is an awkward term that tells nothing about size and is mostly omitted from these pages.) The norm is for a city to have more than 10,000 people, a town to have more than 1,000 and a village to have more than 100. In Manitoba it doesn't always work that way. Many incorporated towns have lost population in the intervening years since incorporation and are now barely hanging on as village-sized communities. Some villages have gained in population, but haven't bothered to become official towns. Others have lost population. There are towns in Manitoba with only a few hundred people and villages over 1,000. Local Urban Districts could also have almost any number of residents. Unincorporated settlements could have under a hundred or more than a thousand inhabitants.

In this book, I use the official designation in first reference for every entry—whether city, town or village—when there is an official designation other than local urban district. After the first reference in each heading, I describe a community with whatever term seems to fit. I may call an official town a "village" in the entry's text. Depending on its size, I may use the term "town" for an official village or a local urban district. For unincorporated communities, the first reference may be as a town, village or rail point, if suitable, but most often I simply use the word "settlement."

Some unincorporated Manitoba settlements that lack the official designation, but still look like a town, with a downtown area and a population of over a thousand people, I call towns here. Most other places in this book are called settlements, no matter if they are village-size, but lack the official designation, or if the only population is widely scattered in small numbers around the locality. Even ghost towns were once settlements, so the term seems appropriate.

A few places are called railway points. Here, the settlements might still be a stopping place along a railroad. Or the name might recall nothing more than a former whistle stop in the days of steam when trains needed regular stopping places, populated or not, to take on loads of wood or coal and water. A few of these places remain along the railroad tracks on the Manitoba map and their stories need to be included in any book about Manitoba community names.

We have to at least know the stories behind the names of the communities where Manitobans live before we can decide which of them are the most important or interesting. We have to know the stories to have favorites. No matter what else, the stories behind Manitoba names should be remembered as long as the names continue to be used.

Alexander

Settlement approximately 20 kilometers west of Brandon on Highway 1

The first post office in this district, named Pulteney, opened in 1881, but in 1885 the Canadian Pacific Railway came through and named the stop Alexander Station after a nearby homesteader, Alexander Speers.

So wrote Robert Douglas in 1933 in *Place-Names of Manitoba*. Later researchers have claimed CPR officials named the station after Sir John Alexander Macdonald, Canada's first prime minister.

Alexander Railroad Station in 1888. By permission of Manitoba Archives: Alexander 2, March 3, 1888, Railway Station, N21560

Alonsa

Village approximately 160 kilometers northwest of Portage la Prairie on Highway 50

When Canadian National Railways reached Alonsa in 1922 Alonzo Phillips surveyed the townsite. In return, railroad officials named the station after him. There's some question about how Mr. Phillips spelled his first name, however. Initially, the town was known as Alonzo, but the spelling was later changed to the current version of Alonsa.

Altamont

Settlement on Highway 23 approximately 50 kilometers northwest of Winkler

The post office here was first named Musselboro, after the first post-master, who was named Mussell. In 1891 the name of the post office was changed to Alta, apparently signifying its high altitude. The name wasn't high enough for some, however, and in 1894 it was changed again, to Altamont, or "high mountain."

The "high mountain" here seems rather wishful thinking. Some points are higher than others, but Altamont is in the midst of gently rolling prairie hills, with nary a mountain in sight.

Altamont homes about 1911. BY PERMISSION OF MANITOBA ARCHIVES: ALTAMONT HOMES 5, N21603

Altona

Town approximately 30 kilometers southeast of Winkler on Highway 30

According to some accounts, Mennonite settlers named this Manitoba community after a town in Germany. The German name was said to refer to an old, fertile plain. Other reports claim the name means "all too near." All too near to what, however, is open to speculation.

A Mennonite settlement in southern Russia was named Altonau, but so far as is known none of the early settlers of Altona, Manitoba came from there. A more likely source can be found in an early East Reserve settlement in Manitoba that initially used the name.

When Mennonite settlers first came to Manitoba from Russia in 1875 they were granted a huge block of land held in reserve for them east of the Red River and north of the Rat River. It soon became obvious that most of the good land in the initial reserve would be taken up with new settlers, so a second reserve on the west side of the Red, known as the West Reserve, was granted. Settlers came to the West Reserve from both Europe and the East Reserve, where some of the land wasn't as fertile as land found west of the Red. Apparently, some of the settlers from the East Reserve brought the name Altona with them when they made the move.

Amaranth

Village approximately 100 kilometers northwest of Portage la Prairie

This Manitoba town was named for another Amaranth in Ontario. A mythical flower called amaranth is said never to fade. Botanists have also named a genus of long-flowering plants "amaranthus."

Amery

Rail point on the Nelson River approximately 250 kilometers south of Churchill on the Hudson Bay Railway

Amery was named after a politician, L.C.M.S. Amery. He had been the federal Secretary of State for Canada from 1919 to 1921. The Hudson Bay Railway gave his name to this stop in 1928. A post office opened here the same year, but then closed again in 1929, after the railroad was completed to Churchill.

Prairie farmers had lobbied hard for a railroad to Hudson Bay ever since the idea first surfaced about 1870. Grain shipped through Hudson Bay and the North Atlantic offered a shorter route to overseas markets than traditional routes through Vancouver or the Great Lakes. But the building of the Hudson Bay Railway was a difficult undertaking that had to overcome all manner of difficulties—geographical, economic and political.

The first federal charters for railroads operating to the shore of Hudson Bay were passed by Parliament in 1880, but one roadblock after another stood in the way of completion from the outset. When the first charters were issued, the northern route was seen as possible competition for the partially completed Canadian Pacific Railway, then on its way to crossing the continent. Prime Minister John A. Macdonald was anxious to complete that line, but he also had to appease the Conservative government then in power in Manitoba.

Macdonald solved the dilemma by chartering a pair of railroad lines to the great bay in the north, knowing full well the competition for financing between the two companies would insure neither line would lay much track anytime soon. Eventually, the two proposed lines merged to avoid competition, but by that time the Canadian Pacific had been completed and railroad mania in the West had subsided. With the railroad boom over, little progress was made on the new, merged railroad to Hudson Bay for several more years.

By the early part of the 20th century, though, the Canadian Northern Railway had built a line as far north as Prince Albert, Saskatchewan. Canadian Northern directors picked a point on that line they called Hudson Bay Junction to build a branch line north to Hudson Bay. By 1910, 141 kilometers of track had been built in a northeasterly direction, as far as The Pas, Manitoba. That same year the Laurier government came out in support of a route to the bay and took over the construction. It looked as if the railroad to Hudson Bay would finally be completed.

But an election in 1911 threw the Liberals out and made Conservative R. L. Borden the new prime minister. Construction on the great northern railroad stopped, at least for a time. Then political pressure in the West intensified and forced Borden to change his policy. He ordered the construction to resume, even though it hadn't been decided if the railroad terminus should be at the mouth of the Nelson River, or at the mouth of the Churchill. Officials opted for the Nelson, probably because it looked closer on the map, and a line across northern Manitoba was completed as far as Kettle Rapids, within 150 kilometers of the great bay.

Before the dream of a railroad to Hudson Bay was finally achieved, World War I intervened and construction stopped cold. During WWI even maintenance over most of the line came to a halt, and the terminal development that had begun at the mouth of the Nelson was abandoned completely.

Once the war ended advocates for the Hudson Bay line started agitating again, but much of the completed work was lost. In some ways the obstacles before the northern railroad were as great as they had been before the war. Nothing happened until late in 1926 when Mackenzie King's new Liberal majority government decided to complete the project.

By then Canadian National Railways had come into existence and the government asked them to rebuild what was left of the old line and complete the railroad to saltwater. The CNR—deciding natural advantages to harbor facilities were better at the mouth of the Churchill River—abandoned the idea of new construction along the final leg of the Nelson River in 1928 and turned the line due north at a point near Amery.

By 1929 the rail line stretched another 250 kilometers to the old fur post on the Churchill River. After nearly sixty years of dreaming and political agitation, advocates for a railroad to Hudson Bay finally had what they wanted. Today, the railroad is owned by OmniTRAX, a Denver-based transportation company.

Angusville

Settlement southwest of Riding Mountain National Park, approximately 150 kilometers northwest of Brandon on Highway 45

Angusville was originally called Snake Creek, and that was the name they used when the post office opened here in 1886. The name was changed to Angusville in 1909 after the Canadian Northern Railway began using that name for a siding constructed here in 1908. The railroad siding was on land purchased from John Angus, a descendent of one of the area's earliest settler families.

A view of Angusville in 1929. BY PERMISSION OF MANITOBA ARCHIVES, ANGUSVILLE 4

Anola

Settlement approximately 20 kilometers east of Winnipeg on Highway 16

The post office at Anola was originally named Richland, and the Grand Trunk Pacific Railway siding was first called Free Port, after a town in Illinois from which a syndicate of early landowners hailed.

The siding became known as Anola in 1912 and the post office took that name in 1923 when it moved closer to the railroad. Robert Douglas, in *Place-Names of Manitoba,* reported the name was invented and that he didn't know the reason behind it. Locals sometimes ascribe the name to the rise in elevation there. The area is on a slight, but perceptible, ridge. According to this theory it's on "a knoll," which gave rise to the name Anola.

Others have suggested that Anola was named after the wife of a railroad official. This theory has some credence since Anola comes at the end of a series of rail points (Elma, Hazel, Vivian) using women's first names. It's likely that the same railroad official named at least two of these towns after one or more daughters. Since all four towns received their names at about the same time, Elma, Hazel, Vivian and Anola may have been sisters. Or perhaps the local legend is correct and Anola was the mother of the other three.

Arborg

Town approximately 50 kilometers northwest of Gimli on Highway 7

Opened in 1902, the original post office at this site was called Ardal. In 1910, when the railroad reached the town, the name was changed to Arborg. Both names are Icelandic. The first means river dale, the second river town; both were fitting descriptions for the new town along the Icelandic River.

Arden

Settlement approximately 90 kilometers northeast of Brandon on Provincial Road 352

Arden was evidently named by Walter R. Baker, the general manager of the Manitoba and Northwestern Railway. Baker initially called the railroad stop Arden Station. He chose the name after the family country home in England of a prominent railroad backer. "Station" was dropped from the name a few years later.

Others have suggested a different origin. According to this theory, the town was named after a cook named Arden, who had worked on one of the construction gangs in the area when the railroad first reached the area. If true, the fellow must have baked wonderful pies to inspire such an honor.

Before the railroad entered the name game, the district had been known as Beautiful Plains.

A horse and buggy on Main Street in Arden in 1910. By permission of Manitoba Archives, Arden – homes 1, N12626

Arizona

Settlement on Provincial Road 352 approximately 55 kilometers east of Brandon

In 1880, thirty years before Arizona entered the American union, two men, Williamson and McKinnon, came up with the name for a remote district of Manitoba. The empty spaces of the region reminded them of the territory that was already using that name in the American southwest.

A post office named Arizona operated here between 1892 and 1904. In 1905 the Canadian Northern Railway christened the station built there "Worby." Both names have been used interchangeably in the district since then, although Arizona is the name on the map.

Arnaud

Settlement approximately 60 kilometers south of Winnipeg on Highway 217

The idea behind Arnaud's name was to honor Father Aulneau, a Jesuit missionary who traveled with La Verendrye in the 1730s. Aulneau was killed by Sioux on Massacre Island in Lake of the Woods on June 8, 1736.

Aulneau died along with nineteen others, including La Verendrye's son. The attack came after La Verendrye had returned, briefly, to the East. The men stayed with a group of Assiniboines at Lake of the Woods. The Assiniboine were enemies of the Sioux and La Verendrye's men, along with Father Aulneau, got caught up in the feud.

Perhaps it's unsurprising that the white men incurred the wrath of the Sioux: one of the reasons La Verendrye's men were with the Assiniboine was to advise them on matters of warfare, and to offer them muskets and powder as trade goods. As things turned out the alliance failed to benefit either La Verendrye's men or the Assiniboine, many of whom were also killed by the Sioux.

Named by Bishop Alexandre-Antonin Taché of St. Boniface, the town of Arnaud was established as a rail point in 1877. The Geographical Board of Canada provided a different story for the name in 1928. They stated the town was named after a "French marshal." Perhaps this was General St. Arnaud, who led French forces during the Crimean War, but it seems unlikely. The Aulneau version of the story seems most reasonable, especially since the next town up the line, Dufrost, was also named by Bishop Taché after a member of La Verendrye's expedition.

In the 20th century, historians re-discovered La Verendrye's Fort St. Charles, near Massacre Island where Father Aulneau and the others met their ends., The letters Father Aulneau sent to relatives in France before his death held the clues to the fort's location. In the letters Aulneau described the little fort on an island in Lake of the Woods. Based on Aulneau's descriptions, and foundation stones still in place from the original structure, the fort was rebuilt in the 1950s.

Arnes

Settlement approximately 20 kilometers north of Gimli on Highway 9

A post office named Arnes opened here in 1877. The name, meaning "river point," is from Icelandic. Its use in Manitoba dates to the first Icelandic settlers to arrive in the province in 1875.

A reserve of land had been set aside for Icelandic settlement that year in an area north of what was then the northern boundary of the province. The area consisted of a strip of land 17 kilometers wide along Lake Winnipeg from Boundary Creek in the south to Hecla Island in the north.

The first settlers arrived in October, but only a few established homesteads before the following spring. The territory, which developed its own government, was divided into four districts: Vidines, Mikleyjar, Fljots and Arnes. It essentially operated as an independent entity until the province of Manitoba was enlarged to take in the territory in 1881. Even then, New Iceland remained under a provisional constitution of its own making until 1887 when it officially became the Rural Municipality of Gimli.

Apparently Kristjon Sigurdson first used the name Arnes for his farm. After Sigurdson's wife and two daughters died of smallpox in 1876, however, he sold the farm. The new owner established a store and post office, and continued to use the name Arnes.

Later, Sigurdar Sigurbjörnsson used the name for a store and post office at his farm. In 1914, Sigurbjörnsson moved the business to be near the new Arnes Station, established with the arrival of the railroad. Sigurbjörnsson operated the store there until his death in 1925.

Arnot

Rail point approximately 70 kilometers east of Thompson on the Hudson Bay line

Arnot was named in 1928 for William Arnot, a Canadian National Railways employee. In the days of steam engines, Arnot was responsible for looking after the railroad's water supply along the Hudson Bay route.

Arrow River

Settlement approximately 80 kilometers northwest of Brandon near Highway 24

The community of Arrow River gets its name from the nearby river. Before the Hudson's Bay Company brought firearms to the area, the native people made arrows from the wood of saskatoon bushes growing near the stream. As early as 1819 Peter Fidler called the river Arrow

Wood Creek, although at least one other report notes that First Nations peoples in the early days of settlement called the stream by another name.

William Elliott, often credited as the town's first settler, said the aboriginal name for the stream was *Wa-hink-a-pa,* or "straight river" (which could refer to the straightness of arrow wood). Elliott's brother James became the town's first postmaster. Born near Guelph, Ontario, the two brothers, first came to Winnipeg in 1873. They then worked as cowboys in southern Manitoba near the North Dakota border before homesteading near present-day Morden. In 1879 William moved farther west, building a dugout in the bank of the Arrow River where he lived during his first winter in the district. James arrived at Arrow River the following spring.

A stone farm house built near Arrow River in 1896 by James Wiggins, photo taken in 1963. BY PERMISSION OF MANITOBA ARCHIVES, ARROW RIVER – HOMES 2

Ashern

Town approximately 160 kilometers north of Winnipeg on Highway 6

Railroad officials named Ashern after the railroad construction crew timekeeper A.S. Hern, running the letters of his name together. Hern was the timekeeper for the railroad construction crew when it arrived at the new siding in 1911.

Before it took its current name, the town was briefly called Seventh Siding and then Dodd's Siding, the latter apparently named after an early settler.

Ashville

Settlement approximately 20 kilometers west of Dauphin on Highway 10

This community got its name from an Irish immigrant, Isaac Ash. Ash homesteaded the land where the townsite was later established. The first post office opened in Ashville in 1901.

Athapap

Settlement approximately 25 kilometers southeast of Flin Flon on Athapapuskow Lake

Athapap was established as a rail point by Canadian National Railways in 1929, on the northern shore of Athapapuskow Lake. The name is a corruption of the Cree name for the lake, which means "rocks on both sides of the water." David Thompson first recorded the name in 1813.

Atikameg Lake

Rail point on the Hudson Bay Railway and Provincial Road 287 approximately 45 kilometers northeast of The Pas

The community of Atikameg Lake was named after a body of water that is now, officially, Clearwater Lake. The lake lies in the heart of Clearwater Provincial Park. The community of Atikameg Lake, originally just a nearby rail point on the Hudson Bay line, became a resort community. It still goes by the aboriginal name for the lake, which is usually translated from the Cree as "Whitefish Lake."

Austin

Village approximately 40 kilometers west of Portage la Prairie on Highway 1

The post office opened at Austin in 1883 or 1884 and took the name of the nearby Canadian Pacific Railway siding. Before the railroad, the district had been known as Three Creeks because the old Saskatchewan Trail crossed three creeks near here.

In 1881 the Marquis of Lorne, then Governor General of Canada, chose the name Austin while traveling in the West with his wife,

Princess Louise Caroline Alberta. CPR officials encouraged him to name six stations between Portage la Prairie and Brandon. He named Austin and nearby Sidney after Sidney Austin, a reporter for the London Graphic who had accompanied the marquis and princess on the journey. Later the Governor General named Lake Louise near Banff, Alberta after his wife. Douglas, Bagot, Chater and MacGregor were other Manitoba stops along the route that he named.

Back

Rail point approximately 110 kilometers south of Churchill on the Hudson Bay line

There ought to be a good story about a name like Back. But the name isn't the result of the railroad crew turning back at this point or the shenanigans of some lost trapper turning back on the trail. The rail point was named after the Arctic explorer Admiral George Back. Back was an officer with Sir John Franklin's exploration of Hudson Bay in 1819 and 1823.

Several Manitoba place names originate with Arctic explorers, although none honor Henry Hudson, the great bay's discoverer. Hudson sailed into what became known as Hudson Bay in 1610. He and his crew sailed as far south as James Bay, but were caught by the freeze up and forced to spend the following winter on the frigid shore. In June, while preparing to set sail once more, part of Hudson's crew mutinied and put their captain adrift on the ice, along with his son and a few other loyal crewmembers. They were never heard from again.

In England, members of the returning crew blamed Hudson. Charged with murder instead of mutiny, the leaders were found innocent. Hudson, of course, never told his side of the story, but his exploration and discovery fueled interest in the possibility of a northern water route across the top of the continent to the Pacific.

Thomas Button, along with Robert Bylot (who piloted the mutineers back to England after Hudson was put overboard in 1611) explored Hudson Bay again in 1612. Button and his men spent the winter of 1612–13 at the mouth of the Nelson River. Button and his crew became the first Europeans not only to set up residence on Manitoba soil, but also the first to enjoy the vigor of a Manitoba winter. Button gave the first European name to what became

Manitoba, calling the west shore of the bay New Wales. He named the icy river after one of his crew, an officer named Nelson, who died during the winter.

Other early explorers on Hudson Bay included William Gibbons in 1615 and William Baffin in 1616. Jens Munk, a Dane, made another attempt to find a passage to the Orient through Hudson Bay in 1619. His failure to discover a Western outlet forced him to winter on the Manitoba shore near the present town of Churchill. Only Munk and two of his crew survived the grueling cold until the following spring. By that time the three survivors were so weak they were unable to remove the dead from their midst. For years afterward the Churchill was known as Munk's River to other northern explorers.

Despite Munk's disaster others came looking for a way to the Orient through Hudson Bay. It was only after the separate voyages of Luke Foxe and Thomas James in 1631 and 1632 that the dream of a Northwest Passage through Hudson Bay was put to rest, although for another century the notion would be periodically revisited. James spent the winter of 1631 and 1632 frozen in at the bottom of Hudson Bay, in the smaller bay that has gone by his name ever since.

Looking for a route to the Orient through Hudson Bay ended, for the most part, with Foxe and James, but within forty years the French explorers and fur traders Radisson and Des Groseilliers rekindled interest in Hudson Bay. They convinced investors in England that there was a fortune to be made trading furs through the huge bay that Henry Hudson had discovered sixty years before.

Bacon Ridge

Settlement approximately 75 kilometers southeast of Dauphin on Provincial Road 278

Bacon Ridge took its name from a time when the first road was constructed through the area. Bacon, it seems, was the only meat the local storekeeper kept in stock. The men building the road honored the settlement with a name commemorating their appreciation for the variety this policy afforded their diet.

Baden

Settlement approximately 90 kilometers north of Swan River on Highway 77

Baden, on the Canadian Northern rail line south of Red Deer Lake, was named for Sir Robert Stephenson Smyth Baden-Powell, a British general during the Boer War in South Africa. He was also a founder of the Boy Scout movement.

Baden-Powell came to prominence when he commanded the 5th Dragoon Guards during the Siege of Mafeking in 1899. During the siege he and 1,200 men successfully defended the town against a Boer force of 9,000. After the war Baden-Powell stayed in South Africa to organize the South African Constabulary. When he returned to England in 1903 he discovered youth leaders and teachers all over the country were using his book *Aids to Scouting*, published during his absence.

Baden-Powell wrote the book to help the army train young soldiers, but youth leaders were using it for young boys. After the leader of the British Boys Brigade asked Baden-Powell to come up with more ideas for training boys in outdoor skills and good citizenship, he set to work rewriting *Aids To Scouting*.

Baden-Powell published his new book, *Scouting for Boys,* in 1908. Soon boys in England, and then around the world, spontaneously organized themselves into scout patrols. Intended as a training guide for existing organizations, Baden-Powell's book spawned a worldwide movement, first for boys, then for girls.

Baden-Powell set up an office in England to handle enquiries coming in from around the globe, looking for information about his "scout troops." The book was translated into several languages. In 1920, at the first International Scout Jamboree, Baden-Powell was acclaimed the "Chief Scout of the World."

Badger

Settlement approximately 65 kilometers southeast of Steinbach on Provincial Road 203

While the settlement took its name from a nearby creek, there seems to be no clear explanation why that stream gained the tag of the ferocious burrowing animal. Some put forth the theory that the creek was named by early Scandinavian settlers who immigrated to Manitoba from the Badger area of Minnesota.

Trappers and lumberjacks moved north from Minnesota in the early years of settlement in this area. That one or more of them would name the creek after a similar stream farther south seems credible. It's also possible that someone saw a badger along the stream and so named the creek.

Bagot

Settlement approximately 30 kilometers west of Portage la Prairie on Highway 1

The Marquis of Lorne, Governor-General of Canada, named the rail point Bagot on the new Canadian Pacific Railway in 1881. The Marquis and his wife, Princess Louise Caroline Alberta, traveled through the Canadian west that year and the CPR offered him the chance to name six railroad stops between Portage la Prairie and Brandon. He named the stop at Bagot after his aide-de-camp, Captain W. R. Bagot. Captain Bagot later became a baron.

Other stops along the route named by the Governor General included Austin, Chater, Sidney, Douglas and MacGregor

Bakers Narrows

Settlement approximately 15 kilometers southeast of Flin Flon on Highway 10

Bakers Narrows is located at a narrows in Lake Papapuskow. A pair of trappers had a cabin here in the early part of the 20th century when prospecting and mining opened in the area. One of the trappers was Baker, and his name has graced Bakers Narrows ever since.

Billy Baker's cabin.
By permission of Manitoba Archives: Campbell, John A., Series IV, 10, Cabin of Billy Baker and Tom Patton, Baker's Narrows

Baldur

Village approximately 115 kilometers southeast of Brandon on Highway 23

Icelandic settlers named their settlement here after Baldur, the Norse god of innocence and the summer sun. Known for his beauty, Baldur personified the nobler qualities of human nature in Scandinavian mythology. Settlers, it seems, thought the surrounding countryside was as richly endowed.

Balmoral

Settlement approximately 35 kilometers north of Winnipeg on Provincial Road 236

In the 1870s an early settler in the district, James Barbour, named this frontier settlement after Balmoral Castle in Scotland, one of Queen Victoria's estates. Her husband Prince Albert bought the original castle, which had been built in the 15th Century, as a gift for his wife. The royal couple leased the castle as a vacation spot for several years before that.

After Albert bought the estate, a new, larger castle was built on the grounds. Since then it has passed down to Victoria's descendents. For the most part, it is a royal summer home and a getaway for hunting and fishing. Prince Charles, it is said, took Princess Diana to Balmoral Castle on their honeymoon, but once they arrived he promptly left her alone and spent most of his time fishing.

Barrows

Rail point approximately 110 kilometers north of Swan River on Highway 77

Originally, Barrows was on a Canadian Northern Railway spur on the south shore of Red Deer Lake, but that settlement is now known as Red Deer Lake. The rail point a few kilometers to the south, once known as Barrows Junction, on the CNR main line, is now called Barrows.

F.G. Barrows was the secretary of the Red Deer Lumber Company, which operated a mill in the area.

Basswood

Settlement approximately 55 kilometers north of Brandon on Highway 16

If early settlers in Basswood possessed a little more knowledge about botany the town probably would have had a different name. Members of the community wanted to name the settlement after the trees that grew along the banks of the nearby creek. The trees were balsam poplars but someone said they were basswoods and apparently no one in the community knew the difference.

Perhaps it's just as well—Basswood is a nicer name for a town than Balsam Poplar.

Beaconia

Settlement on Lake Winnipeg 70 kilometers northeast of Winnipeg near Highway 59

Canadian National Railways established Beaconia in 1918 when they extended the railroad north to several beaches on the east shore of Lake Winnipeg. Until that time the district had been known as Silver Pines, but CNR officials named the station after a nearby beacon. A local wood seller built and used the beacon to guide boats coming down the Red River and into Lake Winnipeg. Cutting firewood was one of the major occupations of the area and the beacon apparently signaled to boats from Winnipeg the location of firewood for ready fuel.

Beach at Beconia in 1961. By permission of Manitoba Archives, Beach at Beconia in 1961.

Beausejour

Town approximately 50 kilometers northeast of Winnipeg on Highway 44

The Canadian Pacific Railway established Beausejour as a rail point in 1877. The station was built on a small, elevated area of sand and gravel surrounded by otherwise marshy country. First Nations peoples knew the area by a name that could be translated as "Stony Prairie."

A likely story is that a French Canadian construction engineer bestowed the name Beausejour to the station. Loosely translated Beausejour from the French as "a good stopping place," the name fits. The station was a good place to stop in the middle of the marshy country around it. The *Geographical Names of Manitoba,* offers a different version, proposing that a Mrs. Armstrong, the wife of the town's surveyor, suggested the name.

The Beausejour Hotel in 1929. BY PERMISSION OF MANITOBA ARCHIVES, BEAUSEJOUR – BUILDINGS, 6, N4680

Belair

Settlement approximately 90 kilometers north of Winnipeg, just off Highway 59

Belair was established in 1916 as a Canadian Northern Railway point and named by the railway's district engineer. Evidently just a pleasant sounding name with no local connection, some have suggested it was inspired by the district's good, clean air blowing from nearby Lake Winnipeg.

Railroad officials hoped its new line would encourage cottage and resort development along the sandy beaches of the Lake Winnipeg shoreline. Whenever possible, they gave stations along the line names to evoke a vacation theme.

Belcher

Rail point approximately 100 kilometers south of Churchill on the Hudson Bay line

Belcher was named for the British naval officer Edward Belcher. Admiral Belcher commanded an expedition that searched in vain for Arctic explorer John Franklin. Belcher discovered what has come to be known as Belcher Channel in Nunavut's high Arctic during the search.

Bellsite

Settlement approximately 60 kilometers north of Swan River on Highway 10

Early settlers near Bellsite, a stopping point on the Canadian National Railways, evidently selected the name because of the proximity of the Bell River. Apparently, the river was named because of a bell-shaped plant that grew in the area. The town was first noted on a map in 1924. The local post office opened in 1928 and closed in 1969.

Belmont

Village approximately 90 kilometers southeast of Brandon on Highway 23

Jams and jellies on display at Belmont fair about 1820.
BY PERMISSION OF
MANITOBA ARCHIVES,
BELMONT – FAIRS I.

One story is that Belmont got its name because the townsite is on a bluff once owned by an early homesteader named Joe Bell, hence Bell's Mount. Douglas, in *Place-Names of Manitoba,* reported that John O. Bell, the district's first settler, suggested the name to Canadian Northern Railway surveyors in 1889. Either way, the town was named after a man named Bell.

Benito

Village approximately 35 kilometers southwest of Swan River on Highway 83

Mrs. Dykeman, the first postmaster, named Benito after a character in a story or novel. It may have been Herman Melville's "Benito Cereno," published in 1856 in *Piazza Tales.*

Berens River

Settlement approximately 270 kilometers north of Winnipeg on the east shore of Lake Winnipeg at the mouth of Berens River

The Hudson's Bay Company established a trading post at the mouth of Berens River in 1814 and named both the river and the post after Joseph Berens, a company governor at the time. Later, the community took the name of the fur post. At least that's one prominent story for the name's origin.

Another tale says the community was named after Chief Jacob Berens when a reserve for the Swampy Cree people of the region was established on Lake Winnipeg by the Canadian government after the signing of Treaty 5. Robert Douglas, in *Place-Names of Manitoba,* reported the Cree name for the river had been *Omimi Sibi,* which means "Pigeon River." Early records call both the community and the river by the translated name. On today's maps, however, Pigeon River lies several kilometers to the south.

Bethany

Settlement approximately 55 kilometers north of Brandon on Provincial Road 471

The Canadian Northern Railway established a rail point here in 1904. A number of early settlers were from Bethany, Ontario and both the station and the first post office were named after that town.

A local legend claims an early minister, Reverend McLeod, named the community after Bethany in the Holy Land.

Beulah
Settlement approximately 90 kilometers northwest of Brandon on Highway 83

One version of Beulah's naming states that an early postmaster took the name from the book *Beulah: A Novel* by Augusta J. Evans. But the Geographic Board of Canada has records indicating the first postmaster, G. H. Rowswell, turned the job of choosing a name for the first post office over to three area women. They chose Beulah from Isaiah 62:4 in the Bible.

Other sources suggest neither is the correct story. Beulah was first settled in the 1880s, long before the first post office, when a number of people speculated that the main line of the Canadian Pacific Railway would be built there. The railroad followed another route, but the people stayed, and according to some reports named the new settlement after a gospel song, "The Land of Beulah."

Bield
Settlement approximately 15 kilometers southeast of Roblin on Highway 5

Bield is located in the lee of a nearby hill, sheltered in a valley between the Duck and Riding mountains. When it came time to choose a name, after the Canadian Northern Railway established a station here in 1913, the first postmaster, Rev. Andrew Chisholm, chose a Scottish word, *bield,* meaning "shelter."

Big Black River
Settlement on the northwest shore of Lake Winnipeg at the mouth of the Mukutawa River

The settlement known as Big Black River was named after the nearby river. The original Cree name, Mukutawa, translates to English as "big black river."

Binscarth

Village approximately 170 kilometers northwest of Brandon on Highway 16

Binscarth took its name from William Bain Scarth, founder and manager of a nearby ranch owned by the Scottish, Ontario and Manitoba Land Company. The ranch was particularly well-known for the pure-bred cattle it raised. The first post office here opened in 1883. In old Norse *bin* means "farm," so Binscarth was Scarth's farm. To carry the old Norse further, *scarth* means a "cleft" or opening in the hills.

Scarth was born in Scotland, but immigrated to Ontario in 1855. He made a fortune in lumber and ship building before coming to Manitoba where he prospered even more during the land boom of the 1880s. Although he ran into financial trouble when the land boom collapsed, he managed to carry on a political career after that. Another Manitoba community, Scarth, is also named after him.

Birch River

Village approximately 40 kilometers north of Swan River on Highway 5

The community here was named after the nearby river, which in turn was named for the birch trees that grow along its banks.

Birds Hill

Settlement off Highway 59 on the northeastern edge of Winnipeg

Birds Hill takes its name from the Hudson's Bay Company factor James Curtis Bird who once owned more than 1,000 acres of land around this site. Once known as the Pine Hills, at least by the time of the spring flood of the Red River in 1852 people were calling the place Bird's Hill. The high ground was one of the areas where people took refuge during flood.

Bird was born in London and joined the Hudson's Bay Company in 1788. He served at York Factory for a few years and then moved to posts along the Saskatchewan River. After the merger of the Hudson's Bay and North West companies Bird was made a chief factor at Red River before his retirement. The company gave him a grant of 1,245 acres of land at what became Birds Hill.

Although his name has lasted as a community place name in Manitoba, as well as a nearby provincial park, Bird had a reputation as a harsh man in the Red River settlement of his day. He was difficult to get along with and generally unpopular throughout the settlement.

Perhaps as a result of this, some reports claim the community was named for Curtis Bird, James Bird's son, who was a medical doctor and a speaker of the Manitoba Legislature. But the name was in use much earlier, so its source has to be with his father.

Birdtail

Settlement approximately 155 kilometers northwest of Brandon on the edge of Waywayseecappo First Nation

The settlement here takes its name from nearby Birdtail Creek, which is a translation of the original Sioux name. According to one early account of a Sioux legend, the creek received the name after a band of Sioux were camped at the stream while on a buffalo hunt. The chief's young son was watching a beautiful bird flying over the creek when suddenly a hawk swooped out of the sky. The hawk snagged the bird with its talons, but the smaller bird broke free and flew away.

As the boy watched a blue feather floated down over the water. The boy reached for the feather, but slipped and fell into the river where he drowned. When the adults recovered the body, he was still clutching the blue tail feather. From that time on the Sioux referred to the creek as the Birdtail.

Birnie

Settlement on Highway 5 near the southeast corner of Riding Mountain National Park

Birnie was named after an early settler, John Birnie, whose homestead furnished the new settlement's townsite. Birnie opened a store, known as Birnie's Place, on the property in the 1880s.

Birtle

Town approximately 135 kilometers northwest of Brandon on Highway 42

Some say the name Birtle derived from a contraction of nearby Birdtail Creek when the community started its life as a stopping place on the

Edmonton Trail. Others claim the settlement was named after a town in England where the countryside is said to resemble that of Birtle.

Another explanation claims that the name comes from an early homesteader. Each of the stories seems equally plausible, although the Bird Tail contraction is my favorite.

A view of Birtle in 1925. BY PERMISSION OF MANITOBA ARCHIVES, BIRTLE 2, N7262

Bissett

Settlement approximately 150 kilometers northeast of Winnipeg on Provincial Road 304

Site of the San Antonio Gold Mine, Bissett took the name of the local member of Parliament, Edgar Bissett, when the post office opened in 1927. As far as anyone knows, Bissett never actually visited the community.

Although the town grew from the discovery of gold and the development of the mine, the man who made the original gold claim here was never honored, in name or money. Alex Desautels filed a claim that led to the development of the first gold mine in 1911, but he was a canoe man and wilderness guide, not a prospector. He was only in the area as an employee of Ephram Pelletier, a retired North West Mounted Police officer who was prospecting for gold in the area and needed a guide.

One day, while Pelletier was away moose hunting, Desautels left their campsite on Rice Lake to do some prospecting of his own on a nearby island. Desautels was mostly killing time waiting for his employer to return, but while he was on the island he discovered some interesting green-colored rock mixed with what appeared to be quartz. The old canoe man took samples of the ore and later filed an official claim. He named his mining claim the San Antonio, evidently because the French name for his patron saint, St. Anthony, had already been taken by another claim and he figured the Spanish version would be just as good.

Not long after filing his claim, while celebrating at a prominent Winnipeg watering hole, Desautels decided he had no interest in gold mining. "Why, for ten cents I'd sell the whole thing," he told Pelletier.

Instead of a dime, Pelletier gave Desautels a dollar. It turned out to be worth millions, but Desautels never expressed any regrets about his loss, preferring, he said, the life of a wilderness canoe man to gold mining and urban luxuries.

Blumenort

Two settlements, one just south of Altona and a second just north of Steinbach

The two Manitoba Blumenorts were Mennonite settlements, one in the West Mennonite Reserve, the other in the East Reserve. Their original settlers used the German words for "flowering place" to name their new hometowns.

In 1998 the Blumenort near Altona began using the designation Blumenort South to help distinguish it from its northern counterpart.

Boggy Creek

Settlement approximately 35 kilometers north of Roblin on Provincial Road 367

Boggy Creek, in the shadows of the Duck Mountains, takes its name from the creek a few kilometers west of the community. The stream flows through a low, boggy countryside along a portion of its course.

Boissevain

Town approximately 65 kilometers south of Brandon on Highway 10

Boissevain was originally named Cherry Creek. It wasn't until the railroad arrived in 1886 that the town picked up its current name. The railroad chose the new name to honor the European financier Adolf Boissevain. Boissevain was the first to sell shares of Canadian Pacific Railway stock in European markets. A CPR branch line still goes through the town.

Bowsman

Village approximately 15 kilometers north of Swan River on Highway 10

Supposedly, when the geologist and mining engineer Joseph B. Tyrell traveled in this area he named the Bowsman River after the bowsman of his canoe, perhaps because of a stop along the river when the bowsman was first one out of the boat to come ashore. That, at least, is a popular story in the locality. The village, then, took its name from the river.

A less circulated reason behind the name claims that the river and community were both named after a local trapper in the area who went by the name of Bowsman Moore. Moore already lived in the area when Tyrell and his bowsman arrived. To my ear this version of the name's origin sounds more credible.

Boyd

Rail point approximately 80 kilometers east of Thompson on the Hudson Bay line

Boyd was named in 1930 after the Canadian flyer J. Errol Boyd, who was the first Canadian pilot to fly the Atlantic. Boyd was born in Toronto in 1891 and became a pilot after flying with the American barnstormer Lincoln Beachy in 1912.

When World War I started, Boyd joined the Royal Naval Air Service. Five months later he was shot down over Belgium. His plane plummeted more than 10,000 feet, but somehow Boyd gained control and guideed it to a crash landing in Holland. On the ground he was at first imprisoned in the neutral country but was eventually returned to North America where he lived in New York, became a songwriter and also worked as a test pilot.

After the war ended Boyd returned to Toronto and went into business, but when one of his songs, "Dreams," became a Broadway hit he returned to New York. Later, he moved to Detroit and went into business there. Charles Lindbergh's solo flight across the Atlantic in 1927 rekindled Boyd's interest in aviation. He took a job in Quebec, flying mail from Montreal to ocean liners about to cross the Atlantic bound for England. After that, Boyd moved to a job with a Mexican airline before moving back to New York in 1929 to fly with Coastal Airways.

In early 1930 the eccentric millionaire Charles A. Levine hired Boyd to pilot his Bellanca Columbia. Boyd flew a record-setting, non-stop flight from New York to Bermuda and back in seventeen hours. After the trip Boyd decided to become the first Canadian pilot to fly the Atlantic. Hearst Newspapers gave him a $10,000 contract for exclusive rights to covering the flight and Boyd took Levine's Columbia to Toronto where he renamed the plane the Maple Leaf.

Weather was poor when Boyd and his navigator, the American Harry Conner, reached Harbour Grace in Newfoundland that October. Officials urged him to wait until spring before making the trip, but Boyd decided to leave immediately. On his first attempt to take off Boyd's airplane, overloaded with fuel, wasn't able to gain enough speed to get off the ground. The tail skid sank into the runway. Undaunted, Boyd climbed down from the plane and enlisted onlookers to come out and push. With the extra help the Maple Leaf was able to start again and rose from the runway. The first Canadian-piloted flight to Europe was underway.

He had planned to land at Plymouth, England, but as the plane neared Europe a fuel pump problem developed in the last reserve tank. It appeared the plane wouldn't have enough fuel to make it to England, so when the Scilly Isles off the coast of Ireland came in sight Boyd decided to land there.

The next morning, with more fuel, he made the three-hour flight to London. After that Boyd and his navigator visited Paris and Berlin. Boyd was not only the first Canadian to fly the Atlantic, he was the first to cross the North Atlantic in the stormy off-season. And because of the late start much of the trip was at night. Since Conner wasn't a pilot, Boyd piloted the craft for the entire distance.

Three years later Boyd made the first nonstop flight between New York City and Haiti, a distance greater than crossing the North Atlantic.

Brandon

City on Highway 1 approximately 180 kilometers west of Winnipeg

Applied to the city, the hills to its south and the Hudson's Bay Company trading post that was once in the area, the name Brandon is sometimes attributed to a wealthy Englishman who was forced to leave home and join the Hudson's Bay Company. Dubbed Lord Brandon on this side of the Atlantic, where he was considered somewhat of a dandy, the young man was stationed near Portage la Prairie, but ran off to live the life of a hermit in what became known as the Brandon Hills. According to the tale Lord Brandon fled his post at Portage la Prairie after falling in love with the wife of another officer in the company.

A more likely explanation is that the first trading post in the area, Brandon House, was named in recognition of the 8th Duke of Hamilton, head of the House of Douglas, who took a seat in the House of Lords in 1782 as the Duke of Brandon. The Douglas family eventually owned controlling shares of Hudson's Bay Company stock.

Both the Brandon Hills and today's city took their names from the original trading post.

Rosser Ave. in Brandon. By permission of Manitoba Archives: Brandon – Streets, Rosser 1, c. 1882, North side of Rosser between 9th and 10th St.

Bridgar

Rail point approximately 50 kilometers southeast of Thompson on the Hudson Bay line

Bridgar was named for John Bridgar, the Hudson's Bay Company governor who attempted to build a post on Hudson Bay at the mouth of the Nelson River in 1682. The French thwarted Bridgar's effort when they captured him and transported him to Quebec City, where they first imprisoned and then later released him.

Brochet

Settlement near the Saskatchewan border approximately 120 kilometers north of Lynn Lake on Reindeer Lake

Brochet is the French word for northern pike. Located on the shores of Reindeer Lake's Brochet Bay, the community takes its name from what is presumably an excellent pike fishing spot.

There is also a village in Manitoba called Lac Brochet approximately 75 kilometers north of Brochet, where the fishing is evidently also good.

Brokenhead

Settlement on the Brokenhead River approximately 70 kilometers northeast of Winnipeg on Highway 12

Brokenhead takes its name from the nearby Brokenhead River. Douglas, in *Manitoba Place-Names,* says the river got its name because there are two streams that could be logically considered its headwaters, thus the head of the river is broken into two parts.

An aboriginal legend reports a more likely origin for the name. According to this story two warriors met near the river and fell into battle. One of the combatants received a head wound and from that time forward the stream was known as the river of the broken head.

Alexander Henry, the younger, was the first European to record the Brokenhead River's existence in 1800. He didn't call it the Brokenhead, though. He called it the Catfish River.

Brookdale

Settlement approximately 25 kilometers northeast of Brandon on Provincial Road 353

The community's first postmaster, Keith Blenkhorne, named Brookdale in 1882. Not surprisingly, the name is derived from the presence of a small nearby brook that flowed from the west through the open prairie, or dale. When a Canadian Pacific Railway line came through the area a few years later, the post office moved a short distance to the rail point, but kept its original name.

Broomhill

Settlement approximately 125 kilometers southwest of Brandon on Provincial Road 345

The first postmaster at Broomhill, a man named Kilkenny, tried to name the community Greenhill because of a nearby grassy knoll. The post office rejected the name because it was already in use. Undeterred, the determined Kilkenny switched to the name Broomhill because, he said, broom grass grew on the green knoll. Postal officials accepted the new name, but Broomhill Post Office permanently closed in 1964.

Brunkild

Settlement approximately 35 kilometers southwest of Winnipeg on Highway 3

Canadian Pacific Railway officials named Brunkild after a character in Norse mythology. Even so, the CPR got things mixed up. The rail point here was supposed to have been named Sperling, after financial backers Sperling and Company.

While recording the location, however, the official in charge mixed up the section numbers, with the result that today's Brunkild became Brunkild instead of Sperling, and a point up the line that was supposed to have been Brunkild is now Sperling.

Bruxelles

*Settlement approximately 110 kilometers southeast of Brandon on
Provincial Road 245*

Bruxelles was named after the capital city of Belgium by Manitoba's
Bishop Taché in 1892. Belgium settlers made up most of the community at that time.

Budd

*Rail point approximately 40 kilometers northwest of The Pas on the
Hudson Bay line*

This rail point was named for Reverend Henry Budd, the first missionary of aboriginal descent in Rupert's Land. The son of a Métis father
and First Nations mother, Budd became a clerk with the Hudson's Bay
Company about 1827 and moved west with the company to the
Columbia River region. Ten years later he returned to Red River to
teach at St. John's Parish school. In 1840, the church sent him to the
Cumberland House district as a missionary and teacher. Two years later
he moved to The Pas where he established the Devon Mission.

Budd was the first aboriginal in North America ordained as a
Church of England minister when he became a deacon in the church in
1850. Three years later he was ordained a priest. An eloquent speaker
and a good farmer, Budd was a prominent clergyman in what was at the
time still the North West Territories. After serving in The Pas, he lived
in the Nipawin area for a few years before returning to The Pas in 1867.

Button

*Rail point approximately 170 kilometers northeast of The Pas on the
Hudson Bay line near Highway 39*

The railroad stop here was named after Admiral Thomas Button, the
first man to raise the British flag over what is now Manitoba. Having
first entered the British Navy in time to take part in the fighting of the
Spanish Armada, Button led an expedition in 1612 seeking a northwest
passage across the top of North America through Hudson Bay. He had
also been charged to look for Henry Hudson, abandoned by his crew in
1611. Button discovered the mouth of the Nelson River and wintered on

what would become part Manitoba's far north. He and his crew were the first Europeans to endure a Manitoba winter and probably would not have survived had it not been for the local ptarmigan. Button and his men killed 21,000 of the birds during their time on the Manitoba shore.

Button spent the following summer aboard ship looking for a North West Passage to the Pacific. Although he failed to find one, be continued to believe in its existence until his death in 1634. (See entry for Back.)

Bylot

Rail point approximately 40 kilometers south of Churchill on the Hudson Bay line

Bylot was named for Robert Bylot, an arctic explorer who served with Henry Hudson, Thomas Button and others. When Hudson organized his expedition to go looking for a North West Passage, Bylot was hired as a deckhand. Bylot was a good choice, but historians have criticized Hudson's hiring practices for producing a crew that was generally thuggish, unqualified and disreputable.

During the voyage Hudson demoted his first mate and gave the job to Bylot. The mate turned out to be a particularly disagreeable sort who later helped lead the mutiny. After starting home the next summer, Hudson undermined his authority even further when he dismissed Bylot and made him a deckhand again. This time Hudson appointed as mate the ship's carpenter, a man who couldn't read and was without navigational skills.

After the mutineers set Hudson adrift on his newly discovered bay, Bylot piloted Hudson's ship back to England. The following year he returned to the Bay as Thomas Button's navigator. Part of that voyage's mission was to look for what might have become of Hudson. No evidence was found.

Calders Dock

Settlement approximately 140 kilometers north of Gimli on Provincial Road 234

The name for Calders Dock and the surrounding area originated from a government dock located on the west side of Lake Winnipeg. The dock apparently took the name Calder from a federal employee who maintained it.

Caliento

Settlement approximately 60 kilometers southeast of Steinbach on Provincial Road 201

There are a couple of versions that explain how Caliento got its name. One story reports that it's from an Icelandic word for village, but there doesn't appear any Icelandic word close enough to the name to make that explanation credible.

Another local legend fits the bill somewhat better: the name derives from the Spanish word for hot, *caliente*. Since Caliento isn't any warmer than anywhere else in this part of the province the explanation seems questionable, but you never know when it comes to names in Manitoba. It may have been a warm day when the name was chosen.

Camper

Settlement approximately 145 kilometers north of Winnipeg on Highway 6

Camper was named after Father Joseph Charles Camper, who worked as a missionary in aboriginal communities in the late 19th and early 20th centuries. The settlement was established as a rail point in 1911. Father Camper died five years later at Fort Alexander.

Camperville

Village approximately 110 kilometers north of Dauphin on Highway 20

Camperville, like the community of Camper, was named after Father Joseph Charles Camper.

Camp Morton

Settlement approximately 8 kilometers north of Gimli on Provincial Road 222

Camp Morton was named for Father Morton, the parish priest from St. Mary's Church in Winnipeg, who established a summer camp for children here. Previously, the CPR stop at Camp Morton had been called Faxa and the local post office was called Haas, after the first postmaster. The name was changed to Camp Morton in 1925.

Carberry

Town approximately 40 kilometers east of Brandon on Highway 5

The American railroad magnate James J. Hill chose this name in 1883 after Carberry Tower in Scotland. Hill was born in Ontario, emigrated to the United States and founded the Great Northern Railway that crossed the American West just south of the Canadian border. He was also a Canadian Pacific Railway director.

When he chose Carberry's name Hill was traveling across Canada on the new, but uncompleted, CPR line with Lord Elphinstone. Carberry Tower was Lord Elphinstone's county seat back in Scotland. Carberry Heights was also part of Elphinstone's estate.

Cardale

Settlement approximately 70 kilometers northwest of Brandon on Provincial Road 355

Cardale was named after John Cardale, an early settler from England and former Reeve of the municipality. He homesteaded near Cardale in 1880.

Cardale came to the area as a young man, married Jessie Stewart and built a fine home on the shores of what became known as Cardale Lakes. The Cardale home became the center of social life for much of the community. Then, in 1909, Jessie Cardale died. John returned to England a little more than three years later.

Carlowrie

Settlement approximately 50 kilometers south of Winnipeg on Provincial Road 218

The settlement of Carlowrie got its start when a general store opened here in the late 19th century. The site was near a traditional crossing place on what was once known as the Riviere du Milieu, or Middle River. At that time travelers on the Crow Wing Trail between Fort Garry and the Mississippi River at Crow Wing and St. Paul in Minnesota crossed the creek somewhere near this spot. The name Middle River came about because the small stream is approximately half way between trail crossing points on the Rat and the Roseau Rivers.

A post office opened here in 1894. A local resident suggested the name Carlowrie by after reading a novel that used the name in the title. Evidently, members of the community liked the suggestion and the post office accepted it. The book was, probably, *Carlowrie, or Among the Lothian Folk* by Annie S. Swan. It had been published ten years earlier.

Dog sled on the Trans Canada Trail near Carlowrie. The trail follows parts of the old Crow Wing Trail. PHOTO BY TED STONE

Carman

Town approximately 65 kilometers southwest of Winnipeg on Highway 3

Carman was named after Reverend Albert Carman, Bishop of the Episcopal Methodist Church in Canada and Chancellor of Albert College in Belleville, Ontario. Manitoba Premier Rodman P. Roblin, who had attended school in Belleville, suggested the name.

Rev. Carman had dedicated a log church here in the community that would later bear his name. Initially, the town called itself Carman City, but later residents opted for the less pretentious name it carries today.

Carrick

Settlement approximately 50 kilometers southeast of Steinbach on Provincial Road 203

Known as Spurgrave before 1908, the community was re-christened when the railroad picked another name for the rail point. Railroad officials named Carrick after Lt. Colonel J. J. Carrick, an Ontario politician who represented Port Arthur in the Ontario Legislative Assembly. Colonel Carrick was also involved in the sale of real estate in Western Canada. The post office continued to use the name Spurgrave until it closed in 1970.

Carroll
Settlement approximately 25 kilometers south of Brandon on Highway 2

The post office here opened in 1884 as Carrolton, but the name was shortened to Carroll a decade later. Douglas, in *Place-Names of Manitoba,* said the community was named after A. H. Carroll, an area resident who was later elected to Parliament. Another story has the name originating with A. C. Carroll, a member of the Manitoba Legislative Assembly in the 1880s.

Cartwright
Village approximately 225 kilometers southeast of Brandon on Highway 3

The community here was first known as Badger Creek, after the near-by stream, but the name was changed to Cartwright when a post office opened in 1882 after the construction of a branch line of the Canadian Pacific Railway. Badger Creek had been located about a mile north, but the town moved closer to the railroad once it arrived. The owner of the new site just happened to be a former federal minister of finance named Richard Cartwright.

Badger Creek and the "old" Cartwright in 1883, before the arrival of the railroad. BY PERMISSION OF MANITOBA ARCHIVES, CARTWRIGHT I, N12933

Cayer

Settlement approximately 90 kilometers east of Dauphin on Provincial Road 481

When postal service began in 1914, the community took the name of its first postmaster, Narcisse Cayer. Cayer had brought his family north from the St. Francis Xavier area of Manitoba about 1911. The Cayers were one of several Métis families to homestead in the area about this time.

Chater

Settlement on the northeast edge of Brandon

Chater was one of half a dozen rail points between Portage La Prairie and Brandon named in 1881 by the Marquis of Lorne, then Governor-General of Canada. He chose the name for his aide de campe, Captain Vernon Chater. The Governor General and his wife, Princess Louise Caroline Alberta, were visiting western Canada at the time. The Province of Alberta and Lake Louise in Banff National Park would each bear the name of the Princess. The Governor General also named Douglas, Sidney, Austin, MacGregor and Bagot in Manitoba.

Chatfield

Settlement approximately 160 kilometers north of Winnipeg on Highway 17

Chatfield's first postmaster, George Chatfield, used his name for his post office when he opened it in 1903 and Chatfield has been on the map ever since. In 1905 the post office moved closer to the new rail line.

Born in England, Postmaster Chatfield came to Canada in 1880 settling near the future town of Chatfield about 1899. Chatfield farmed and worked for the Immigration Department as a land locator for immigrants who wanted to homestead in the Interlake region of Manitoba.

Chortitz

Settlement 5 kilometers southwest of Winkler near Schanzenfeld

Chortitz takes its name from Chortitza, the first district in Russia settled by Mennonites from Germany more than 200 years ago. Located in present-day Ukraine, the area around Chortitza became a center of Mennonite culture in the region. The Chortiza Oak, a huge tree several hundred years old, was important in Ukrainian and Mennonite folklore. Newlyweds, supposedly, walked around the tree three times to bring good luck to the marriage.

In the 1870s Mennonite settlers from the Chortitza area of what was then Russia arrived in Manitoba and founded a new community, and they gave it the same name as their old hometown.

Churchill

Town on Hudson Bay near the mouth of the Churchill River

The first Fort Churchill was built up the river from the present town by the Hudson's Bay Company in 1688, but the French captured and burned it the following year. Captain John Abraham of the Hudson's Bay Company named the river, which provided the name for the fort and the town, for Lord John Churchill, the first Duke of Marlborough. The duke was an ancestor of the United Kingdom's World War II prime minister, Sir Winston Churchill, and the Hudson's Bay Company's governor between 1685 and 1692. More than 250 years later, his descendent, Sir Winston, accepted the post of Grand Seigneur with the company, the only commercial undertaking the British leader undertook in his retirement.

The HBC's Captain Abraham was on Hudson Bay looking for a new site for a fur post to compete with the French when he named the river. Previously the Churchill had been known as Munk's River, after the Danish navigator, Jens Munk, spent the winter here in 1619 after ice closed the bay before he could escape to the open Atlantic. Out of a crew of 64, only Munk and two of his comrades survived to sail from the Manitoba coast the following spring.

The HBC built a stone fortress, Fort Prince of Wales, at the mouth of the Churchill in the mid 1700s. Although it was the most fortified post on Hudson Bay, chief trader Samuel Hearne surrendered without a fight when French forces arrived in 1782. The French took Hearne and his men, along with Hudson's Bay Company personnel from York Factory, as prisoners and sent them home to England just before freeze-up.

Both personally and professionally the events of 1782 turned out to be the tragedy of Hearne's life. Hearne came to prominence after two epic journeys exploring the far north., In 1769 he led an expedition to look for copper deposits to confirm stories told by Chipewyan First Nations traders about interior mineral deposits.

Hearne's Chipewyan friend Matonabbee was crucial to Hearne and the success of the mission that saw them cross the tundra on foot to the Coppermine River. From there they followed the river to the Arctic Ocean. Hearne was the first European to see Great Slave Lake, and the first to reach the Arctic Ocean overland through the interior. While no copper deposits were ever mined by the HBC, Hearne's three years of traveling back and forth across the high arctic, as recorded in his journals, was one of the most remarkable feats in the history of North American exploration. So remarkable, in fact, that academics have discussed for years the possibility that Hearne embellished his journals to help later book sales.

After a brief return to Fort Prince of Wales at the end of his exploration expeditions, Hearne traveled southwest, up the Churchill River system to Cumberland House, where he established the HBC's first inland trading post in 1774. One of the reasons Hearne was anxious to establish the inland post, it is said, was because he despised Moses Norton, the chief trader at Fort Prince of Wales under whom he would have had to serve had he remained at the fort.

After Norton's death the following year, Hearne was made the fort's new chief trader. Once back at Fort Prince of Wales he promptly fell in love with Norton's sixteen-year-old daughter, Mary. The following six years appeared to be the happiest of Hearne's life. He and Mary kept countless animals as pets, including beavers, foxes and squirrels. He enjoyed reading essays by Voltaire and he studied the ways of the Chipewyan people. Helped by his friend Matonabbee, trade increased on the Churchill to record levels.

Then in August of 1782 the French arrived and destroyed the stone fort. Hearne's wife fled to the safety of her mother's people. The French sent Hearne back to England. When he returned the following summer, he discovered Mary had starved to death the previous winter.

In addition, Matonabbee, distraught at Hearne's capture and what he assumed to have been his execution by the French, committed suicide. Hearne never recovered from these twin tragedies. He built a small trading post he called Fort Churchill up river from the old fort, but the death of his wife and friend had drained his enthusiasm for the north.

In 1787, Hearne left the Manitoba shore forever. After his departure, Fort Churchill and the little settlement surrounding it never amounted to more than a minor HBC outpost. When the Hudson's Bay Railway reached the community in the 1920s Churchill became a true seaport and town.

Charles and Ann Lindbergh visit Churchill in August, 1931. BY PERMISSION OF MANITOBA ARCHIVES, CAMPBELL COLLECTION, CHURCHILL 145 – 147, N13166.

Clandeboye

Settlement approximately 10 kilometers northwest of Selkirk on Highway 9

An early settler, Mary Muckle, suggested the name of Clandeboye when she moved to the area in about 1870. Muckle said the area reminded her of Sir Walter Scott's expression, "the lovely woods of Clandeboye."

Clanwilliam

Settlement approximately 60 kilometers north of Brandon on Provincial Road 262

Settlers in the Clanwilliam area in the early 1880s wanted to name their community Lamontagne, probably because of its proximity to the Riding Mountains to the north. When the proposed name for the new post office reached Ottawa, however, postal officials rejected it and named the new community after the 4th Earl of Clanwilliam instead.

The post office opened in 1882, but moved a few kilometers west in 1902 to be closer to the new Canadian Northern Railway line. Canadian rancher Pat Burns was one of the Clanwilliam area's earliest homesteaders.

After arriving in Manitoba in 1878, Burns walked more than one hundred sixty kilometers from Winnipeg the following summer to find the land where he established his first ranch. It was on this homestead that Burns first went into the cattle business. Later, he moved to Alberta, established several large cattle ranches in the foothills of the Rocky Mountains, started the Burns meat-packing company and helped organize the first Calgary Stampede in 1912.

Clarkleigh

Settlement approximately 65 kilometers northwest of Winnipeg on Highway 6

James Clark settled in the area in 1881 and opened the first post office here four years later.

Clearwater

Settlement approximately 90 kilometers west of Winkler on Highway 3A

According to legend this name is descriptive of the crystal clear water found in the area's streams and creeks. Settlers found the pristine streams of the area a pleasant contrast to the murky Red River and they wanted to advertise their good fortune to others.

Cooks Creek

Settlement approximately 20 kilometers northeast of Winnipeg on Provincial Road 212

The post office at Cooks Creek took its name from the nearby creek. The creek, in turn, came by the name because early settler Joseph Cook lived at the mouth of the stream, on the Red River. The post office opened at Cooks Creek in 1873. It closed in 1970.

Douglas, in *Place-Names of Manitoba,* reported the creek got its name because Robert and Charles Cook lived in a cabin near the mouth of the stream. These Cooks were, perhaps, later settlers or descendents of Joseph Cook.

Cormorant

Rail point approximately 60 kilometers northeast of The Pas on the Hudson's Bay line

The rail point of Cormorant was named after a nearby settlement. The settlement, on the southeast shore of Cormorant Lake, took its name from the lake. A cormorant is a bird species common to the area and is a translation of the original aboriginal name for the body of water.

In 1928 the name was used at a rail point a few kilometers up the line from the present site, but it was switched later to the current location in order to be closer to the original settlement of Cormorant. The old rail point Cormorant became the whistle stop now called Dering.

Cottonwoods

Settlement near Sprucewoods approximately 10 kilometers east of Brandon on Provincial Road 340

Despite the similarities in name there is no connection between the naming of Cottonwoods and the nearby settlement of Sprucewoods. The latter's name derived from a community club that formed at the edge of what is now the Spruce Woods Provincial Forest. Cottonwoods, a more recent settlement, took its name from the real estate development that first sold lots here.

One of the most recent additions to the Manitoba map, the property was primarily unproductive farmland developed for small acreage owners beginning about 1970. Parcels of land were sold in what the developers called Cottonwood Acres. Apparently there were cottonwood trees in the area, but some have suggested the name was a way to distinguish the new community from nearby Sprucewoods. Popular usage shortened the name to Cottonwoods almost immediately.

Coulter

Settlement approximately 160 kilometers southwest of Brandon on Provincial Road 251

Today's Coulter originated as a Canadian Pacific Railway stop and post office in 1905. It was probably named for the first postmaster in nearby Coultervale, also known at one time as Coulter. The Coultervale post office opened in 1893 as Coulter, changed its name to Coultervale in 1898 and closed in 1927.

Cranberry Portage

Village approximately 50 kilometers south of Flin Flon Highway 10

Cranberry Portage was established as a rail point and named after an historic canoe portage here between the first Cranberry Lake and Goose Lake. The original aboriginal name may have been "cranberry-carrying place."

Cranberry Portage linked streams flowing into the Nelson River system to the north with the Saskatchewan River system to the south and west.

Crandall

Settlement approximately 90 kilometers northwest of Brandon on Highway 24

Crandall originated as Carlingville, named after the Carling Beverage Company, a Winnipeg brewer. As such, it might have been the only town in the country named after a beer company. The Carling Company made a financial contribution to start a school here.

The Canadian Pacific Railway apparently didn't like the name. In 1901 the CPR changed the town's name to Crandall or Crandell—there was some confusion about the spelling because the railroad station spelled it one way and the post office another. The name may have derived from a local doctor, J. B. Crandall, or perhaps a railroad construction worker, Morley Crandell, but the truth has been lost in history.

The confusion could have been avoided, of course, had the railroad stuck with the community's choice of a beer company as a name.

Crane River

Settlement approximately 80 kilometers northeast of Dauphin on Provincial Road 481

The community here takes its name from the nearby river and bay on Lake Manitoba. Crane River and Crane Bay, named after the sandhill cranes of the region, are translations from the aboriginal names in use when Europeans first came to the region.

Chesnaye

Rail point approximately 75 kilometers south of Churchill on the Hudson Bay line

This rail point was named in 1929 for Aubert de la Chesnaye, the founder of the Compagnie du Nord. De la Chesnaye's fur trading company competed with the Hudson's Bay Company, establishing posts on Hudson Bay to encourage trade in the same manner as the larger company, beginning in 1682.

For several years, French posts on the Hudson Bay coast considerably outnumbered those of the English company. It was only after the Treaty of Utrecht in 1713 that the Hudson's Bay Company began to develop the upper hand, although fierce competition from the French and later other Montreal traders continued until the 19th century.

Cromer

Settlement approximately 90 kilometers west of Brandon on Provincial Road 255

Cromer is said to have been named for Evelyn Baring, a British financier and the first Earl of Cromer, when the Canadian Northern Railway line went through the area in 1906. Another story behind the name alleges that the railroad stop was named after Cromer, England. Before the railroad arrived, the community here was known as Elm Valley.

The H.J. Chandler Livery Stable and a meat market at Cromer about 1900. By permission of Manitoba Archives, Cromer 1, N943

Cross Lake

Village approximately 130 kilometers south of Thompson on Cross Lake

The village here takes its name from the nearby lake. The name of the lake probably stems from fur-trading days when the main trade route from Hudson Bay along the Nelson River had to cross the lake.

Robert Douglas, in *Place-Names of Manitoba,* reported the Cree name for Cross Lake is *Pimichicomow,* and he gives the meaning as "lies athwart."

Crystal City

Village approximately 80 kilometers west of Winkler on Highway 3

Ontario settlers with the Rock Lake Colonization Company arrived at Crystal Creek in the late 1870s. Surveyors named the nearby creek Crystal Creek because of the clear water. The community took its ambitious name from the creek.

Harvesting about 1905 on a farm near Crystal City. By permission of Manitoba Archives, Crystal City – farms 5.

Culross

Settlement approximately 50 kilometers west of Winnipeg on Highway 2

The Canadian Pacific Railway established Culross in 1898. Local people suggested Oakridge, a descriptive name for the new community, but the CPR decided to name the stop after a village in Perthshire, Scotland instead.

Culross, Scotland was the hometown of one of the CPR's construction engineers. The Manitoba village was laid out on land that had originally been given to Edouard Piele in a Métis land grant in 1882.

Cypress River

Settlement approximately 90 kilometers southeast of Brandon on Highway 3

The community of Cypress River takes its name from the nearby river. Since cypress trees are not native to Manitoba, and none grow along the river, the real question is how the river got its name. Apparently early French-Canadian fur traders called the river Notre Dame de Cypres, perhaps because spruce trees in the area reminded them of the cypress trees found in the east.

Dacotah

Settlement approximately 20 kilometers west of Winnipeg just off Highway 1

A local legend claims a number of early settlers in the area hailed from what was then Dakota Territory in the western United States. Dakota Territory has become the two states of North and South Dakota, just below of the Manitoba border, but the spelling of the American states and former territory differs from the spelling of the Manitoba community. This suggests that the settlement's name derives from the Dacotah, or Lakota, First Nation.

But even the Lakota name has engendered some controversy over the years. When Europeans first arrived in western North America, the Lakota people were tagged with the name *Sioux,* still in common use today. The term comes from the Ojibwa *No-do-wa-sioux*, which means "enemy" or "snake people." Understandably, many Lakota prefer their own name, in their own language. The word means an "allied" or "leagued" people.

Dallas

Settlement between Peguis and Fisher River first nations approximately 170 kilometers north of Winnipeg on Provincial Road 224

There are a lot of stories about how the name of Dallas was chosen. One theory is that the Dallas Post Office was named after an early settler named Dalaszynski. Another report claims Rev. William H. Prince, a descendent of Chief Peguis, chose the name to honor the first postmaster, James Asham. Asham's nickname was "Dill." Make Dill into Dall, add the first two letters of the last name and you have Dallas.

The true story of the name, however, is that James Asham chose the name Dallas himself. Aboriginal people in the area wanted the community known as *Megiso,* which means "eagle's nest" in the Ojibwa language. Postal officials turned down the request for that name, however, and sent Asham a list of acceptable names, asking him to pick one. Asham, perhaps noting the connection to his name, or perhaps not, chose Dallas. He said later that he chose the name because it was short and easy to spell.

Dalny

Settlement approximately 150 kilometers southwest of Brandon just off Provincial Road 251

Dalny, a former rail point, was named in the early part of the twentieth century after a Chinese seaport with that name. The Chinese city gained prominence during the Russo-Japanese War of 1904–05. Formerly, the Manitoba community was known as Corona.

Dand

Settlement approximately 100 kilometers southwest of Brandon on Highway 21

Dand was named after Thomas Dand and his son James. The senior Dand came to North America to look after the railroad interests of the Duke of Devonshire. Eventually, the two Dands filed for homesteads in southwestern Manitoba near what was then known as Lampman. The community derived its original name from the Canadian Confederation poet Archibald Lampman, but after the Dands arrived—and before a Canadian Pacific branch line was built in the area—the town re-named itself after the Dand homesteaders.

Darlingford

Village approximately 30 kilometers west of Winkler on Highway 3

According to a local legend the name is a combination of the first part of "Darlington" and "ford," as a stream crossing. Several of the town's early homesteaders came from Darlington, Ontario and they had to ford the Pembina River in order to get to their new home. Hence, the new district became Darlingford.

As it turns out, the local legend is untrue. According to Canadian Pacific Railway records, the town was named after C. R. Darlingford, one of the railroad's early engineers.

Dauphin

City north of Riding Mountain National Park on Highway 10

In France, the title *dauphin* was reserved for the king's oldest son. In 1739 La Verendrye named Dauphin Lake after that member of the French royalty. A year later he established Fort Dauphin nearby.

Cars parked in front of King's Hotel in Dauphin in 1956. By permission of Manitoba Archives, Dauphin – buildings 12, N10044.

A community near the present town first used the name Dauphin, but when the railroad bypassed that place many of its residents, along with others, moved to a site on the railroad and named the new community Dauphin as well. For a time, there were two communities named Dauphin, one on the railroad, and "Old Dauphin," which was sometimes known as "Dog Town."

Dauphin River

Settlement approximately 75 kilometers northeast of Gypsumville at the mouth of Dauphin River on Lake Winnipeg

The community takes its name from the river. It can be surmised that the river—with the earliest known reference to this name on Peter Fidler's map of 1809—derived its name because it was on a route that led from Lake Winnipeg to Fort Dauphin.

Decker

Settlement approximately 100 kilometers northwest of Brandon on Provincial Road 355

Decker came into existence when the Canadian Northern Railway named the stop here after W. H. Decker, who owned the land where the townsite was developed. As a member of the Canadian Northern survey crew, it was, perhaps, not entirely surprising that Decker would own land where the railroad would locate a station.

According to at least one account the community was at first known as Deckers, but the *s* was dropped after animosity developed over the choice of the location of the railroad station. As one early resident reportedly explained, it was "bad enough to have the old man's name [for the town], let alone the whole family."

Deepdale

Settlement approximately 110 kilometers west of Dauphin on Provincial Road 593

James "Boggy" Johnston owned a local farm called Deepdale when the Canadian Northern Railway arrived in the area in the early part of the twentieth century. It is thought the Johnston farm was named after one or the other of the two Deepdales found in England.

Deerwood

Settlement approximately 45 kilometers northwest of Winkler on Highway 23

Deerwood was named by Northern Pacific Railway officials after a large number of deer were seen crossing the tracks along a wooded area here. The community was first noted as a rail point in 1891. A post office opened in 1895 and closed in 1968.

Deleau

Settlement approximately 75 kilometers southwest of Brandon on Highway 2

Deleau was named after one of its early settlers, Sebastien Deleau, who came to the area in the late 1880s. When the Canadian Pacific Railway line came through a few years later Deleau sold land to the railroad for the establishment of a station and townsite. The first post office opened here in 1893.

Deloraine

Town approximately 125 kilometers southwest of Brandon on Highway 3

Deloraine first appeared on the Manitoba map in the 1880s, a few kilometers southeast of its present location. Unhappy with community's original name of Zulu, residents changed it to Deloraine, after a locale in Scotland. When Canadian Pacific tracks bypassed the town, the community, like so many others, picked up and moved to its present location in order to be on the railroad.

Delta Beach

Settlement approximately 20 kilometers north of Portage la Prairie on Provincial Road 240 on the south shore of Lake Manitoba

The marshy, delta-like shores at the south end of Lake Manitoba account for the name, although the geography is not a traditional delta and the marshy shores are far from what most consider a traditional beach.

Denbeigh Point
Settlement approximately 75 kilometers southwest of Grand Rapids on the northeast shore of Lake Winnipegosis

The community here was named after the finger-like point of land extending into Lake Winnipegosis. Formerly called Long Point, the peninsula was apparently renamed after Jim Denby, a man who lived in the area during World War I. A Dominion of Canada land surveyor named Plunkett named the point after staying with Denby in what was, perhaps, his fishing cabin.

Dering
Rail point approximately 60 kilometers northeast of The Pas on the Hudson Bay line

Dering was named after the Hudson's Bay Company ship that Captain John Young sailed into Hudson Bay in 1689. The ship was christened in honor of Sir Edward Dering, a Hudson's Bay Company deputy governor. Originally called Cormorant, the rail point assumed the name Dering when the Cormorant was taken by the settlement to the southwest near Cormorant Lake.

Essentially an armed freighter, the *Dering* was involved in one of the Hudson's Bay Company's biggest naval battles in 1697. Along with another company ship, the *Hudson's Bay,* and the Royal Navy frigate *Hampshire,* the *Dering* came across the French ship *Pelican* near the mouth of the Nelson River. The commander of the *Pelican* assumed the three ships were three other French ships he believed in the area, and sailed towards the *Dering* instead of fleeing.

By the time the French Captain d'Iberville realized his mistake it was too late. Caught between the English fort guarding the River at York Factory and the three English ships in the Bay, the *Pelican* had almost no chance for escape. With no real option open except to fight the French crew prepared for battle.

Outgunned and shorthanded as well, d'Iberville attacked. The first barrage tore the *Pelican*'s rigging from the ship, but the battle still raged for four hours. A shot from the Dering blew off the *Pelican*'s prow, leaving her to appear dead on the water. D'Iberville refused to surrender when the captain of the Hampshire, John Fletcher, sailed alongside.

In tribute to the Frenchman's courage Fletcher proposed a toast across the gap between the two vessels. Each captain held a glass of wine in salute to the other, but the battle resumed.

D'Iberville fired a broadside into the English ship's hull, puncturing it at the waterline. Within three ship lengths, the Hampshire struck a shoal and sank. D'Iberville maneuvered towards the Hudson's Bay and began firing. The English ship, amidst drowning sailors from the *Hampshire,* surrendered. Meanwhile, the *Dering* fled for the shelter of the Nelson River.

All was not well for d'Iberville and the crew of the *Pelican,* however. Before the crew could board the *Hudson's Bay* an afternoon storm came up and blew both surviving ships aground. With the *Pelican's* lifeboats shot away in the battle, the only survivors were those who managed to swim ashore. A few days later additional French ships arrived and the English survivors at York Factory surrendered.

Domain

Settlement approximately 20 kilometers southwest of Winnipeg on Provincial Road 330

This community went by a number of names in its early years, including Shanawan, which the Canadian Pacific used for its station until 1914. At that point, because of the possibility of confusion with the similarly named Shaunavan, Saskatchewan, the CPR changed the station name here to Selborne.

In 1915 the CPR changed the name again, this time to Domain. The post office, however, continued to use the name Shanawan. Mail came addressed to people at the Shanawan Post Office in Domain, Manitoba.

By 1933, residents had tired of having two names for their community, so they petitioned postal officials in Ottawa to make the name of the post office the same as the railroad station. The request was granted, but no one seems to know today why railroad officials chose the name Domain, although it was certainly in their domain to do it.

Dominion City

Village approximately 65 kilometers south of Winnipeg on Provincial Road 200

Dominion City took its name from the heady days of the boom when nearly every community on a new railroad saw visions of greatness in its future. Known earlier as Roseau Crossing the community sat at a river crossing on a trail to Pembina that later became known as St. Mary's Road. Several places on the river had the name Roseau, however, and the local postmaster changed the name to Panza, mostly to avoid confusion with a new post office called Roseau upriver in the United States.

Even with the postal name change the community was still generally known as Roseau Crossing. Finally, in 1880, the community called a meeting to settle the name question once and for all. Roseau Crossing seemed the most popular name, but a good number of people wanted to call the town Fort Roseau. The townsite is only a few kilometers from where La Verendrye's Fort Roseau once stood. (The La Verendrye fort, which dates back to the 1730s, was the first fur post on the Canadian prairies.)

Replica of a sturgeon pulled from the Roseau River near Dominion City. The fish was the largest sturgeon ever caught in Manitoba. PHOTO BY TED STONE.

The aboriginal people of the area, many of whom attended the meeting, wanted to keep their name for the district, *Ahgomaque*. Others lobbied Roseau City, insisting that the town would grow.

The meeting went on all morning before a break for refreshments brought in from the local hotel. In addition to the food, the refreshments included a keg of beer, but still the controversy over a new name continued. Then, about mid-afternoon, just as the crowd prepared for yet another vote, somebody in the back of the room called out, "How about Dominion City?"

Either everybody liked the name, or else the continued debate had worn them out. For whatever the reason, they chose Dominion City on the next ballot.

Douglas
Settlement south of Highway 1 approximately 10 kilometers east of Brandon

Douglas was one of several towns along the Canadian Pacific Railway named in 1882 by the Marquis of Lorne, who was the Governor General of Canada at the time. The Governor General named five rail points in Manitoba east of Brandon for other people, but when he came to Douglas he named it after himself. The Marquis' full name was John Douglas Sutherland Campbell.

Other rail points named by the Governor General before arriving at Douglas were Sidney, Austin, Bagot, MacGregor and Chater.

Dropmore
Settlement approximately 25 kilometers south of Roblin on Provincial Road 482

Dropmore is said to have received its name when the Canadian Northern Railway finally arrived in the ranching country west of the Riding Mountains in 1909. As the last work crew left the new rail point a group of local men gathered in a caboose on the siding to celebrate the event. Undoubtedly they discussed a name for the new community. One thing led to another until, at one point, they decided to have a "drop more" from a bottle before choosing the town's name.

A less-likely version of the name's origin has it that a Canadian Northern official drank a glass of milk while visiting a local resident.

The official promised that the new station would have a name as soon as they could come up with a suitable appellation. As he finished the milk the resident—you guessed it—offered him a drop more. That's it, the official cried, and the new town was named.

Somehow, a drop more from the first bottle seems the more likely source.

Drybrough

Rail point approximately 50 kilometers south of Lynn Lake on the Sherritt–Lynn Lake line

In 1954 railroad officials suggested the name Drybrough for what was then a Canadian National Railways stop. after the post office rejected the first proposed name. Initially CNR officials wanted to use the name MacLachlan, after a former Hudson Bay Railway manager, but post office minions feared the name might be confused with McLaughlin, Alberta.

The railroad chose Drybrough in honor of John Drybrough, the director of the nearby Sherritt-Gordon Mine.

Duck Bay

Settlement approximately 110 kilometers east of Swan River on Provincial Road 272

The community of Duck Bay, on a Lake Winnipegosis peninsula, took its name from the nearby bay. That name apparently derived from the aboriginal name, although there was an intermediate step using the French *Baie de Canard*. The original name undoubtedly comes from the abundance of ducks in the area, but whether the ducks were on the bay or the nearby Duck River, which flows into the bay, is lost to history

Duck Lake Post

Settlement approximately 60 kilometers south of the Nunavut Territorial border on Little Duck Lake

Duck Lake Post is the most northerly settlement noted on Manitoba provincial highway maps. A private trading post here took the name of the nearby lake. Later, the Hudson's Bay Company bought Duck Lake Post. Although the HBC called its new trading post by another name, the community continued to go by the name Duck Lake Post.

Duck River

Settlement approximately 110 kilometers north of Dauphin on Provincial Road 489

It seems inexplicable that the settlement of Duck River, located on the Garland River, just below its mouth on the Pine River, has the name it does. Today the waterway known as Duck River lies a few kilometers north, but over the years there has been plenty of confusion surrounding the name of the river and the small bay into which it flows. At different times, different adjacent creeks have been combined on maps and called Duck River and North Duck River. Succeeding maps have recorded several Duck Creeks in the area. Even Sagemace Bay, the large bay near the community of Duck River, was once known as Duck Bay, so it's not surprising for the settlement to have picked up the name it has somewhere along the way.

Dufrost

Settlement approximately 40 kilometers south of Winnipeg on Highway 23

In 1877 Bishop Taché of St. Boniface named Dufrost after La Verendrye's nephew, Christophe Dufrost de la Jameraye. De la Jameraye died in 1735 while traveling between Fort Maurepas near Lake Winnipeg and Fort St. Charles on Lake of the Woods. He met his end after suffering from an unknown illness, southwest of present-day Dufrost, near junction of the Roseau and Red rivers.

Pierre Gaultier de Varennes Sieur de La Verendrye began his exploration of Western Canada and United States in 1731 under a mandate from the French government. His primary task was to find a western sea that could be used as an outlet to the Pacific. He was given no money to complete this task, but the French government did grant him a monopoly on the fur trade in the West. As a result he established trading posts from Lake of the Woods to the Saskatchewan River.

But LaVerendrye was just the commander. It was Dufrost and LaVerendrye's eldest son, Jean Baptiste, who blazed the trail, or in this case, paddled the canoe route. LaVerendrye made it as far as Fort St. Charles on Lake of the Woods in 1732, but Dufrost and Jean Baptiste followed the traditional aboriginal route to the Red River by paddling down the Roseau. They built Fort Roseau on the west side of the Red, opposite the mouth of the Roseau River near the present town of Letellier. The fort was the first European fur post built on the Canadian prairies, although LaVerendrye wouldn't visit the site for several years.

On May 10, 1735 Dufrost succumbed to an illness while at Fort Roseau. His close friend and cousin, Jean Baptiste, would be killed in a battle with a Sioux war party on Massacre Island in Lake of the Woods the same summer.

While La Verendrye never found a western sea he did push the exploration of New France farther west than ever before. More than half a century before the American explorers Lewis and Clark would reach the same site, he traveled from the Assiniboine River near present-day Portage la Prairie to visit the Mandan on the Missouri River. Two of LaVerendrye's sons probably traveled as far west as Wyoming and they may have been the first Europeans to see the northern Rocky Mountains.

La Verendrye returned to Quebec in 1744. He died in 1749, while preparing for another trip to the West.

Fort St. Charles, built by La Verendrye in the 1730s, and rebuilt by the Minnesota Historical Society on the same foundation in the 1950s. PHOTO BY TED STONE.

Dugald

Settlement approximately 10 kilometers east of Winnipeg on Highway 15

The post office opened here in 1879 with the name Sunnyside, but in 1892 it was renamed Dugald after Dugald Gillespie, the community's postmaster at the time. Postmaster Gillespie arrived in the area around 1880 from Ontario.

Dunlop

Settlement approximately 130 kilometers south of Thompson on Highway 6

The whistle stop of Dunlop on the Hudson Bay Railway was originally named Winston, after Winston Churchill, the British Chancellor of the Exchequer in 1916 when the railroad reached this point. The name was rejected, however, and it was renamed Dunlop after W. D. Dunlop of Yorkton, Saskatchewan, a long-time advocate for a railroad to Hudson Bay.

Dunnottar

Village approximately 35 kilometers north of Selkirk on Provincial Road 232

Dunnottar is an amalgamated village that includes the resort communities of Matlock, Ponemah and Whytewold inside its official boundaries. Alex Melville chose the name in the early part of the twentieth century after a castle in Scotland. Melville arrived in the area from that country in 1902.

Dunrea

Settlement approximately 75 kilometers south of Brandon on Highway 23

Dunrea is a combined name, taken from the last name of the community's first settler and postmaster, Adam Dunlop, and another early settler with the last name of Rae. Both Rae and Dunlop sold the land for the community to the Canadian Northern Railway.

East Braintree

Settlement approximately 110 kilometers east of Winnipeg on Highway 1

Originally Braintree when the post office opened in 1919, the name changed to East Braintree a year later. Evidently the postal officials requested the name change to avoid confusion with a similarly named rail point on the Greater Winnipeg Water District Railway.

A man named Victor Watson or Victor Wilson suggested the original. He was an American who had reportedly come west to the area from the community of Braintree, Massachusetts.

Easterville

Settlement approximately 200 kilometers southeast of The Pas on Provincial Road 327

Residents in this planned community named their settlement in 1964 after Donald Easter, a longtime chief of the Chemawawin First Nation in northern Manitoba. Members of the community were relocated to this site on the south shore of Cedar Lake when their homes were flooded by a hydroelectric dam on the Saskatchewan River at Grand Rapids.

East Selkirk

Settlement approximately 30 kilometers north of Winnipeg just off Highway 59

The community took its name from geographical orientation. It's on the east side of the Red River, opposite the city of Selkirk. Thomas Douglas, the Earl of Selkirk, founded a settlement of Scottish people on the Red River south of here in 1811.

A stone house at East Selkirk built about 1945 in a photo taken in 1960.
By permission of Manitoba Archives, East Selkirk 1

Ebor

Settlement approximately 100 kilometers west of Brandon on Provincial Road 255

The first post office at Ebor opened in 1904 with the name Sproule. The name changed to Ebor Station in 1907 after a Canadian Pacific Railway branch line passed through the community. The CPR apparently borrowed the name from a post office north of the rail point. That Ebor may well have received its name in a rather underhanded fashion.

According to the local story, the new community had planned to call itself Ramona, after a well-known native woman in the area. But the man in charge of sending the papers to the postal department was from York, England. He surreptitiously changed the name to Ebor. Eboracum was the Roman name for York, and that city had been the Roman capital in Britain for 400 years.

The community of Ebor dropped the "Station" from its name in 1909. The post office closed in 1970.

Eddystone

Settlement approximately 55 kilometers east of Dauphin on Highway 68

Eddystone assumed its name from the local school district, which in turn was named after a Hudson's Bay Company supply ship. Named after the Eddystone Reef near Plymouth, England, the Eddytsone traveled regularly between England and Hudson Bay. .

For HBC traders at York Factory on Hudson Bay the late summer arrival of the ship delivering trade goods and supplies was the major event of the year. These supplies then had to last the men of the post until the following year. Within a few days, the ship would be unloaded and then packed with furs for the return trip to England. Crewmembers were always anxious to leave before ice formed on the great northern bay, blocking the route back to the North Atlantic.

Eden

Settlement approximately 100 kilometers northeast of Portage la Prairie on Highway 5

Early settlers in Eden must have thought highly of their new home. After all, they named it Eden. The choice for the name fell to a Mrs.

McCracken, deemed to be the oldest woman in the town in 1877. According to Mrs. McCracken, her new home, with its bountiful crops, was more like the Garden of Eden than anyplace else she had ever lived.

Edrans

Settlement approximately 70 kilometers west of Portage la Prairie on Provincial Road 352

The name of the community and surrounding school district (Edrans Union) derived from an estate in Ireland that was owned by the family of John Bredin. An early settler in the area, Bredin owned the property that the Canadian Pacific Railway chose for the townsite.

Elie

Settlement approximately 25 kilometers west of Winnipeg on Highway 1

There are several stories about the naming of Elie. Douglas, in *Place-Names of Manitoba,* said the town was named for Elie Chamberland, who opened a store in the new community in 1899. Elie Dufresne also operated a store here, and his tombstone bears the inscription "Founder of Elie."

Records from the Canadian Permanent Committee on Geographical Names indicate that Elie Chamberlain and Elie Dufresne chose the town's name jointly. The two storekeepers apparently got together and named the new town after themselves.

Elkhorn

Village approximately 90 kilometers west of Brandon on Highway 1

A Canadian Pacific Railway surveyor named the rail point Elkhorn when he came through the area with a survey party in 1882. The survey crew was mapping the rail line ahead of construction workers on the main line of the CPR when someone in the crew discovered a large set of elk antlers nearby. Until that time the district had been known as Flat Creek.

Elma

Settlement approximately 75 kilometers east of Winnipeg on Highway 15

A prominent story about this community is that Elma started as a logging camp before the arrival of the railroad. According to this tale, its name derived from an island in the Whitemouth River covered with elm trees.

A more likely explanation, however, connects the naming of Elma to the arrival of the Grand Trunk Pacific Railway. One of the railroad officials engaged in the construction work named the new siding after his daughter. This seems particularly credible since a series of stops on this section of the railroad line (Elma, Hazel, Vivian and Anola) have female first names. It's possible that the railroad official had four daughters. Evidence points to someone involved in railroad construction naming at least one other of the four towns after his daughter.

While the community went by the name of Elma, the post office here used another name for most of its existence. Until residents asked for a change in 1991, the local post office address was Janow, after the first postmaster, Janow Gilewicz.

Elm Creek

Settlement 55 kilometers west of Winnipeg on Highway 2

Elm Creek started as a rail point named after the nearby creek. At that time the little stream now known as Elm River was called Elm Creek. Before that it was *Riviere aux Ormes,* the French version of Elm River.

Railway station at Elm Creek in 1908. By permission of Manitoba Archives, Elm Creek 4

This area was originally within a Métis land reserve, established when Manitoba became a province. Most of the Métis land claims in the area were rescinded, however, when settlers from Ontario came in with the railroads. These settlers began homesteading throughout the area in the 1880s.

Elphinstone

Settlement approximately 90 kilometers northwest of Brandon on Highway 45

Elphinstone was a Hudson's Bay Company trading post named for the 15th Lord Elphinstone by the company's factor here. Initially the name of the post was Riding Mountain House.

The name change occurred after the HBC moved the post southeast from its location at Riding Mountain in 1878. Lord Elphinstone visited the following year, as a director for the new Canadian Pacific Railway, and he purchased an 8,000-acre cattle ranch nearby. After that purchase, the factor renamed the post Elphinstone. This probably took place about 1880.

Elva

Settlement approximately 160 kilometers southwest of Brandon on Highway 3

Elva was named in 1889 after Elva Modiland, the first baby girl of European descent born in the district. Modiland, in turn, had been named after a young aboriginal girl who visited the family's home sometime before the birth.

Emerson

Town approximately 100 kilometers south of Winnipeg on Highway 75

Named for the American writer Ralph Waldo Emerson, the town was founded by two American businessmen, Thomas Carney and William Fairbanks. Emerson was Fairbanks's favorite writer.

The two men obtained land at Emerson under a colonization grant from the Manitoba government in 1873. The area where the Red River crosses the U.S. border had been inhabited on both sides of the national divide since the late 1790s.

For a time, the new town of Emerson languished. In 1874 there was only one hotel in the community, a small plywood building with a canvas roof. The land office was apparently no bigger than a small grain bin. Through most of the 1870s the streets were mostly mud after the snow melted in the spring. Then the railroad finally arrived.

Carney and Fairbanks established the town in the first place because of the proposed railroad between Winnipeg and St. Paul. It was the first town inside Manitoba on the St. Paul, Minneapolis & Manitoba Railway , so the community immediately began to grow once the trains started to run. For a decade, in fact, Emerson experienced something of a boom before settling back down to the traditional role of a quiet country town.

Europeans had inhabited the area around the Emerson in one way or another since the fur-trade days. The first Canadian post office opened on the west side of the Red River in 1871, sharing the name Pembina with the American settlement across the border. Later, the Canadian post office became "West Lynn," a name that continued even after Emerson appeared on the east side of the river. Emerson and West Lynn amalgamated as a town in 1889, so the community eventually grew to encompass land north of the 49th parallel on both sides of the river.

Flood at Emerson. By permission of Manitoba Archives: Emerson 14, flood, April 1897

In late 1797, a North West Company trader built the first fur post in the area on the east side of the river, just south of what became the international boundary. Although the 49th parallel became the official border demarcation in 1801, the actual boundary was somewhat unclear for more than half a century after that. It wasn't until after Manitoba became a province that a boundary commission surveyed the border we know today.

One story has it that when the border was finally established a local saloon straddled the international line. According to the tale, a white line was painted through the middle of the saloon, separating Manitoba on the north side and North Dakota on the south, and business went on as usual.

Erickson

Town approximately 70 kilometers north of Brandon on Highway 10

Erickson began as a station on the Canadian Northern Railway line in 1905. The Avista post office nearby opened in 1908, named after a town in Sweden. The name changed to Erickson after moving closer to the railroad the same year.

The rail point was named after Albert Erickson, an early settler. Erickson owned the land where the station was established. He was also the community's postmaster.

Eriksdale

Village approximately 125 kilometers north of Winnipeg on Highway 6

The Canadian Northern Railway established Eriksdale in 1911. Members of the community at first wanted to name the settlement Erikson, after Swedish settler Jonas Erik Erikson, although some talked of naming the new town Lairdsville, after the owners of a local boarding house. Erikson had homesteaded the land at the townsite and he was allegedly the first settler in the area.

In the end, residents decided on Erikson. Then someone pointed out there was already a town in Manitoba named Erickson. After further discussion, residents changed their choice to Eriksdale, still in Erikson's honor.

Erinview

Settlement approximately 60 kilometers northwest of Winnipeg on Provincial Road 415

The open green countryside here today looks much the way it must have when Irish settlers first came to the area and called it Erinview, meaning "beautiful view" or "Ireland view." The last post office here closed in the 1960s.

Ethelbert

Village approximately 60 kilometers northwest of Dauphin on Highway 10

K. J. Mackenzie, the Canadian Northern Railway's superintendent of construction, named Ethelbert after his niece, Ethel Bertha Mackenzie. At least that's the story Robert Douglas tells in *Place-Names of Manitoba*. Other sources report that Mackenzie named the community after two young girl nieces, Ethel and Bertha, and a community legend records that it was a niece, Ethel, and a nephew, Bert.

One thing is clear: the father of the child, or children, was Mackenzie's brother Sir William Mackenzie, president of the Canadian Northern Railway.

Fairfax

Settlement approximately 55 kilometers south of Brandon on Highway 23

When they petitioned the government for a post office in 1885, residents of the settlement here called their community Crown, the name of the area school district since the early 1880s. Word came back from Ottawa granting the community its post office, but the government didn't like the name. Officials named the new post office Fairfax instead. Nobody knows why, but when the railroad came through a few years later they stuck with the post office name for the new station. The community has been Fairfax ever since.

Fairford

Settlement approximately 225 kilometers north of Winnipeg just off Highway 6

The aboriginal people named the community and river here Partridge Crop, because the variety of reeds and grasses growing here were as diverse as the seeds found in a partridge's crop. Lying just outside today's Fairford First Nation, the community was once the site of a Hudson's Bay Company trading post and a church mission.

The name of the community changed from Partridge Crop to Fairford in 1851 when the church became known as Fairford Mission. The church chose the name because Fairford, England was the birthplace of Reverend Abraham Cowley, the missionary stationed here at the time.

Falcon Lake

Settlement approximately 125 kilometers east of Winnipeg on Highway 1

Falcon Lake is a resort community named for the nearby lake. The lake, in turn, was named after Pierre Falcon, the Métis bard best known for his song "La Chanson de la Grenouillère," or "La Bataille des Sept Chênes," which celebrated the Métis victory over the English in the Battle of Seven Oaks. The song has sometimes been called the Métis national anthem.

Toniata Beach at Falcon Lake in 1956. BY PERMISSION OF MANITOBA ARCHIVES, FALCON LAKE 11, N21240

Falcon, born in the Swan River district of Rupert's Land in 1793, was an employee of the North West Company, and later the Hudson's Bay Company after the merger of the two firms in 1821. He was also an early settler in Grantown, which eventually became known as St. François Xavier.

Only a few of Falcon's songs have survived, celebrating the adventures of the Métis at the height of the fur-trade era. Among the songs remaining from oral tradition are "La Bataille des Sept Chênes" ("The Battle of Seven Oaks"), "La Général Dickson" ("General Dickson Song"), and "Les Tribulations d'un Roi Malheureux" ("Misfortunes of an Unlucky King"). The book *Songs of Old Manitoba,* by Margaret Arnett MacLeod, published in 1960, contains all of Falcon's known songs.

Fannystelle

Settlement approximately 35 kilometers west of Winnipeg on Highway 2

Fanny Rivers worked among the poor of Paris in the nineteenth century before she arrived at the idea of resettling some of the city's most destitute people in the Canadian west. Through her work she met the Countess of Albufera. The countess and her husband arranged to help finance the settlement of some of these poor people in Canada.

Although Rivers died before the establishment of Fannystelle in 1889, the countess helped found the town and had a large mansion built there. She named the community Fannystelle, or Fanny's Star, after her friend. A memorial to Rivers, a Protestant, was erected in the Roman Catholic Cemetery in the community.

Faulkner

Settlement approximately 200 kilometers north of Winnipeg on Provincial Road 239

The Canadian Northern Railway established Faulkner in 1914 as a stop on a branch line in the Manitoba Interlake. Almost as soon as the railroad arrived the Canadian Elevator Company built a grain elevator on the siding and an official of the company, Franklin Faulkner, traveled regularly to the new settlement to oversee company business. He always stopped in at Payne's Store, at the time the new community's post office as well as its general store.

Henry Payne, the proprietor, and Faulkner got along well and Payne named the post office and community after his friend.

Finger

Rail point approximately 40 kilometers northeast of The Pas on Provincial Road 287

Herman Finger was a pioneer lumberman in the area around The Pas. He negotiated a spur line to his lumber company (a firm that later became The Pas Lumber Company) in 1910, and he became the community's first mayor after the town's incorporation in 1912.

The name Finger was first applied to the Hudson Bay Railway point here in 1928. Until then the settlement near the stop was known as *Matis,* the Cree word for Flint.

Firdale

Settlement approximately 60 kilometers west of Portage la Prairie on Provincial Road 352

The settlement at Firdale was first known as China in the 1890s. Attempting to farm the sandy soil of the locality, an early settler claimed somebody might be able to grow tea here, like they did in China, but wheat was out of the question. The Grand Trunk Railway arrived at the community in 1908, and named the station Firdale.

The name was chosen instead of China because of the evergreen trees that grew in the neighboring sand hills, and because the railroad named its stops in alphabetical sequence along that section of track west of Portage la Prairie. Other alphabetical stops included Arona, Bloom, Caye, Deer, Exira, Gregg, Harte and Ingelow. The names continued in the same fashion until the line reached Zenata in Saskatchewan. The arbitrary way the railroad assigned the names, often planting them on existing communities, alienated many residents. In later years a number of the towns renamed themselves to their own suiting. Other rail points have disappeared.

Fisher Branch

Settlement approximately 140 kilometers north of Winnipeg on Highway 17

Fisher Branch took its name from the nearby East Branch of the Fisher River, which flows north into the Fisher River (see next entry).

Fisher River

Settlement approximately 200 kilometers north of Winnipeg on Provincial Road 224

Fisher River took its name from the nearby Fisher River. The river, in turn, took its name from the fur-bearing animal in the marten family. Originally the waterway had the Cree name *Ochakeweo* (*Ochak* is the Cree word for fisher). In French it was *Rivière aux Pecans*, and then was eventually anglicized to Fisher River.

Fishing River

Settlement approximately 30 kilometers north of Dauphin just off Highway 20

The Fishing River flows by the settlement into the Mossy River a few kilometers to the east, just before that river empties into Lake Dauphin. Presumably the art of angling has been practiced successfully on the river for some time.

Flin Flon

City approximately 150 kilometers north of The Pas on Highway 10

Flin Flon is blessed with what is probably one of the most distinctive and interesting names in North America, and it all started with a dime novel found along a northern trail. The gold rush in northern Manitoba in the early years of the twentieth century had pretty much run its course by the time Tom Creighton discovered a promising out-cropping near Ross Lake in 1915. Creighton (also the namesake of nearby Creighton, Saskatchewan) called his claim the "Flin Flon" after the main character in the book he'd found lying on the trail two years before.

The novel, *Sunless City* by J. E. Preston-Muddock, was about Flintabbettey Flonatin, (Flin Flon) a crazy professor who found a passageway under a lake that led to a city at the center of the earth where the streets were paved with gold, and coins were tin. Flonatin failed to gain any riches for himself in the fictional tale, but Creighton's find by the northern lake reminded him of the book's city of gold. He named his claim after the fictional Flonatin and his discovery led to the building of the largest copper mine in Manitoba, as well as today's city of Flin Flon. Unlike Flonatin, Creighton reaped some financial gain from his discovery.

Main Street Flin Flon in 1930s. By permission of Manitoba Archives, Campbell, John A. Collection, 149, Flin Flon, north end, Main Street, c. 1939.

Fork River

Settlement approximately 40 kilometers north of Dauphin on Highway 20

When the Fork River Post Office opened in 1897 it was called *Minnokin,* the Cree name for the nearby river, which loosely translated meant "many berries" or a "place that produces well." The community changed the name to Fork River, the English name for the river, two years later. About a half mile from its mouth, the waterway is blocked by large boulders that divide the channel into several fork-like streams.

Forrest

Settlement approximately 8 kilometers north of Brandon on Highway 10

The Great North-West Central Railway reached Forrest in 1890, prompting residents of the nearby settlement of Humesville to move their community to the new rail point. The station here was named for the Great North-West Central's railroad inspector, H. F. Forrest. The Great North-West Central was later taken over by the Canadian Pacific.

Humesville, first settled about 1881, began when homesteader Alexander Hume donated land for a church and began selling lots. By the time the community that bore his name relocated to the railroad at Forrest, he had already moved on to California. According to at least one report Hume became a millionaire in the early years of the twentieth century buying and selling land in Hollywood.

Fort Alexander

Settlement approximately 120 kilometers northeast of Winnipeg on Highway 11

Several trading posts existed near the mouth of the Winnipeg River in the vicinity of today's community of Fort Alexander, beginning with the French Fort Maurepas, built by La Verendrye in 1739. In 1792 the North West Company built a fort known over the years by several names, including Sieur's Fort, Winnipeg House and Bas de la Rivière, which was on the south side of the river near here.

Sometime around 1800 the Hudson's Bay Company also began to maintain trading posts nearby. After the amalgamation of the two fur companies in 1821, the Hudson's Bay Company built a new post that operated in the community until 1940, evidently rebuilding the fort in 1857. In use for the HBC post here since the 1840s, the name Fort Alexander apparently honors the Canadian explorer Alexander Mackenzie. Mackenzie traveled the Winnipeg River in 1793 on a journey that took him across the North American continent to the Pacific Ocean more than a decade before Merriweather Lewis and William Clark repeated the achievement in the United States.

The Sagkeeng First Nation used the name Fort Alexander when a treaty was signed with the Canadian government in 1871. A post office with the same name opened here the same year.

Fortier

Settlement approximately 20 kilometers east of Portage la Prairie on Highway 1

The Canadian Northern Railway point here was first officially called Willow Range when a post office opened in 1898. For a decade before that the rail point had been called Blake's Siding. Then in 1909 the name was changed to Fortier, after the Reverend Joseph Fortier, a local minister who also served as the local postmaster.

Fox Mine

Settlement approximately 45 kilometers southwest of Lynn Lake on Provincial Road 396

Fox Mine is a mining community established in 1970 when Fox Lake Mine began operating. Locally the community is sometimes called Fox Lake or Fox Lake Mine despite the official designation. The mine was named after nearby Lake Mukasew. Translated from the Cree, a *mukasew* is a fox.

Foxwarren

Settlement approximately 160 kilometers northwest of Brandon on Highway 16

There have been several explanations for the origin of this community's name, but Robert Douglas put forward the most likely reason in *Place-Names of Manitoba* in 1933. The town was named after the English estate of W. J. Barnebe. Barnebe visited Manitoba in the early 1880s, before Foxwarren was named, and he wrote a book called *Life and Labour in the Far, Far West,* published in 1884. Barnebe's son also lived in the area about this time. The Foxwarren Post Office opened in 1889.

Franklin

Settlement approximately 55 kilometers northeast of Brandon on Highway 16

First known as Bridge Creek, residents petitioned to change the name in 1890. Apparently they chose the new name to commemorate

Benjamin Franklin, the U.S. inventor, publisher and statesman during and after the American War of Independence.

Some have argued the Arctic Explorer Sir John Franklin inspired the name, but this appears to be an explanation that grew in popularity in more recent years.

Fraserwood

Settlement approximately 70 kilometers north of Winnipeg on Highway 7

A man named Wood and a woman named Fraser owned the first two businesses in Fraserwood. The first post office was Kreuzberg in 1910, but in 1918, after Fraser and Wood married, residents renamed their community Fraserwood in their honor. In addition to running a store, Fraser was the community's postmaster, which probably also had something to do with the naming of the town.

Freshford

Rail point approximately 16 kilometers south of The Pas on Highway 10

This point was first noted on the Canadian Northern Railway line in 1911. As one of a series of stops south of The Pas named for towns in the British Isles, it's unknown if the original Freshford is the one in Ireland or England. Other points nearby are named for the Scottish locations of Whithorn, Turnberry, Westray and Cantyre.

Garden Hill

Settlement approximately 600 kilometers northeast of Winnipeg on the north shore of Island Lake

The four settlements of First Nations people in this area were once one band, mostly living at a community known as Old Post. When the band decided to split up, first into three groups, then into four, one of the new settlements was in an area known as *Buskwinnukgoosesink,* which means "a bare island." The name referred to a small island near Garden Hill where the Hudson's Bay Company kept their dogs during the summer. Over the years, the dogs completely denuded the island of its vegetation, even the trees.

The new community of Garden Hill chose the present site not because of the nearby bare island, but rather because the settlement is on a rise overlooking the lake and seemed a good place to grow gardens. They called the new place *Kistigan Wachink,* the "garden on a big hill." Anglicized, the community became Garden Hill.

Gardenton

Settlement approximately 90 kilometers southeast of Winnipeg on Provincial Road 209

An early Ukrainian settlement in western Canada, Gardenton is the home of the first Greek Orthodox Church built in North America. Ukrainian settlement here began about 1896. Construction on the church was completed in 1899. The local post office opened in 1905.

In unpublished research available at the University of Manitoba's Archives and Special Collections, the late Aileen Garland suggested that the town might have been named for Gardner, an early non-Ukrainian. According to Penny Ham, in *Place Names of Manitoba,* however, the name derived from a combination of the words garden and town.

Garland

Settlement approximately 75 kilometers north of Dauphin on Highway 10

The Lake Manitoba Railway and Canal Company established Garland as a rail point in 1900. David Blythe Hanna named the town after his wife, the former Maggie Garland of Portage la Prairie. Hanna eventually became president of the Canadian Northern Railway, and while in that position he named the new railroad stop of Hanna, Alberta after himself.

After emigrating from Scotland, Hanna started in the railroad business in Montreal as a clerk with the Grand Trunk Railway. He moved west with the Grand Trunk, becoming a Superintendent on the Lake Manitoba Line, then president of Canadian Northern and finally president of Canadian National Railways when several lines combined to form the new national railroad. In addition to Hanna, Alberta, a street in Toronto was also named for the former railroad magnate after he retired there.

Garson

Village approximately 30 kilometers northeast of Winnipeg on Highway 44

William Garson opened a stone quarry near here about 1900 and when the Canadian Pacific established a rail point nearby in 1902 they called the station Garson Quarry. A post office using the same name also opened that year, but when the community was incorporated in 1915 residents chose to name the town Lyall.

Even with the new name, however, people continued to call the place Garson, so to avoid confusion the name was officially adopted in 1927. William Garson was also the father of Stuart Garson, who became premier of Manitoba in 1943 and remained in office until 1948.

Gilbert Plains

Town approximately 30 kilometers west of Dauphin on Highway 5

A Métis man named Gilbert Ross had already settled in the Gilbert Plains region when the first homesteaders began moving into the region, and as a consequence the area was first known as "Gilbert's Plain" or "the Gilbert Plains."

Ross lived undisturbed on the plains through the first half of the 1880s, but in the summer of 1886 Glenlyon Campbell traded a pony for Ross's log house and the land around it. Campbell moved in and planted a crop. In the following years other settlers, too, moved to the area and Campbell was well on his way to becoming one of the province's most prominent ranchers and farmers.

Main Street Gilbert Plains. By permission of Manitoba Archives: Gilbert Plains 17, c. 1912.

The Gilbert Plains post office opened in 1892 after the railroad arrived, taking its name from the surrounding plains. Campbell left

Manitoba twice before his death. In 1897 he led an expedition through what is now northern Alberta and the North West Territories on a grueling trek to Dawson City during the Yukon Gold Rush. The second time, he organized a regiment to go overseas during World War I. He was killed in France Oct. 20, 1917, three days before his fifty-fourth birthday.

Gillam

Town approximately 300 kilometers south of Churchill on Provincial Road 280

Named for an early Hudson Bay trader and sea captain, Zachariah Gillam and his son, Ben Gillam, the community of Gillam began as a rail point and Hudson's Bay Company trading post in 1927. Gillams father and son captained trading ships on Hudson Bay, beginning when the elder Gillam took command of the *Nonsuch* in 1668.

Captain Ben Gillam arrived in the great northern bay on *Batchelor's Delight,* out of Boston, and built a trading post on an island just upstream from the mouth of the Nelson River (Gillam Island) in 1682. The French had already established a trading post nearby, on the Hayes River, and the elder Gillam, captaining the *Prince Rupert,* soon arrived at the mouth of the river to establish his own post for the Hudson's Bay Company. The *Prince Rupert* sank before the elder Gillam could come ashore, however, and the French outmaneuvered both the English and American traders for the season's trade.

Gimli

Town approximately 75 kilometers north of Winnipeg on Highway 9

The first Icelandic settlers established and named the community in 1875 upon their arrival in what was then known as New Iceland. At that time Gimli and the New Iceland settlement lay just outside Manitoba's borders in what was then the North West Territories. The settlement's name derived from the Hall of Gimli, the residence of Odin, father of the gods in Norse mythology.

New Iceland had its own constitution and governed itself independently of Manitoba until after the province expanded its borders for the first time in 1881. New Iceland kept its local government until 1887, when a municipality was established in the area to conform to other Manitoba locations. Later the old area of New Iceland divided into a second municipality.

Viking at Gimli. PHOTO BY TED STONE.

Giroux

Settlement approximately 10 kilometers northeast of Steinbach on Provincial Road 310

Named after Father L. R. Giroux, a priest at the nearby parish of Ste. Anne, the post office at Giroux opened in 1884. When the railroad arrived nearby in 1898, the community and post office migrated a short distance to that site. The railroad intended to name the station Steinbach Station, because it was the closest point to the thriving young city of Steinbach, but nearby residents persuaded Grand Trunk officials by to use the name Giroux.

According to its original plans, the railroad would have preferred to go right through the town of Steinbach. But local officials there rejected the proposal for reasons that are unclear today.

Gladstone

Town approximately 60 kilometers northwest of Portage la Prairie on Highway 16

Gladstone was either named after a horse or the British Prime Minister. At one time known as Third Crossing, because it was at the third crossing of the Whitemud River on the Saskatchewan Trail, by the 1870s the name Palestine had replaced Third Crossing.

The name Gladstone came into use in the 1880s when the town was incorporated. Legend has it that local politician Corydon P. Brown had a horse he called Gladstone. Brown said the animal always knew its own mind, like Prime Minister W. E. Gladstone of Great Britain. The town, in turn, took the name of Brown's horse.

Others say that the town was named after Gladstone the man. While this may be true, the horse explanation is by far the better story.

Two children show off sewing skills in an early 4-H Club at Gladstone. BY PERMISSION OF MANITOBA ARCHIVES, 4-H CLUBS 119, N4302.

Glenboro

Village approximately 75 kilometers southeast of Brandon on Highway 2

Jonas Christie and James Duncan were the first two settlers in what became Glenboro. They arrived in 1879 and homesteaded the following year, after the Homestead Act was passed. When the two men discovered the Canadian Pacific Railway planned a rail point near the common boundary of their properties they began selling lots. Duncan provided the name. He chose the word glen to represent the "glens" of his native Scotland and then added "boro" to indicate the site's new status as a town.

Glenella

Settlement approximately 100 kilometers northwest of Portage la Prairie on Provincial Road 462

D. D. Mann was a vice president of the Canadian Northern Railway in 1897. He named the railroad stop here after his sister-in-law, Ella Williams. To the Scottish "glen" he added her first name and the town became Glenella.

Glenlea

Settlement approximately 20 kilometers south of Winnipeg on Highway 75

Glenlea's first postmaster, C. H. Mackwatt, named the community in 1891 after his nearby farm. It is thought the name was also that of Mackwatt's rural home in Scotland.

Glenora

Settlement approximately 100 kilometers southeast of Brandon on Provincial Road 253

In the 1880s the Ogilvie Milling Company owned three sections of land near what became the community of Glenora. New settlers were anxious for the company to build a grain elevator in the area, and perhaps even a mill. At that time, the company's flour bags were marked "Glenora," after the firm's Glenora Mill in Montreal, so the town, post office, rail point and school district here all took the name on the flour bag.

Gods Lake / Gods Lake Narrows / Gods River

Settlements approximately 250 kilometers southeast of Thompson on Elk Island in Gods Lake, on the southeast shore of the lake at the narrows, and on the lake's north shore at the mouth of Gods River

The names are probably translations of the Cree word *Manitou* or "spirit." Swampy Cree First-Nations people still live in the communities on Gods Lake. The Hudson's Bay Company built a post, Gods Lake House, on the north shore of the lake about 1825 and it operated intermittently until about 1922 when it moved to a site on Elk Island, where

Gods Lake Mine had opened. When the mine closed the HBC moved its operations to Gods Lake Narrows, where it had operated other trading posts intermittently over the years.

Goodlands

Settlement approximately 140 kilometers southwest of Brandon on Provincial Road 251

The name Goodlands doesn't have anything to do with the quality of the soil in this community at the edge of the Turtle Mountains. The village here was named for its first postmaster, Herbert Goodland. The Canadian Pacific established a rail point here in 1899.

Grahamdale

Settlement approximately 195 kilometers north of Winnipeg on Highway 6

A Canadian Northern Railway branch line reached Grahamdale in 1911. The post office probably opened a year or two later. It's unknown for certain if the community was named after Samuel Graham, the first postmaster, or J. W. Graham, a fuel-wood and lumber dealer in the area. The smart money, though, would bet on the postmaster.

Grand Beach / Grand Marais

Settlements on Lake Winnipeg approximately 90 kilometers north of Winnipeg on Highway 59

Grand Beach in 1952. By permission of Manitoba Archives, Grand Beach 1, N5706.

The Canadian Northern Railway established Grand Beach as a stop in 1916 and began developing the area as a resort community. It's thought that La Verendrye camped nearby and gave the location the name *Grand Marais,* or "large marsh," when he first reached Lake Winnipeg in the 1730s.

The nearby community of Grand Marais kept its French name while the railroad used the descriptive Grand Beach to entice visitors. The spot has also been known as Hunters Point and Grand Marais Point.

Grand Rapids
Town approximately 350 kilometers north of Winnipeg on Highway 6 near the mouth of the Saskatchewan River on Lake Winnipeg

Not long after the French fur post here, Fort Bourbon, was destroyed, the Hudson's Bay Company built Grand Rapids House at the foot of the rapids about 1778. The HBC apparently built a second post after the amalgamation of the Hudson's Bay and North West companies in 1821. During the 1960s a large hydroelectric power dam was built at Grand Rapids to exploit the natural drop in the Saskatchewan River towards the lake at the rapids. The name, probably translated from the Cree, is purely descriptive.

Grande-Clairière
Settlement approximately 85 kilometers southwest of Brandon on Provincial Road 541

The post office opened in Grande-Clairière in 1890. It closed in 1967. The words are French for "big clearing," a name given to it by the noted missionary and colonizer Abbé Jean-Isidore Gaire, who helped the first settlers in the area build a church here in 1888.

Abbé Gaire came to St. Boniface from France in May of 1888, but he had no desire to stay in that city. He had come to Canada to help establish French-speaking settlers in homesteads on the prairies. By July he had moved on to western Manitoba where he gathered nearly 50 families, some from Europe and some Métis, to establish a parish in a "big clearing" where Abbe Gaire intended to build a church.

That winter he returned to France where he recruited 80 more families to immigrate. Two years of good crops encouraged friends and relatives of these settlers to come to Manitoba as well. As new homesteads became harder to find around Grande-Clairière Abbe Gaire moved farther west, establishing new communities for French-speaking immigrants. In the following 14 years, he helped establish 11 more settlements on the Canadian prairies.

Grande Pointe

Settlement approximately 10 kilometers south of Winnipeg on Highway 59

Grande Pointe, French for "big point," was named after a point of woods on a bend in the Seine River. Traders used the spot as a camping spot on one branch of the ox-cart trail, sometimes known as the Crow Wing Trail, between Fort Garry and the Mississippi River in Minnesota. The trail came into use in the early 1840s when tension between Métis traders and the Sioux tribes made travel on trails west of the Red River dangerous.

The Crow Wing Trail, also called the Woods Trail, followed the heavily wooded ridges on the east side of the Red River valley. In its early years the trail led to the settlement of Crow Wing, Minnesota, on the Mississippi River north of the city known today as St. Paul but then called "Pig's Eye."

Pierre "Pig's Eye" Parrant was a former Red River trader who moved south and opened a saloon near the United States Army post at Fort Snelling. The post commander didn't care to have Pig's Eye so close to the fort, presumably because of the distractions his tavern offered the soldiers, so he drove the trader and the assembly of Red River refugees who lived nearby farther upstream. Pig's Eye set up his saloon in what is today downtown St. Paul.

Because Pig's Eye opened his establishment below the falls on the Mississippi, the settlement that grew up around him was accessible to steamboat traffic. Furs and hides carried south from Fort Garry along the Woods Trail reached the Mississippi River at Crow Wing, but the final leg of the journey continued downriver to what became the largest trading center in the region.

Grandview

Town approximately 45 kilometers west of Dauphin on Highway 5

Settlement in the Grandview area began about 1890, but the coming of the railroad a few years later truly established the community. Legend has it that what we know as Grandview today was just a water stop in 1901 when a passenger got off the train to stretch. Looking up at the surrounding countryside he exclaimed: "Oh, what a grand view."

It's just as likely railroad officials gave the name to the community because it describes the astonishingly grand view of prairie and hills here.

Granville Lake

Settlement approximately 75 kilometers southeast of Lynn Lake on Grandville Lake

Robert Douglas, in *Place-Names of Manitoba,* reports that Granville Lake was named after the fourth Earl of Granville, the British diplomat Granville Leveson-Gower. Only circumstantial evidence supports this assertion, however, so the lake, the location of a Hudson's Bay Company outpost for many years, could just as easily have been named for a local trader or trapper. The community, of course, shares the name of the lake and the nearby Granville Falls.

Graysville

Settlement approximately 10 kilometers west of Carman on Provincial Road 245

George Gray settled in this area about 1880. The post office opened in 1904 as Graysville, but the community had also been known as Grays and Grays Siding until that time.

Great Falls

Settlement approximately 135 kilometers northeast of Winnipeg on Highway 11

The Great Falls on the Winnipeg River were part of a series of falls along the river before the construction of a hydroelectric dam here. Today's community developed with the construction of the dam. The post office opened in 1922 and took the name of the falls, that the construction of the dam largely destroyed.

Before the dams went up in the twentieth century, the Winnipeg River was a major fur-trade route that linked the prairies with eastern

Canada through Lake of the Woods and the Great Lakes system. One of La Verendrye's sons first mapped the river in the 1740s.

Hydroelectric dam at Great Falls on the Winnipeg River. PHOTO BY TED STONE.

Green Ridge

Settlement approximately 75 kilometers south of Winnipeg near Provincial Road 218

A post office opened in Green Ridge in 1879 and operated for a number of years. The name is descriptive, taken from a long, north-south ridge that runs intermittently through Manitoba and Minnesota east of the Red River. The ridge is one of the ancient beaches left by Lake Agassiz before it disappeared several thousand years ago.

Lake Agassiz formed from melt waters after the glaciers retreated about 10,000 years ago. On maps, the huge lake often occupies an immense area of land, from Lake Superior to Saskatchewan and from South Dakota north to Hudson's Bay. Although the lake at one time or another covered all of this ground, it never covered it all at the same time. The lake in the southern areas had mostly drained or dried up by the time the glacier had melted enough to create more lake in the northern areas.

As the big lake dried, it left smaller lakes behind. Some of these lakes eventually disappeared too, but others, such as Red Lake in Minnesota, Lake Winnipeg in Manitoba and Lake of the Woods on the Canada–U.S. border remain.

Staggering amounts of water from the disappearing glaciers, water from thousands of feet of ice, transformed the countryside. There was so much water the warming climate became much more humid than it is here today. It was so humid with the increasing temperatures and melting ice that a spruce forest grew up on the northern plains in the wake of the glacier.

As the great lake slowly retreated it left a series of great ridges, old shorelines like the one that passes through Green Ridge and nearby Ridgeville today. The climate became drier and the forests disappeared, replaced by prairies.

The Red River Valley, west of Green Ridge, is the bed of the 100-kilometer-wide remnant of the old lake before the water's final retreat. The concentrated glacial sediment from the disappearing lake has given the Red River Valley some of the deepest and richest top-soil in the world.

Greenway

Settlement approximately 125 kilometers southeast of Brandon on Highway 23

Established in 1891, Greenway was named after Manitoba's premier at that time, Thomas Greenway. Greenway was born in England, but immigrated to Ontario with his parents in 1846. Before leaving Ontario he sat as a Member of Parliament first as a Conservative and then a Liberal. In the late 1870s he bought an 800-acre farm in Manitoba and led a group of Ontario settlers west.

Under the auspices of the Rock Lake Colonization Company, Greenway's settlers homesteaded near his farm, close to what became the town of Crystal City. The new settlers helped elect Greenway to the Manitoba Legislative Assembly in the first election held in the province after he arrived.

In 1888 Greenway led the Liberals to a majority government and was re-elected three times before losing to the Conservatives in 1899. After a few years of lackluster performance in opposition, Greenway left provincial politics and won a seat for the Liberals in the 1904 federal election. Greenway's government in Manitoba is probably best remembered for eliminating the dual English-Roman Catholic school system during the 1890s.

The post office closed in Greenway in 1971.

Gretna

Town approximately 50 kilometers southeast of Winkler on Highway 30

The first European name given to this location on the Manitoba–North Dakota border was "Smugglers Point." The Pembina River in North Dakota bends north toward the border here and meets a treed coulee extending south from the Canadian side. The point provided a perfect cover for smugglers, and traditionally it served as such. As early as 1864 a saloon and customs house located on the American side of the border used the name Smugglers Point. A Canadian Customs Preventive Station with the same name was established in the mid-1870s.

Gretna was named in 1882 when the Canadian Pacific Railway arrived. W.W. Ogilvie traveled to the location of what was to be the new town to select a site for a grain elevator near the railroad. He named the new rail point Gretna, after Gretna Green, a border community in his native Scotland.

A tavern and restaurant called Smugglers Point operated until recently on the American side of the border here.

Griswold

Settlement approximately 40 kilometers west of Brandon on Highway 1

Griswold Station was established as a Canadian Pacific Railway stop in 1881. It was named, apparently, after friends of T. L. Rosser, the CPR's chief engineer. The post office opened in 1884 and the word "station" was dropped from the name in 1890.

Rosser was later fired from his position as chief engineer, along with A.B. Stickney, the railroad's general superintendent, because the two became more interested in real-estate speculation than railroad building. Rosser and Stickney's actions, of course, didn't involve a lot of speculation. They knew the railroad's route, and where the stations would be located, so they invested in land that would increase in value as soon as the railroad arrived.

Given the generally lax attitude at that time about people from business and politics profiting from inside information, Rosser and Stickney must have indulged in blatant and abundant market manipulation. Or perhaps the two men's business activities got in the way of someone else, with more power, who preferred to make the money.

Gross Isle

Settlement approximately 20 kilometers northwest of Winnipeg on Highway 6

Gross Isle was apparently a large wooded area, or "big island" of trees surrounded by swamp when French-speaking Métis gave the area the name in the early 1800s. During a flood of the Red and Assiniboine rivers in the spring of 1852 a number of refugees with homes closer to the Assiniboine camped at Grosse Isle for several weeks to avoid floodwaters.

Later, settlers in the new community adopted the name when the Canadian Northern Railway established a rail point here in 1904.

Grunthal

Settlement approximately 25 kilometers southwest of Steinbach on Provincial Road 205

The spelling of Grunthal has been anglicized somewhat from Gruenthal, which is German for "Green Valley." Mennonite settlers chose the name because of the way one of ancient Lake Agassiz's beach ridges on the west side of the town rises above the relatively flat landscape of the area.

The community was first settled in the late 1870s. A post office was established in 1898.

Gull Harbour

Settlement approximately 100 kilometers north of Gimli on Highway 8

Once a small Icelandic settlement, Gull Harbour on Hecla Island in Hecla Island Provincial Park is now home to a luxury resort, golf course, marina, motel and restaurant, as well as nearby vacation homes.

In the 1970s the government of Manitoba expropriated land on Hecla Island to create the provincial park. The few people who still lived there were dispersed. Years later, cottage and summer-home lots went on the market again. Today the provincial park and vacation-home settlement has turned the island into one of Manitoba's most well-known vacation areas.

Descriptive of the gulls that frequent the area, Gull Harbour's name has been used for the nearby harbor for at least 100 years and applied to the island settlement for at least 50.

Gull Harbour on Hecla Island. Photo by Ted Stone.

Gunton

Settlement approximately 40 kilometers north of Winnipeg on Highway 7

The Canadian Pacific Railway established a siding here in 1905 when the CPR branch line arrived and a quarry opened. The post office opened the following year, initially as Gunview, but then changed to Gunton the same year. The first postmaster, Donald Gunn, named the settlement after himself.

Gypsumville

Settlement approximately 245 kilometers north of Winnipeg on Provincial Road 513

Gypsumville gets its name from nearby Gypsum Lake and the gypsum deposits found there. The lake was named about 1890 when mining of gypsum from the area first began. At that time, a short railroad line was built to Lake Manitoba and the gypsum was barged to the railroad at the south end of the lake.

A post office was established in nearby Gypsumville in 1905 and the Canadian Northern Railway arrived in 1912, providing direct access to the south.

Hadashville

Settlement approximately 80 kilometers east of Winnipeg on Highway 11

Hadashville's first postmaster Charlie Hadash came to eastern Manitoba from North Dakota while the Greater Winnipeg Water District Railway was under construction. Hadash first opened a store and post office just to the north of the present town, at today's Medika, where the line was supposed to go. That post office was called Hadashville as well, but when the railroad changed its route, Hadash abandoned his first store site and moved his business to the new railroad line, and he brought the post office with its name of Hadashville with him.

Halbstadt

Settlement approximately 55 kilometers southeast of Winkler near Provincial Road 421

The name of the Mennonite settlement means "half town" in German. Evidently, even at its birth, Halbstadt was a very small place that didn't expect to get much bigger.

Halcrow

Rail point approximately 75 kilometers northeast of The Pas on Provincial Road 287

Railroad officials named Halcrow in 1928 after Gideon Halcrow, an officer of the Hudson's Bay Company. For about ten years previously the siding on the Hudson Bay Railway stop had been called Persley, after a village in Scotland.

Hallboro

Settlement approximately 105 kilometers northwest of Portage la Prairie on Highway 5

When the local post office opened in 1913, Hallboro was named after an early settler, John Hall. Hall owned land where the townsite was established when the railroad came through in 1904. He had settled here in the late 1870s and later became mayor of Neepawa. The Hallboro post office closed in 1968.

Hamiota

Town approximately 75 kilometers northwest of Brandon on Highway 21

There's some controversy over just how Hamiota got its name. One thing is sure: the community started out as Oak River. But when the first post office opened in 1882 residents chose the name Hamilton instead of Oak River. The plan was to name the community after an early settler named Thomas Hamilton, or perhaps, several settlers in the area with that last name.

Two years later, however, the name was changed to Hamiota after the postal department decided Hamilton was no longer acceptable. Evidently, postal officials wanted to avoid getting Hamiota's mail mixed up with the letters meant for Hamilton, Ontario.

Some reports indicate that the name of Hamiota derives from the combination of the Sioux word *ota*, which means "many," with the first four letters of Hamilton, denoting the many Hamiltons who lived in the community. Another credible report argues the choice of the name Hamiota had no particular reason at all. People just liked the name Miniota, a town a few kilometers to the west, and opted to give their community a name that sounded something like it.

The Hamiota Band in 1910. By permission of Manitoba Archives, Hamiota 1, N10891.

Harding

Settlement approximately 50 kilometers northwest of Brandon on Provincial Road 259

Harding was originally a Canadian Pacific Railway point called Parr Siding. To confuse matters more the post office that opened here in 1904 used the name Earl Grey, but only for a short time. The next year postal officials changed the name to Harding, with no clear explanation as to why.

There's some evidence to suggest the name of the rail point had changed from Parr Siding, or perhaps Parr Side, to Harding Station by the time the post office opened, but records aren't clear on the point. Harding Station, perhaps, was a name generally used in the community despite the official name of Parr Siding. For whatever reason, though, the railroad stop became Harding Station and the post office, probably in the interest of uniformity, changed its name to Harding soon afterwards.

Hartney

Town approximately 80 kilometers southwest of Brandon on Highway 21

The town's first postmaster, James H. Hartney, named the town after himself in 1885 when the post office opened. Hartney had homesteaded here three years before. In addition to his postal duties Hartney operated a large farm and ran a general store along with the post office.

Later, Hartney moved to Toronto where he became an immigration agent.

Harwill

Settlement approximately 175 kilometers north of Winnipeg on the western edge of Peguis First Nation

The name of this community is a combination of the first three letters of Harry with the first four letters of William. Early settlers Harry Francis and William Kinsman arrived to the area in 1911. The post office opened five years later using the combined name of the two pioneers. It closed in 1964.

Haskett

Settlement approximately 20 kilometers south of Winkler on Highway 32

The name comes from C. T. Haskett, who owned the townsite when the railroad arrived. A post office using the name opened in 1908. The settlement, just north of the North Dakota border, was once a rail point for the Great Northern Railway. Haskett eventually moved to the United States. The post office closed in 1971.

Haywood

Settlement approximately 70 kilometers west of Winnipeg on Highway 2

Haywood must have been a pretty spot when the Canadian Northern Railway reached here in 1894. The community received the name because of the alternating areas of trees and meadows in the countryside around the new rail point.

At least that's the most common story. Another report has it that the railroad stop took the name of a community benefactor, a man whose first or last name was Haywood. Whatever the reason, when the first post office opened here after the turn of the century, it too was named Haywood.

Hazel

Settlement approximately 50 kilometers east of Winnipeg on Highway 15

The name for this rail point established by the Grand Trunk Pacific Railway in 1911 has nothing to do with the hazel nuts that grow wild in this part of Manitoba. It derived from the daughter of a railroad official or contractor involved in the construction of the rail line here. Originally, the stop was known as Hazel Station, but the second word was dropped from the name sometime later.

Hazelridge / Hazelglen

Settlements approximately 35 and 40 kilometers, respectively, northeast of Winnipeg on Provincial Road 213 and Highway 12

Unlike Hazel, Hazelridge and Hazelglen are apparently both descriptive names that note the profusion of hazelnut bushes that grow in the area.

The Canadian Pacific Railway established Hazelridge as a rail point in 1904. The Hazelridge post pffice opened the same year. The post office was renamed Klondyke from 1909 until 1915 when it closed, but the community's original name continued.

Apparently first applied to the school district there, the name for nearby Hazelglen was used for a post office in the community for just over 30 years, beginning in 1936.

Headingley

Settlement on Highway 1 on the west side of Winnipeg

English missionary Reverend Griffith O. Corbett, who lived at Red River between 1851 and 1865, established a mission here that became the original settlement of Headingley. He named the place after his former parish in England. A post office opened here in 1871. Later it became a railroad stop.

Heaman

Rail point approximately 130 kilometers northeast of Flin Flon on the Sherritt–Lynn Lake line

Heaman was named after a former chief engineer of Canadian National Railways, J. A. Heaman. Heaman had held the same position with the Grand Trunk Pacific Railway before it became part of the Canadian National system. Today Colorado-based transportation company OmniTrax owns the former CNR lines in northern Manitoba.

Hecla

Settlement approximately 80 kilometers north of Gimli on Highway 8 on Hecla Island in today's Hecla/Grindstone Provincial Park

Settlers first came to Hecla Island in 1876 as part of the New Iceland settlement just north of what was then the northern boundary of Manitoba. At first, the new settlers called their island Mikley, the Icelandic word for big or magnificent. Things were tough the first few years, and the island didn't always seem so magnificent. Over time, the settlers began to call the island Hecla, after a volcano in Iceland said to be the "entrance to hell." Eventually, not only the island in Lake Winnipeg, but the settlement as well, became Hecla.

In the 1970s the government of Manitoba expropriated land at Hecla Island to create a provincial park. The few people who still lived there were dispersed. Later, cottage and summer-home lots in the village went on the market again. Today the provincial park and vacation-home settlement has turned into one of Manitoba's most well-known vacation areas.

Heming Lake
Rail point approximately 50 kilometers northeast of Flin Flon on the Sherritt–Lynn Lake rail line

This railroad stop was named in 1929 after nearby Heming Lake. The lake was named for Canadian author Arthur Heming, who wrote a number of books about northern travel.

Herb Lake / Herb Lake Landing
Nearby settlements approximately 135 kilometers east of Flin Flon on Wekusko Lake

In the Cree language, *wekusko* means "herb" or "sweetgrass." The two communities on the lake use the translated name. The lake kept the aboriginal name. Presumably, sweet grass grows in the area. The communities developed along with mining activity in the area.

Herchmer
Rail point approximately 155 kilometers south of Churchill on the Hudson Bay line

This railway stop was named in 1928 after Lawrence W. Herchmer, a former commissioner of the Royal Northwest Mounted Police. He was also a supply officer for the International Boundary Commission that surveyed the Canadian and American border at the 49th Parallel in 1872.

In 1874 he opened a brewery in Winnipeg, but a couple of years later he became an Indian agent in western Manitoba and then the inspector for Indian agencies throughout the North West Territories. A year later, in 1886, he was named commissioner of the North West Mounted Police.

While with the NWMP, a number of accusations concerning corruption were leveled at Herchmer. Though nothing was ever proved against him, Herchmer resigned from the force and enlisted for service in the Boer War.

A post office opened at Herchmer in 1929, but closed the same year.

Herriot

Rail point approximately 180 kilometers northeast of Flin Flon on the Sherritt–Lynn Lake rail line

G. H. Herriot was one of the original surveyors to run base lines and meridians along Hudson Bay. A creek and an island in northern Manitoba also takes his name.

High Bluff

Settlement approximately 10 kilometers northeast of Portage la Prairie just off Highway 26

In the West, the word *bluff* means a stand of trees rather than a headland or cliff. Named probably in the 1860s, High Bluff uses the Western definition. Not long after naming, the area became the birthplace of a short-lived republic on the Canadian plains.

Located just outside the jurisdiction of the Hudson's Bay Company's Council of Assiniboia at Fort Garry, the four hundred or so settlers in the Portage la Prairie area had no organized governmental institutions when Thomas Spence arrived in the High Bluff vicinity about 1867. Spence was a politician in the making and was soon elected to the quasi-legal local government in the area. He persuaded the local council to create an office of president and then elect him to the post. Spence at first called the region between Assiniboia and the 100th meridian Caledonia, but then changed it to the Republic of Manitobah.

Spence notified the Colonial Office in London of these events, but heard nothing in response for several months. During this time Spence and his followers jeopardized the budding republic's future when they ran into trouble trying to collect taxes. Spence first tested his taxing authority at the Hudson's Bay Company trading post, but the officer there refused to pay up and Spence had to look elsewhere.

A shoemaker named McPherson complained that any money paid to the new government in taxes would just go to buy whiskey for members of the government, so Spence had the man arrested and charged with treason. A hasty trial convened in one of the settlement's log cabins, but there was seldom order in the courtroom. At one point revolvers were drawn and fired and Spence, the president of the new republic, took shelter under a table while McPherson escaped with some of his friends.

In the ensuing weeks of 1868 the new republic collapsed. A letter from the Colonial Office denied the upstart government any legitimacy other than enacting local ordinances. Still ambitious for politics, Spence found an outlet the following year during the Red River Rebellion, when he was arrested for a brief time by the Métis. He later became the clerk of the Manitoba Legislative Assembly.

Highrock

Settlement approximately 150 kilometers northeast of Flin Flon on the east shore of Highrock Lake

The name here comes from the two high rocks on opposite shores of this lake on the Churchill River. The name is an anglicized version of the aboriginal name.

The nearby community of Prayer River also takes its name from an aboriginal word, *ayamilesiti*. Members of the Mathias Colomb First Nation settled at Highrock Lake and Prayer River. After a fire in the region during 1960s many residents of these communities relocated to band land at Pukatawagan. Others, mostly relying on fishing and trapping, still live at Highrock Lake.

Hilbre

Settlement approximately 190 kilometers north of Winnipeg on Highway 6

Some people say the name Hilbre derives from its location on somewhat higher ground than its surroundings. The geography doesn't really support this theory, however, because the landscape is generally flat despite its location on an area of limestone. How any rise of land became a hill and led to the name Hilbre is also somewhat unclear. Others speculate that the name may have referred to the Hilbre Islands off the British coast, but no link has ever been shown.

A local story offers a more likely explanation: a railroad construction worker was killed in the area, and the name for the station here honors the fallen worker. Another local account claims the first stationmaster was named Hilbre. Then the postmaster simply used Hilbre Station for the postal name. The timing fits the theory. The railroad arrived in Hilbre in 1911. The community's first postmaster, Florence McNamee, submitted the name Hilbre as the postal address when the post office opened in 1914.

Hillside Beach

Settlement approximately 100 kilometers north of Winnipeg just off Highway 59 near Lake Winnipeg

The Hillside Beach post office opened here in 1919, with a name somewhat descriptive of the area. There's also a Hillside Bay and Hillside Point nearby on Lake Winnipeg. After 1959 the post office was only open summers before it closed permanently in 1969.

Hnausa

Settlement approximately 100 kilometers north of Winnipeg on Provincial Road 222

Hnausa is from an Icelandic word that means rough or uneven. The Interlake Development Council claimed in 1973 the community's name stems from the Icelandic hnasu, which means lump of sod-topped earth. According to the IDC, Reverend Magnus Skaptason came up with the name for the new settlement."

But Skaptason apparently came from a place called Hnausa in Iceland. If he gave the settlement a name, one might suppose he simply named it for his birthplace, old rough and uneven Hnausa.

Hockin

Rail point approximately 50 kilometers south of Thompson on the Hudson Bay line

Hockin was named in 1928 after Northwest Mounted Police Corporal Charles Home Sterling Hockin. Corporal Hockin was killed in the line of duty on October 29, 1897 in a battle with a Cree named Voice of the Great Spirit, or Almighty Voice, and two young followers.

Almighty Voice was arrested in the fall of 1895 for stealing and butchering a cow near Duck Lake in what is today Saskatchewan, but then was the North West Territories. Unfortunately for everyone, Almighty Voice broke out of the Duck Lake jail soon after his arrest, killing Sergeant Colin Colebrook in his escape.

For nearly two years Almighty Voice evaded the police, but was finally cornered in a poplar bluff with two young relatives from the One Arrow Reserve near Batoche in the fall of 1897. Almighty Voice and his two cousins fought off a force of 100 police and volunteers for two days, killing Hockin, who commanded the force, along with Constable John Randolph Kerr and Ernest Grundy, the Duck Lake postmaster.

Eventually the Mounties bombarded Almighty Voice's fortified position in the bluff with cannon fire, killing the three and ending what has been described as the last armed conflict between aboriginals and a military force in North America.

Hodgson

Settlement approximately 150 kilometers north of Winnipeg on Highway 17

Henry Hodgson was the first postmaster here, and he named the post office after himself. Hodgson, an early homesteader in the district, sold land to the Canadian Northern Railway for the new community's town site and railway station, which also took the name Hodgson.

Although Hodgson held the first postal contract and named the community, his brother-in-law, Jack Bush, actually ran the first post office.

Holland

Settlement approximately 110 kilometers southeast of Brandon on Highway 2

Contrary to what many people may think, Holland does not take its name from the European country. The town was named after A. C. Holland, who ran the first post office here. Holland arrived before the railroad and opened his post office about 1880. When it finally arrived he had to move the post office just over a kilometer west of its original location in order to be on the rail line.

A steam train arrives in Holland. By permission of Manitoba Archives, Holland 3.

Hollow Water

Settlement approximately 160 kilometers northeast of Winnipeg on Lake Winnipeg

A long time ago, according to a Cree legend, a river flowing west from the land of many hills emptied into a great lake where it ran into a hole in the water and disappeared. The Wanipigow River, which flows into Lake Winnipeg at Hollow Water, is the river of the legend. *Wanipigow* is a Cree word that means "hole in water" or "hollow water," from which the community and the Hollow Water First Nation derive their names. Wanipigow is also the name of a nearby lake on the river.

Holmfield

Settlement approximately 95 kilometers southeast of Brandon on Provincial Road 458

Originally called Long River, after a local stream, the village name changed with the arrival of the Canadian Pacific Railway in 1885. The new name was chosen in honor of a village in Scotland. The first post office opened here in 1886.

Homewood

Settlement approximately 25 kilometers east of Winnipeg on Highway 2

The story is that Homewood was named for the estate of former Manitoba Premier Rodmond P. Roblin who had a summer residence about a kilometer out of the town.

Roblin had been born in Ontario and came to Manitoba in the 1870s to work as a cheese buyer in Winnipeg and then as a merchant in Carman. After moving back to Winnipeg he entered the legislature in 1888 as an independent. In 1892 he ran unsuccessfully as a Conservative, but in 1896 he ran again and won. Shortly afterward the Conservatives elected him leader. He became premier in October of 1900.

While he was premier Haywood was supposedly dubbed after Roblin's summer home, but Roblin's son said later that his father's nearby farm had nothing to do with the name. The farm, he said, had been called Maplewood, not Homewood.

A post office opened in the community as Haywood in 1905. It had been a rail point with the same name before that. Perhaps, a railroad official had mistakenly thought Roblin's home was Homewood.

Hone

A rail point approximately 175 kilometers north of Flin Flon on the Sherritt–Lynn Lake rail line

Hone was named for Jack Hone, a pioneer aviator in northern Manitoba. He was a recipient of the Distinguished Flying Cross during World War II.

Horndean

Settlement approximately 20 kilometers east of Winkler on Highway 14

This rail point dates from 1911. The post office opened in 1912. The name derives from a village in Scotland.

Ile des Chênes

Settlement approximately 20 kilometers south of Winnipeg on Highway 59

Ile des Chênes was an "island of oaks" in the surrounding prairie for French-speaking freighters traveling one branch of the Crow Wing Trail between Fort Garry and St. Paul in the mid-19th Century. When animosity was at its fiercest between the Métis and Sioux, Métis traders took the route for its cover, and they often called it the Woods Trail or the Ridge Trail.

Traditionally, traders used a trail on the open prairie well west of the Red River, but cart trains in the open country were vulnerable to attack from Sioux warriors. In the early 1840s traders established the Crow Wing Trail east of the river, in Ojibwa territory. The new trail, much of the way through forested areas, was more difficult, but safer than the prairie trails to the west.

Inglis

Settlement just west of Riding Mountain National Park approximately 190 kilometers northwest of Brandon on Provincial Road 592

Inglis was established as a rail point at the end of a Canadian Pacific branch line in 1923. Manitoba Premier T. C. Norris suggested the name, after the man who drove the last spike on the tracks to town.

Inwood

Settlement approximately 65 kilometers north of Winnipeg on Highway 17

First known as Cossette, after an early settler who became the first postmaster in 1906, the community here changed to Inwood the same year. The name is said to have originated because the settlement is "in the woods" or "in wood" and not on the prairie.

Another story claims that the community took the new name when the railroad arrived, but the contraction that created the name is the same. The trains went "in the woods" beyond the town before turning around. Somehow, according to this theory, the name Inwood derived from this observation.

Isabella

Settlement approximately 110 kilometers northwest of Brandon on Provincial Road 474 and 355

Isabella Taylor was the oldest woman in the settlement when the post office was named here in 1906. Taylor came from Scotland in the 1870s to keep house for her son. Before the post office opened her home was an unofficial distribution point for the mail of area residents.

Island Lake

Settlement approximately 600 kilometers northeast of Winnipeg

The Hudson's Bay Company first established a post on Island Lake in 1824. The name comes from the many islands in the lake Samuel Hearne noted the lake was "entirely full of islands" in 1772.

Another explanation maintains the name originated with a particular island known as *Pascunegas,* which means "bald-headed island," or *Buskwinnukgoosesink,* which means a "bare island." The Hudson's Bay Company once kept dogs on this island during in the summer months and over the years the dogs completely denuded the island of its vegetation, even the trees. The lake became "Bare Island Lake" and then simply Island Lake.

An early North West Company post called Lac des Isles lends credence to the lake of many islands theory. The four settlements of First Nations people in this area were once one band, living at a community known as Old Post.

The Hudson Bay post at Island Lake in 1925. By permission of Manitoba Archives, Island Lake 1, N12926.

Jacam

Rail point approximately 275 kilometers south of Churchill on the Hudson Bay line

Railroad officials intended to call the railway point here *Kinapic*, a Cree word for snake, but in 1928 the Canadian National officially established the stop on its Hudson Bay line as Jacam, after J. A. Campbell. Campbell was a former Member of Parliament from The Pas who had, at one time, served as the Commissioner for Northern Manitoba.

Jackhead

Settlement approximately 225 kilometers north of Winnipeg on the west side of Lake Winnipeg at Kinonjeoshtegon First Nation

The nearby Jackhead River has been labeled with some variety of name for northern pike (or a part there of) since the area was first mapped. A jack, or jackfish, is a nickname for a northern pike and pike fishing is, or was at one time, presumably good along the Jackfish River, or at nearby Jackhead Point. Alexander Henry, the elder, recorded the name *Tete de Brochet,* or "Pike Head," in 1775. Peter Fidler noted in 1820 that a band of hunters generally resided along Lake Winnipeg at the Jack Head.

Jenpeg

Settlement approximately 200 kilometers south of Thompson on Provincial Road 373

The name Jenpeg came about years before construction actually started on a Manitoba hydroelectric dam here. When initial planning for a dam on the Nelson River to regulate water levels on Lake Winnipeg was underway an engineer at Manitoba Hydro named the proposed hydroelectric station after two water resource branch employees, Jenny Kitkoski and Peggy Johnston. When the dam was built in the 1970s, the community that grew up to house construction workers took on the name of the hydroelectric station.

Jetait

Rail point approximately 90 kilometers south of Lynn Lake on the Sherritt–Lynn Lake line

Canadian National Railways named this rail point after Captain James Edward Tait, killed during World War I. Tait was awarded the Military Cross and the Victoria Cross after dying in the Battle of Amiens in 1918. Before the war Tait participated in the original surveying for a route for the Hudson Bay Railway.

Justice

Settlement approximately 20 kilometers northeast of Brandon on Provincial Road 468

Justice is a noble concept, but the Grand Trunk Pacific Railway selected the name in 1908 to fit with a series of stations west of Portage la Prairie. Each station along the line follows consecutive letters of the alphabet. The first three were Arona, Bloom and Caye, followed by Deer, Exira and Firdale. The alphabetical phenomenon went all the way to Zanata, Saskatchewan. Angered at the arbitrary assignations, many of the towns along the line renamed themselves to the liking of local residents rather than railroad officials.

Kaleida

Settlement approximately 35 kilometers west of Winkler on Provincial Road 528

A horse and buggy going over the Pembina Bridge at Kaleida in 1911. By permission of Manitoba Archives, Kaleida 3, N1361.

In the 1880s settlers got together to name the new community and the school district here. Area residents met in the home of George Reilly. At one point during the meeting Reilly opened his front door, looked out and commented that a person would be unlikely to see a more beautiful scene, even in a kaleidoscope. The group had an epiphany and they chose the name Kaleida.

Kane

Settlement approximately 30 kilometers northeast of Winkler on Highway 23

Established as a rail point in 1911, Kane derived its name from local settler Robert Kane, who owned the station and townsite land. Kane later sold out and returned to the United States. A post office opened here in 1920, closed briefly in 1930, reopened again the same year and closed for good in 1970.

Katrime

Settlement approximately 30 kilometers northeast of Portage la Prairie on Provincial Road 350

In 1901 Scottish settlers suggested Loch Katrime in Scotland as the source for the name of the rail point here. The railroad obliged. A post office opened using the name in 1907, and closed in 1970.

Kellett

Rail point approximately 150 kilometers south of Churchill on the Hudson Bay Railway

Kellett was named in 1929 for Vice-Admiral Henry Kellett who explored the Canadian arctic in the 1850s. Kellett took part in four separate voyages between 1848 and 1853 looking for what had become of the Franklin Expedition.

On one of these voyages Kellett rescued Robert McClure. McClure had been icebound for nearly two years, but Kellett's ship also became icebound before leaving the arctic, so McClure spent a third winter in the ice. In 1849 Kellett became the first European to see and chart Ostrov Vrangelya in the Chukchi Sea off the Siberian coast. In addition to the Manitoba rail point, Cape Kellett on the easternmost point of Banks Island bears his name. He died in Clonacody in 1871.

Kelloe

Settlement approximately 135 kilometers northwest of Brandon on Highway 16

Kelloe gained its name in 1887 from a woman's estate in either Scotland or, perhaps, Ireland. The woman appears to have been a large investor in the Manitoba and Northwestern Railway which first established Kelloe Station. The post office dropped the word *station* in 1905 and closed in 1958.

Kelsey

Settlement approximately 85 kilometers northeast of Thompson at the end of a Hudson Bay Railway branch line

Kelsey is the site of a hydroelectric generating station that powers the International Nickle Company's mining and smelting operations in Thompson. Constructed in the late 1950s and early 1960s, the dam and generating station site was named after Henry Kelsey, an employee of the Hudson's Bay Company who explored the prairies in the early 1690s.

Kelsey's mission was to encourage aboriginal people from the prairies to trade at the English fort on Hudson Bay, but in the process he became the first European to visit and describe the northern prairies. Kelsey paddled up the river system from York Factory, and traveled overland, perhaps as far as western Saskatchewan.

Kelsey's fame as an explorer owes much to the journals he kept of his travels on the prairies. Partly written in rhyme, his journals put the distance he may have traveled west and south of Hudson Bay somewhat in question. Though unscientific and lacking detail, his records seem to indicate that he traveled up the Hayes River to the Fox and then to the Saskatchewan, probably as far as Battleford. His journals describe encounters with bison and the peoples of the area.

Traveling with an Assiniboine guide, Kelsey sought to encourage the Assiniboine and Gros Ventre to go to Hudson Bay to trade along with the Cree, who monopolized the northern trade with the inland peoples at that time. Kelsey returned to York Factory in 1692 to complete a long career with the HBC. All his life he claimed he never received credit for his discoveries in the Canadian West.

Kelwood

Settlement approximately 155 kilometers northwest of Portage la Prairie on Highway 5

Kelwood originated as the Glensmith Station rail point in 1904. The post office became Kelwood the following year. There are several theories about the name's source, most suggesting a combination of two names.

The name may combine that of Angus Wood, the first postmaster, with that of another early settler in the area named Kelly.

Kenton

Settlement approximately 60 kilometers northwest of Brandon on Highway 21

The first post office near here, called Ralphton, opened in 1884. Ten years later it moved to a new location nearby and new postmaster Annie Kent changed the name to Kenton. Kent and her husband homesteaded here in 1881. In 1904, after the Great North-West Central Railway went through, the Kenton Post Office moved to the railroad site and the new community growing there.

Kenville

Settlement approximately 15 kilometers south of Swan River on Highway 83

The story goes that Kenville, a rail point on the Canadian Northern established in 1906, took its name from the middle syllable of William Mackenzie's name. Mackenzie, with his partner Donald Mann, was a co-founder of the Canadian Northern.

Kettle Rapids

Rail point approximately 215 kilometers north east of Thompson on the Hudson Bay line

Nearby Kettle Rapids lent its name to this rail stop on the Hudson Bay Railway. The name for the rapids is a translation of the original aboriginal name. Some have speculated the rapids earned the name because the water appeared to be boiling, as if in a kettle on a fire.

Another explanation holds that the rapids made it necessary for travelers on the river to portage. According to this theory it was a "kettle-carrying place." Early literature supports the latter version of the name's origins.

The Kettle River (which joins the Nelson near here) and Kettle Lake upstream were also probably named after the rapids. There is now a large hydroelectric dam here.

Killarney

Town approximately 100 kilometers southeast of Brandon on Highway 18

The town of Killarney and the nearby lake take their names from a village and lake in Ireland. Apparently the name derives from Celtic words indicating a church among the black thorn bushes. The name came into use for the community here in the early 1880s. Apparently early homesteader and land guide John Sidney O'Brien hailed from the Killarney Lakes area of Ireland and the lake here reminded him of home.

According to the local legend O'Brien sat on the shore of the as-yet-unnamed lake one day, homesick for Ireland, sipping from a bottle of spirits brewed in his native country. After a time, O'Brien got up and walked to the water's edge where he poured what remained of the bottle into the lake. As he watched the Irish Whisky mix with Manitoba lake water O'Brien christened the lake "Killarney" after his former home across the sea.

Killarney Lake. By permission of Manitoba Archives: Kilarney Lake 4, c. 1956.

Kinosota

Settlement approximately 90 kilometers southeast of Dauphin near
Provincial Road 278

The post office here adopted the name Kinosota in 1889, but before that the settlement was known by the name of a local Hudson's Bay Company fort called Manitoba House. Established at the Kinosota site about 1828, the trading post continued to operate until 1910 when the company sold the post to an independent trader. Some abandoned buildings from the HBC post still stand in the community.

The original name of Manitoba House probably has its origins in the Cree, or a similar Ojibwa word, and means something akin "spirit narrows" or "spirit voice." This refers to the *Manitou* or "Great Spirit" living at the nearby Lake Manitoba narrows just to the north.

Evidence of the Manitou manifests itself because the water makes unusual noises as it passes between the rocky shores where the lake narrows. Some doubt remains whether this is the source of the name for the lake and province, however, because the Assiniboine called the lake *Minni-toba,* or "Lake of the Prairies. "

Kinosota too could be from the Assiniboine. An early postmaster in the community claimed the name was a Sioux word and the Assiniboine spoke a Siouxian language. A community history book credits the name Kinosota to an aboriginal word that means "probably strong," although the book does not mention which aboriginal language is the source.

Some have said that Kinosota is from the Cree words *Kim-is-gay-ak* that mean "lots of grass." An abundance of grass apparently grew along Reedy Creek at the time the name was chosen. Others have said Kinosota is from Cree or Ojibwa words having to do with fish. *Kinosao* means fish in Cree, *kino-je* in Ojibwa.

The settlement used some form of the name "Manito-bah" or "Manito-wapaw" for most of the 19TH century. Manitoba premier John Norquay suggested the new name of Kinosota. After all, a town in Manitoba named Manitoba would have a postal address of "Manitoba, Manitoba," although the post office spelling at the time of the name change was "Manito-wapta, Manitoba."

That Norquay suggested the new name gives no clue to its origin. The province's first Métis premier, Norquay could speak French and English as well as Ojibwa, Cree and Assiniboine. He had also studied

Greek and Latin. The name could easily derive from two aboriginal languages. The obvious example would be "Kino-sota" from a combination of Cree and Assiniboine words meaning "lots of fish." In Cree *kino-saskaw* would also be "lots of fish."

Kleefeld

Settlement approximately 20 kilometers west of Steinbach on Provincial Road 216

Kleefeld was apparently a community name for a German settlement in Russia. The community in Manitoba was first listed as Gruenfeld, the German equivalent of Green Field, in 1878, but it became Kleefeld when the post office opened in 1896. Apparently, a post office had already established a Gruenfeld somewhere else. *Kleefeld* is German for "clover field."

Kola

Settlement approximately 105 kilometers west of Brandon on Provincial Road 257

First applied to a district west of Virden near the Saskatchewan border in the 1880s, the name Kola Barton came from an English manor house. Several post offices and the school district in the area operated under the name. Then in 1910 the Kola Post Office changed its name to Butler Station, after the rail point established nearby. The Butler Station Post office then became simply Butler in 1954 and then closed permanently in 1966. Meanwhile the name Kola lived on, as the school district for a time, and then a community name that's still on the map.

Komarno

Settlement approximately 55 kilometers north of Winnipeg on Highway 7

Settlers from the Ukraine in the Komarno district had to put up with a lot of hardships when they homesteaded here in the early years of the 20TH century. The land was rocky, often marshy, and the winters cold. What was immediately evident to the new immigrants, though, was something they called *komarna,* a Ukrainian phrase that meant "too many mosquitoes."

The Komarno Post Office opened in 1907. Today, a huge statue of a mosquito greets visitors on their way into the community.

La Broquerie

Settlement approximately 15 kilometers east of Steinbach on Highway 52

Settlers first came into the countryside around La Broquerie in the late 1870s. The community was named in 1881 when a post office opened. Joseph de la Broquerie was Archbishop Taché's uncle and guardian.

Evidently, Alphonse La Rivière, the member of Manitoba legislature for St. Boniface, suggested the name, in an attempt to please the archbishop, who presumably had suggested the name to him. The Rural Municipality of La Broquerie also took the name when established in 1883.

Lac Brochet

Settlement approximately 200 kilometers north of Lynn Lake

Lac Brochet is a comparatively new community in Manitoba's far north. Beginning in about 1970 a number Chipewyan people from Brochet moved about seventy-five kilometers farther north. The settlement takes its name from the nearby lake, which is French for "Pike Lake." The Northlands First Nation was established here in 1987.

Lac du Bonnet

Town approximately 80 kilometers northeast of Winnipeg on Highway 11

The North West Company established Lac du Bonnet House on the Winnipeg River about 1800. They chose the name because of the bonnet-like shape of the nearby lake. After the North West Company merged with the Hudson's Bay Company in 1821 a post continued in the same location, but was usually called Indian Cap Fort.

The town was established about 1900 as a rail point and post office, although initially the two were about eight kilometers apart. Walter Wardop, an early storeowner and the town's first postmaster, chose the name at that time.

Ladywood

Settlement approximately 35 kilometers east of Selkirk on Highway 12

The settlement of Ladywood and the local school district were named for a local storekeeper whose last name was Wood. She was instrumental in establishing a school in the area and, in tribute, the community honored this lady Wood by attaching her name to the school. When the post office opened in 1905 it took the name of the school district.

Lake Francis

Settlement approximately 50 kilometers northwest of Winnipeg on Highway 6

The lake nearby this settlement was perhaps named by William Wagner, a provincial land surveyor who later became a member of the Manitoba legislature. Wagner surveyed the southern shore of Lake Manitoba. Lake Francis is a marshy body of water so close to the Lake Manitoba shore it's almost as if it has spilled out of the bigger lake.

According to the most common theory, Wagner named the lake after his infant son, Francis. But there's some evidence the name was already used locally when Wagner arrived and it's possible he merely noted a name that was already in common use. Some apparent early names for the lake, Lac Francois and St. Francis Lake, lend credence to this theory. Another early post office in the area was listed as St. Francis Station. The first post office using the name Lake Francis opened in 1881.

Lakeland

Settlement approximately 50 kilometers northwest of Portage la Prairie near Highway 50

Henry Youle Hind noted this spot in 1858 with the name "Awaki's Place," but he did not provide an explanation. Hind was in the west leading an expedition to explore the region's potential for agricultural and mineral development at the time and he probably encountered someone named Awaki living in the area.

The name Lakeland probably came about because of nearby Lake Manitoba. A post office opened here using the name in 1888.

Lamprey

Rail point approximately 50 kilometers south of Churchill on the Hudson Bay line

Lamprey began as a railway stop in 1929. Evidently, the railroad intended to use the name Munk, after the Danish explorer James Munk, for the station here, but discovered they had already used it somewhere else on the line.

Munk was commander of two ships caught by winter ice on the great northern bay sooner than he expected. He spent the season near the mouth of the Churchill River in 1619. Before spring most of his men had died of what may have been scurvy.

Only Munk and two others remained alive to sail the smaller of his two ships, the *Lamprenen*, back to Denmark the following summer. When the railroad couldn't use the name Munk for the stop here they substituted an anglicized version of the name of the ship.

Landmark

Settlement approximately 35 kilometers southeast of Winnipeg on Provincial Road 206

When the post office opened in Landmark in 1923 the community was called Prairie Rose. Postal authorities in Ottawa, however, substituted the name Landmark for the community's choice. No reason was given for the name change. Since then the settlement has gone by several names, including Prairie Rose, Linden and Landmark, but the latter name appears to have won out, both officially and in general usage.

Langruth

Settlement approximately 55 kilometers northwest of Portage la Prairie on Highway 50

G. W. Langdon and his wife Ruth Langdon owned the land that became the Langruth townsite when the Canadian Northern Railway arrived in 1911. Apparently Mr. Langdon was known as "Lang" and Mrs. Langdon as "Ruth." So the town became Langruth.

La Perouse

Rail point approximately 60 kilometers south of Thompson on the Hudson Bay line

La Perouse was the French admiral who captured the English fur post Fort Prince of Wales at the mouth of the Churchill River on Hudson Bay in 1782. The capture of the fort was not a huge military event since La Perouse encountered no opposition from British Commander, Samuel Hearne. Historians generally agree that Hearne's surrender without a fight was probably the prudent response, since the Hudson's Bay chief trader would have been unlikely to mount a successful defense.

Evidently the railroad intended to name the stop here *Mistik,* the Cree word meaning "tree." For unknown reasons, however, it opted for La Perouse instead. La Perouse's full name was Jean François Galaup, Comte de la Perouse.

La Rivière

Settlement approximately 55 kilometers west of Winkler on Highway 3

Ski resort at LaRiviere today. PHOTO BY TED STONE.

The Canadian Pacific arrived in the Pembina Valley here in 1886. A post office opened the following year. If there's any town in Manitoba that deserves the name La Rivière it's this one. The Pembina River has carved a spectacular valley through the surrounding escarpment here, with the town at the bottom. Most people assume the name refers to the stream that cut such a spectacular valley.

But apparently, the name La Rivière doesn't refer to the beauty of its location along the river at all. Both the rail point and post office were named after Alphonse La Rivière, a member of the Manitoba legislature from St. Boniface in the 1880s. La Rivière went on to become a member of parliament and senator.

La Rochelle
Settlement approximately 50 kilometers south of Winnipeg on Highway 59

La Rochelle is only five kilometers north of St. Malo and the first post office to open here, in 1890, took that name. Two years later the name was changed to La Borderie. In 1897 it became La Rochelle. A resident who had been a newspaper editor in La Rochelle, France before moving to Manitoba suggested the name. The post office at La Rochelle closed in 1968.

La Salle
Settlement approximately 10 kilometers southwest of Winnipeg on Provincial Road 330

There are a number of salt springs along the little, muddy river now generally known as the La Salle. Early maps of Manitoba noted the nature of the river with names such as "Dirty River" or *La Sale Rivière*. David Thompson called it the "Salt" or "Bad Water River." Some called it the "Muddy River." The English and French names were apparently translations of aboriginal names for the river.

When the CPR crossed the river here in 1882, instead of *La Sale,* French for "dirty" or "salted," they named the rail point La Salle Station, after Robert Cavalier Sieur de la Salle, the famous French explorer who discovered and explored the Mississippi River from its upper reaches to its mouth in 1682.

At first, the community was called St. Hyacinthe de la Salle because a priest from the College of St. Hyacinthe bought land here to encourage immigration. Later, the name was shortened to La Salle. It's not known if the CPR mistakenly took the name La Salle, thinking it the name of the river, or if someone consciously cleaned up the name. At any rate, once the community became known as La Salle, people began to call the river by the same name.

Some reports indicate that the river was being called La Salle instead of La Sale even before the arrival of the railroad simply because it was easier for the English-speaking population in the area to pronounce.

Lauder

Settlement approximately 100 kilometers southwest of Brandon on Provincial Road 345

Before the Canadian Pacific Railway arrived in 1891 the community here went by the name Grand Bend. It's thought the name came from a bend in the road at a nearby ravine. Grand Bend School District was established in 1889. Two years later the railroad sidetracked the priginal name when it called their new station Lauder after Archdeacon John Strutt Lauder, rector of Christ Church in Ottawa.

Long before the first settlers came to the Grand Bend area, an independent fur trader named Joseph Desjarlais established a trading post on the north bank of the Souris River almost directly north of present day Lauder. Desjarlais's post was no small operation. The fort, built about 1836, was evidently fifty meters wide and almost seventy meters long. It operated successfully for about twenty years, with a workforce of up to seventy-five men. Horses and livestock were kept, and some farming took place to help maintain the post.

Desjarlais operated in opposition to the Hudson's Bay Company. He competed with the larger company for furs, and then sold his goods across the border where he could make more money. For unexplained reasons Fort Desjarlais burned to the ground in 1858 and Desjarlais moved south to build another trading post in American territory. Many of the men who worked for him, however, stayed and established themselves on land in the area, becoming some of southwestern Manitoba's earliest farmers and ranchers.

Laurie River

Settlement approximately 65 kilometers south of Lynn Lake on the Laurie River

The community here, named after the nearby river, is located at a large hydroelectric dam site. The Cree called the river *Muskwawikum,* meaning the bear's spine. Laurie River gets its name from Laurie Lake, where the river begins on the Manitoba-Saskatchewan border. The lake, in turn, received its name from Patrick Laurie, a former publisher of the Battleford Herald in Saskatchewan.

Laurier

Settlement approximately 70 kilometers southeast of Dauphin on Provincial Road 480

Before the railroad came in 1897 the little community here went by the name Fosberry, but railroad officials named their new station Laurier, for Wilfred Laurier, Canada's Prime Minister at the time. Prime Minister Laurier evidently sent the village a note thanking the community, along with money for the local school to buy band instruments. After the money arrived, the name stuck.

Lavinia

Settlement approximately 100 kilometers northwest of Brandon on Provincial Road 355

Lavinia takes its name from an early settler in the area, Lavinia Hoy. Some records indicate Alfred Lief, a local resident and grain buyer, suggested the name and the Canadian Northern Railway applied it to its new station.

Leaf Rapids

Town approximately 220 kilometers northwest of Thompson on Provincial Road 391

Originally established for employees of Ruttan Lake Mine, the town of Leaf Rapids was named after nearby rapids on the Churchill River. The name for the rapids was probably a translation of an aboriginal name. Peter Fidler called the place Weed Portage in 1807.

Lena

Settlement approximately 110 kilometers southeast of Brandon on Highway 18

A Hudson's Bay Company fort named Lena's House operated near here for a short time beginning in 1801. It's unclear exactly where Lena's House was located—it may even have been below the present international boundary—but it operated as an outpost for Brandon House for at least one winter and, perhaps, more.

Independent traders from Montreal were eating into the bigger company's profits. In an attempt to take back some of the trade, John McKay, the factor at Brandon House on the Souris River, had Lena's House built as an outpost on the eastern edge of the Turtle Mountains.

Lena at the U.S. boundary on Highway 18 about 1960. BY PERMISSION OF MANITOBA ARCHIVES, LENA 1.

On Nov. 24, 1801 he appointed Henry Lena to oversee the new post. Lena took along nine men from Brandon House, but within a couple of months the XY Company built a post nearby. Lena complained to McKay that the XY post sat on the road the Assiniboine would need to take from the mountains to Lena's House. There was also concern that Lena's House was vulnerable to attack from Sioux tribes farther south. It's unclear how long Lena's House operated under these unfavorable conditions, but it probably wasn't long.

The Lena Post Office opened 70 years later, and then closed in 1968. The Lena customs point still operates a few kilometers south of the settlement on the international boundary.

Lenswood

Settlement approximately 45 kilometers northeast of Swan River on Provincial Road 268

When World War I started, many of the settlers in this newly established area enlisted in the army and went overseas. When the survivors returned they named the community Lenswood. The name commemorated the Battle of Lens, where several of the area's young men died, and linked the battle to the heavily wooded area where the soldiers had settled.

Letellier

Settlement approximately 50 kilometers south of Winnipeg on Highway 75

This community was originally named Catherine, after local landowner Catherine Wright. The post office opened in 1881 with the address Catherine Station, but not long after the name changed to Letellier. The new name was for Luc Letellier de St. Just, the lieutenant governor of Quebec.

The railroad chose the townsite. The community lies only a short distance west of the Red River, near where Ft. Roseau must have been located. Built in 1832 by La Verendrye's oldest son Jean Baptiste and La Verendrye's trusted lieutenant Christophe Dufrost La Jemeraye, Fort Roseau became the first fur post on the Canadian Prairies.

Between 1732 and 1740, when La Verendrye moved Fort Maurepas from the Red River at present-day Winnipeg to the lower reaches of the Winnipeg River, the route up the Roseau to the Red provided La Verendrye's primary access to his posts in western Canada. After

1740, traders generally followed the more difficult, but faster, Winnipeg River system.

Sign at Lettellier notes the first arrival of fur traders in Western Canada. PHOTO BY TED STONE.

Libau

Settlement approximately 60 kilometers north of Winnipeg on Highway 59

Latvian immigrants named the post office and rail point after a town in Latvia. The post office had originally gone by the name Kreiger, after first postmaster, Julius Kreiger. After Kreiger left the position, in 1906, residents suggested the name be changed to Libau.

Little Grand Rapids

Settlement approximately 260 kilometers northeast of Winnipeg, just north of Atakaki Provincial Park

The Hudson's Bay Company opened a trading post here in the 1840s. The aboriginal people who lived here then called the nearby rapids *Meeseepawistik,* or the "big little-rapids."

The company followed suit, sort of, and called their fur post Little Grand Rapids House. Today, the community, on Fishing Lake, lies at the northern edge of the Little Grand Rapids First Nation.

Lockport

Settlement 15 kilometers north of Winnipeg on Highway 44

Lockport took its name from a lock on the Red River built here in 1902 to enable larger boats to pass the St. Andrews Rapids. The lock opened navigation between Lake Winnipeg and communities upstream on the river, particularly Winnipeg.

Lorette

Settlement approximately 20 kilometers southeast of Winnipeg on Provincial Road 207

Métis settlers began moving to this area in the 1850s. St. Boniface's Bishop Taché apparently named the new community in gratitude to a priest from Notre Dame de Lorette in France. The priest made several large donations to the Manitoba Catholic community, particularly for St. Boniface Cathedral.

Lowe Farm

Settlement approximately 40 kilometers northeast of Winkler on Highway 23

Lowe Farm was named for the nearby farm of John Lowe, a Member of Parliament and one-time the deputy minister of agriculture in Ontario. Lowe's farm included more than 15,000 acres of land. It was one of only a few of the so-called "Bonanza farms" established north of the American border in the last two decades of the nineteenth century.

Lowe began buying land in this area in the late 1870s and early 1880s, at Lowe Farm and other areas nearby, including town lots in Emerson and Morris. He also owned part of the townsite for Pembina Crossing. But none of his real estate holdings in Manitoba, where heavy steam tractors tended to get bogged down in the Red River gumbo, were ever profitable.

Lowe made a few dollars profit on his farm in 1882 and a little over a thousand dollars in 1884, but 1886 and 1887 were drought years on the

Prairies and Lowe couldn't put together the money to pay the interest on his loan. After 1889, when the Northern Pacific arrived, the former deputy-minister of agriculture began selling off parts of his property to keep the farm afloat. He refinanced a couple of times, but by 1890 he'd lost $10,000 on his farming operations and by 1895 he owed something in the neighborhood of $150,000 on his property, more than twice his original debt.

In one last bid at refinancing the property Lowe's land was transferred to his creditor in 1898, with a five-year provision for paying off the loan or losing the property permanently. Lowe lost the property. By that time, the Municipality of Morris had begun listing Lowe Farm, with the new residents who had bought property there, as a separate village. A post office opened there in 1901.

Luke

Rail point approximately 310 kilometers southeast of Churchill on the Hudson Bay line

Luke was named in 1928 after Luke Clemens, one of the more colorful characters of the north. Clemens was a mail carrier and fur trader who traveled the north and claimed to be a relative of the American author Mark Twain. Twain's real name, of course, was Samuel Clemens, so perhaps Luke was telling the truth.

Lundar

Settlement approximately 85 kilometers northwest of Winnipeg on Highway 6

Lundar was a mistake. The post office here opened in 1890, named Lundi by postmaster Henrick Johnson. *Lundi* is the Icelandic word for "meadow" and was the name of the farm where Johnson's wife was raised in Iceland.

Somehow, when the name Lundi got to Ottawa, however, postal officials mixed things up. When the postal guide came out, Lundi had become Lundar. As mistakes in Ottawa go, the name switch wasn't too serious, so nobody complained and the new name stuck.

Lyddal

Rail point approximately 80 kilometers southwest of Thompson on the Hudson Bay line

At first, the Canadian National Railways planned to use the Cree word for "moon" to name this whistle stop near Halfway Lake. But then officials opted for Lyddal instead. William Lyddal had been a Hudson's Bay Company Governor of Rupert's Land in the seventeenth century.

Lyleton

Settlement approximately 160 kilometers southwest of Brandon on Provincial Road 261

Lyleton took its name from one of area's first settlers, and its first postmaster, Andrew Lyle. Lyle homesteaded near here in 1881 and he operated the post office out of his home. In 1900, the post office moved to another farm, near where the Canadian Pacific extended its line in 1902, but the name stuck.

Lynn Lake

Town approximately 315 kilometers northwest of Thompson on Provincial Road 391

The mining town of Lynn Lake was named after the nearby lake. The lake was named after Lynn Smith, the chief engineer of Sherritt-Gordon Mines. Many of the town's first buildings were originally built more than two hundred kilometers south in Sherridon. When the Sherridon mine closed most of the community there was trucked piece by piece and building by building over the frozen muskeg north to the new mine at Lynn Lake. The move took three winters to complete.

Macdonald

Settlement approximately 10 kilometers northwest of Portage la Prairie on Highway 16

Situated on Willow Bend Creek, McDonald grew up around the creek's crossing point on the Carlton Trail. Settlers here called their community

A Miner underground at Lynn Lake in 1950. BY PERMISSION OF MANITOBA ARCHIVES, LYNN LAKE 5, N17221.

Drumconner in the early 1880s. It had been named after a village in Ireland. When the post office opened in 1894, it, too, was called Drumconner. But when the Canadian Pacific Railway line came through a few years later, railroad officials called the new station "Macdonald," after Canada's first prime minister, John A. Macdonald.

Sure enough, people began calling the place Macdonald. With a post office going by one name and a community going by another name, there was bound to be confusion and by 1895 residents of Macdonald were tired of it. They petitioned the postal department in Ottawa to change the name of the local post office to Macdonald.

MacGregor

Village approximately 35 kilometers west of Portage la Prairie on Highway 1

MacGregor was one of the six stops along the new Canadian Pacific Railway named by John Douglas Sutherland Campbell, the Marquis of Lorne, the Governor General of Canada. The marquis was traveling in

Canada on a railroad tour with his wife, Princess Louise Caroline Alberta, when CPR officials told him he could name half a dozen unchristened stops between Portage la Prairie and Brandon.

Rev. James Macgregor was the vicar of St. Cuthburts Church in Edinburgh, Scotland, and a member of the Governor General's entourage at the time. The governor general named another rail point, Douglas, after himself. Later, the Province of Alberta and Lake Louise would be named for the princess.

Mafeking

Settlement approximately 70 kilometers north of Swan River on Highway 10

Mafeking was named after a town in South Africa during the construction of the Canadian Northern Railway. While the railroad was under construction, the British endured a siege of the South African town of Mafeking for 217 days during the Boer War. Colonel Robert Baden-Powell and 1,200 men successfully defended the town against a Boer force of 9,000 men.

Makaroff

Settlement approximately 125 kilometers west of Dauphin on Provincial Road 484

The Canadian Northern Railway created the rail point of McLean Siding here in 1900. The community changed its name in 1904 after the news came in that the Russian Admiral Serge O. Makaroff had gone down with his ship, the Petropavlovsk, during the Russo-Japanese War.

Apparently, the *Petropavlovsk* was torpedoed accidentally by another Russian cruiser.

Makinak

Settlement approximately 90 kilometers north of Neepawa on Provincial Road 480 and Provincial Road 582

The only thing known for sure about the origin of the name for Makinak is that it is from an aboriginal word. In *Place-Names of Manitoba* Douglas said the name is from the Cree word *mikinac,* meaning "turtle." As evidence, he cites the Turtle River a few kilometers east of the community.

But another possible explanation could be the Ojibwa word, *mikin-ak,* or "good trail." The authors of *Ghost Towns of Manitoba* promote this veriosn because of a gravel ridge that goes through the townsite. This ridge was once part of an aboriginal trail that crossed the region.

It should also be noted that the Ojibwa word for turtle is also *mikinak.*

Main Street in early Makinak. By permission of Manitoba Archives, Makinak 3, N5140/N147.

Mallard
Settlement approximately 150 kilometers northeast of Dauphin at the south end of Waterhen Lake

The settlement probably took its name from a nearby lake. The lake was named after the duck species common in the area and throughout much of North America.

Manigotagan
Settlement approximately 200 kilometers northeast of Winnipeg on the east side of Lake Winnipeg just off Provincial Road 304

Once long ago a Cree chief was standing near what is now Manigotagan when he heard a moose call in the distance. The sound of the moose was strange to the chief's ears. It sounded as if there was something wrong with the animal's throat. After that people began calling the river Manigotagan, or Bad Throat River. The community later took the name of the river. The first post office opened here in 1890.

Manitou

Town approximately 45 kilometers west of Winkler on Highway 3

Manitou took its name from an aboriginal word that means a spirit or god. It's also an abbreviated version of the name of the province. The townsite was first planned to be a short distance to the north in anticipation of the coming of the railroad and the original town was to be called, rather presumptuously, Manitoba City.

Manitoba City's short life came about after a Canadian Pacific Railway contractor named John Stewart discovered the location of the future rail point. Stewart bought a half-section of land there and drew up plans. Soon, he had sold more than 40 lots in his town and new buildings appeared.

Everything appeared to be unfolding as it should. Then in the spring of 1882, with the approaching railroad coming into sight, investors purchased a half-section of land next to Stewart's and also began laying out a townsite. Unfortunately for Stewart one of competing site's new owners was H. A. Jukes, a lawyer from Toronto who worked for the CPR engineering department.

Pioneer home at Manitau used today for tourist information center. Photo by Ted Stone.

As railroad construction moved closer, instead of swinging north through Stewart's property it angled to the more southerly route through the land owned by the Jukes group. The railroad built its new station here.

Jukes had apparently sold the CPR every other available lot in his town site for one dollar each. A similar deal had been worked out with the Ogilvie Grain and Milling Company to build an elevator there.

Grateful to railroad officials, Jukes asked CPR land commissioner Andrew McTavish to give the new town site a name. McTavish decided Manitoba City was too long, so he shortened it to Manito. The spelling later changed to conform to the aboriginal word.

Manson
Settlement approximately 175 kilometers west of Brandon on Highway 41

Established as a rail point on a Canadian Pacific Railway branch line in 1904, Manson was named for the company's assistant to the vice president, James Manson.

Marchand
Settlement approximately 20 kilometers east of Steinbach on Provincial Road 210

The Canadian Northern Railway established Marchand as a rail point in 1901 and named it for a well-known hunter in the area.

Margaret
Settlement approximately 65 kilometers south of Brandon on Highway 23

In 1891, settlers at Margaret wanted to name their new town Greenfield, a name used for the local country school here for a number of years. But when the post office pointed out that another community by that name already existed, local residents put the matter to a vote.

After the counting was done, the town had decided to name itself after Margaret Nixon, the wife of the local postmaster. When the railroad arrived it gave the place the name Margaret Siding, but that too soon changed to Margaret.

Mariapolis

Settlement approximately 125 kilometers south of Brandon on Highway 23

When the French-speaking Belgium settlers around today's Mariapolis got together to give their new town a name in 1891 they decided on Ste. Marie. But officials from the railroad rejected the name, saying they "already had enough saints." Since they couldn't get the name Ste. Marie the residents opted for Mariapolis, denoting Marie's city.

Marquette

Settlement approximately 40 kilometers northwest of Winnipeg on Provincial Road 221

The Canadian Pacific Railway named Marquette for Father Jacques Marquette, the Jesuit missionary who explored the Mississippi River with Louis Jolliet in the 1670s. Initially Marquette Station in 1882, the CPR later shortened the name to Marquette. There was already a post office called Bai St. Paul here when the railroad arrived, but the name Marquette took root and ten years later, in 1891, the post office name changed to Marquette as well.

Matago

Rail point approximately 55 kilometers southeast of Thompson on the Hudson Bay line

Matago is a Cree word that means limestone, a mineral common in the area. The rail point was named in 1928.

Mather

Settlement approximately 105 kilometers west of Winkler on Highway 3

Keewatin Flour Mills considered erecting a flourmill at Mather in 1897, when the Canadian Pacific Railway arrived here. A company official even promised residents of the new rail point that he would build a mill if they named the town after him. The next year people saw to it that the new post office was named Mather, after the company official, but in the years to come no flourmill materialized. The promise went unfulfilled, but the name of the town remained the same.

Matheson Island

Settlement approximately 220 kilometers north of Winnipeg on Matheson Island in Lake Winnipeg

Matheson Island used to be called Snake Island, but people who lived in the community didn't like having an address with that name. They opted to name their island after the lighthouse keeper, whose beacon on nearby Black Bear Island they could see. The name change became official in 1903, but a local post office didn't open until 1926.

Home on the lake shore at Matheson Island about 1964. By permission of Manitoba Archives, Matheson Island 3.

Matlock

Settlement approximately 60 kilometers north of Winnipeg on Provincial Road 232

When they established a rail point here in 1910, railroad officials named Matlock after a town in England. Today, Matlock is part of the larger community of Dunnottar, an amalgamated village that also includes the resort communities of Ponemah and Whytewold. Dunnottar was named by Alex Melville in the early part of the 20th century after a castle in Scotland.

McArthur Falls

Settlement approximately 95 kilometers northeast of Winnipeg on Highway 11

McArthur Falls takes its name from the nearby falls in the Winnipeg River. Ironically, the hydroelectricity-generating dam built here covered the falls that provided the name. Once the plant was in operation McArthur Falls disappeared under the higher water caused by the dam. Even more ironically, the falls were named after J. D. McArthur, a contractor involved in the construction of the dam.

McAuley

Settlement approximately 140 kilometers northwest of Brandon on Highway 41

George W. McAuley was apparently an early settler in the area who happened to be the landowner of the site the Canadian Pacific chose for a rail point in 1904. McAuley also became the first postmaster for the new town that bore his name.

McConnell

Settlement approximately 100 kilometers northwest of Brandon just off Provincial Road 355

A.D. McConnell was an early settler in this area. After being elected to the Canadian parliament, McConnell lobbied for a branch line of the railroad to the area. Once the railroad was built, Canadian Northern Railway officials named the new station McConnell.

Until that time the community here was known as Viola Dale, after Mable Viola, the daughter of an early settler. After the railroad renamed the town the local post office followed the railroad's lead and changed its name from Viola Dale to McConnell.

McCreary

Village approximately 160 kilometers northwest of Portage la Prairie on Highway 5

The Canadian Northern Railway named McCreary in 1898, after initially calling the town Elliot. Mr. Elliot was a prominent Winnipeg lawyer. The post office already used the name somewhere else, so the railroad renamed its stop here after Elliot's law partner, William F. McCreary.

A Winnipeg alderman, then elected mayor in 1897, McCreary was elected to Parliament in 1900. He had also been a commissioner of immigration, encouraging Western immigration, particularly to Manitoba.

M'Clintock

Rail point approximately 110 kilometers south of Churchill on the Hudson Bay line

Captain Francis Leopold M'Clintock was an arctic explorer who joined the Royal Navy in 1831. In 1848 M'Clintock led his first arctic expedition as the captain of the *Intrepid*. Then, in 1855, Lady Franklin commissioned him to search for her husband. The arctic explorer John Franklin disappeared in the Canadian Arctic while searching for a Northwest Passage by sea across the top of the continent.

M'Clintock set out in the *Fox* and eventually found graves, belongings and the remains of the ships used on Franklin's expedition. He also discovered a cairn in which he found a written record confirming Franklin's death.

M'Clintock's voyage proved that the Franklin expedition had nearly crossed the Canadian Arctic from East to West. After his return to England M'Clintock published a successful account of his findings, ran as Tory candidate in Drogheda 1868, and was promoted to the rank of

Vice-Admiral. Today, in addition to his name at this rail point on the Manitoba map, there is a M'Clintock Channel in the Arctic Ocean. The channel divides Victoria Island from Prince of Wales Island, leading into Franklin Strait.

McMunn

Settlement approximately 95 kilometers east of Winnipeg just off Highway 1

The community here was established as a rail point on the Greater Winnipeg Water District Railway. When the post office opened in 1918 it took the name of its new postmaster, James A. McMunn. McMunn had settled in the district in 1914 and was also a justice of the peace. The post office closed in 1970.

McTavish

Settlement approximately 40 kilometers south of Winnipeg on Provincial Road 330

The Canadian Pacific Railway established McTavish as a rail point on a branch line in 1895. J. H. McTavish, the railroad's chief land commissioner, had accepted a petition from local farmers requesting his help to get a railroad to the community. When their petition was granted the farmers suggested the name McTavish for the new station.

McTavish was an accountant with the Hudson's Bay Company and a member of the Manitoba legislature before joining the CPR.

McVeigh

Rail point approximately 20 kilometers south of Lynn Lake on the Sherritt–Lynn Lake line

Prospector Austin McVeigh discovered the Lynn Lake mineral deposits that led to the development of several mines in the area. The station here was named after him in 1953. A lake in this area was also named after McVeigh.

Meadow Portage

Settlement approximately 110 kilometers northeast of Dauphin on Provincial Road 276

The community of Meadow Portage is named after the portage here between lakes Manitoba and Winnipegosis. The name describes the local landscape. The passage between the lakes here has been used for hundreds, and perhaps thousands, of years. The earliest historical reference to the portage goes back to 1809 when Peter Fidler noted it as the "barren ground portage."

Thompson called it the "Meadow Portage" on his maps of the area four years later. J. B. Tyrrell called it the "meadow carrying place." All of the names used were undoubtedly translations of the name aboriginal people in the area had been using for generations.

Medard

Rail point approximately 100 kilometers southwest of Thompson on the Hudson Bay railway

Canadian National Railways named Medard after the French fur trader and explorer Médard Chouart Des Groseilliers. Along with his brother-in-law Pierre-Espirit Radisson, Des Groseilliers explored some of the great unknown beyond Lake Superior in the mid-1600s. Drawing mostly from geography learned from the aboriginal people of the region, the two men came to the conclusion that Hudson Bay offered a shortcut for Europeans to the fur territory that lay waiting to be discovered in the heartland of North America.

Ignored by their fellow countrymen in France, Des Groseilliers and Radisson convinced the English of the merits of organizing a fur-trading enterprise through Hudson Bay. The result was the establishment of the Hudson's Bay Company in 1669.

Médard Chouart Des Groseilliers was born in France, but came to Canada in the 1640s. Having established himself as a fur trader, Groseillier invited his young brother-in-law along on a trade expedition north of Lake Superior in 1660. Business in the region was good, but when the pair returned to Quebec with the idea of trading through Hudson Bay they were jailed by authorities for trading without a license. The two men decided to deal with the English, or perhaps the Dutch, instead.

After their release from prison they went first to New England and then to London to promote the notion of trading through the great bay in the north. In succeeding years, after the Hudson's Bay Company was established, the two men worked alternately for competing English or French interests.

Medika

Settlement approximately 85 kilometers east of Winnipeg on Provincial Road 507

The settlement here was originally Hadashville, after the first post-master and early settler Charles Hadash. When news got out that the railroad tracks for the proposed Greater Winnipeg Water District Railway would be a few kilometers south, Hadash moved to a new spot on the rail line. That also became known as Hadashville. The set-tlers who remained named the original community Medika. They took the name from a town in the Ukraine from where many of the people in the area originated.

Medora

Settlement approximately 120 kilometers southwest of Brandon on Highway 3

When the first surveyors came through this part of the province they stayed for a time while they did their work at the home of Medora May Campbell. Campbell had moved west with her husband from Ontario in 1872. In her honor, the surveyors used the name Medora for this region and the local school district adopted it when it was organized. A couple of early post offices in the area also adopted the name. When the railroad came through they initially used the name Medora Station, as did the local post office. Later the name was shortened.

Meleb

Settlement approximately 80 kilometers north of Winnipeg on Highway 7

When the Canadian Pacific Railway arrived here in 1911 two local set-tlers, one named Melnik and one named Leibman, donated a portion of their land for the station. In recognition of their donation the railroad named the station after them, using three letters from the initial part of their last names.

Melita

Town approximately 220 kilometers southwest of Brandon on Highway 3

Settlers here first wanted to name their town Manchester, after the city in England. Postal officials in Ottawa, however, rejected it, apparently because it was already in use somewhere else. Ottawa sent back a list of possible names for the community to use and local people decided residents would vote on the town's new name after church the following Sunday.

That weekend, though, the Sunday school superintendent's lesson was about Melita, the island, now called Malta, where the apostle Paul was shipwrecked. Since the residents didn't care for any of the names on Ottawa's list, the Sunday school superintendent suggested Melita.

The community agreed, and so did postal officials.

Menisino

Settlement approximately 70 kilometers southeast of Steinbach on Provincial Road 201

A legend has it that the name Menisino is from aboriginal words that mean a place with crooked, sandy roads. Despite the legend, however, no records survive to document how the name was determined. It's also unclear what aboriginal words could lead to that name.

A simpler, and more likely, explanation is that the name derives from one aboriginal word, not several. In the Ojibwa language *minisino* means "warrior," or "hero." Either would be a fitting name for a new town.

A Department of Interior map first noted Menisino in 1907.

A log Pentecostal church built about 1931 at Menisino in a photograph taken in 1964. By permission of Manitoba Archives, Menisino Corner – churches i.

Menzie

*Settlement approximately 120 kilometers northwest of Brandon on
Highway 45*

Menzie was apparently named after an early settler in the area, John E.
Menzies. A School district also used the name without dropping the "s."

Miami

Settlement approximately 25 kilometers northwest of Morden on Highway 23

The postal department in Ottawa assigned the name Miami to the community, but not because the climate is akin to Miami, Florida. The name
comes from the Miami, a North American First Nation of the
Algonquian family, indigenous to southern Michigan, Indiana and Ohio.

The tribe is now extinct. The name may have meant "mother" in the Miami language.

Middlebro

Settlement approximately 120 kilometers southeast of Steinbach on Highway 12

It has been suggested that Middlebro is named after the village of Middlebrough, England, but the community here appears to have been first given the name Middleboro about 1920.

The change in spelling from "-boro" to "bro" didn't come about because of any affinity to the English town. The change was a mistake. The rail point was misspelled as Middlebro on a Department of Interior map about 1922 and the altered spelling stuck.

The residents were probably so happy to have the new name they didn't care how anyone spelled it. For the initial years of its life the community had been called Gravel Pit, because gravel used during the construction of the railroad was stored here. For town promoters, after being called Gravel Pit, the spelling of Middlebro probably seemed inconsequential.

Millwood

Settlement approximately 180 kilometers northwest of Brandon on Provincial Road 579

Supposedly the first business in Millwood before the railroad arrived was a sawmill in a heavily wooded area here. Later, the sawmill owners built a dam and gristmill.

Another, less likely explanation claims that a local settler, Henry Millwood Mould, lobbied an influential railway worker until he was allowed to name the new rail point.

Today, Millwood has all but vanished. The authors of *Ghost Towns of Manitoba* trace its demise to one of the original mill operators, a man named Mitchell. According to this story Mitchell got into an argument with the Superintendent of the Manitoba and Northwestern Railway during a game of cricket. Afterwards, the railroad superintendent cancelled the already-planned spur line into the new town. Supposedly, the railroad boss remarked that he would deny the town its railroad and turn it into a sheep trail instead.

Milner Ridge

Settlement approximately 75 kilometers northeast of Winnipeg on Provincial Road 214

In 1901, during the Boer War in South Africa, the Canadian Northern Railway named its station here after Viscount Milner. Milner was the British governor of South Africa at the time.

A few years later a post office opened as Cedarkine, but in 1929 the community added the CPR name to a prominent local land feature and officially became Milner Ridge. The village post office closed in 1964.

Miniota

Settlement approximately 100 kilometers northwest of Brandon on Highway 83

The name Miniota originally applied to the vicinity around the present town while it was still part of the North West Territories. One of the original surveyors in the region, a man named Bulger, was the first to note the name.

After surveying the area Bulger told W. A. Doyle that he'd had the best drink of water he'd ever tasted from a spring here. Together, Doyle and Bulger decided on the name Miniota for the area. The name comes from two Sioux words *minni* and *ota*. Together the words mean "plenty of water," or "several watering places."

Doyle went on to become the first warden of Miniota County. After that, the name was applied to the municipality and then to the community when the Canadian Pacific Railway arrived.

Minitonas

Town approximately 15 kilometers east of Swan River on Highway 10

Minitonas was named after nearby Minitonas Hill. The Saulteaux named the hill for the "little spirit" or "little spirits" who evidently live there. Some references call the translation "isolated hill," because it is some distance south of the more prominent hills of the Duck Mountains.

Minnedosa

Town approximately 45 kilometers north of Brandon on Highway 10

Several names were in use in this area before the name Minnedosa was chosen for the community. For a time it was known as Fourth Crossing, because it was the fourth major river crossing on the Edmonton Trail. Then it changed to Tanner's Crossing, because an early Métis settler named John Tanner provided a ferry across the Little Saskatchewan River here and later established a store. The first post office was known as Little Saskatchewan.

Tanner, who was also the area's first postmaster, and Joseph Armitage, another early settler, gave the community the name Minnedosa. It comes from the Sioux words for the crossing, which means "rushing water." The Little Saskatchewan was named from Cree words for "rapid river," so naming the community Minnedosa from the Sioux language was another way to note the fast-flowing river nearby.

Apparently Armitage particularly liked the name because Minnie was his wife's name. When his daughter was born in 1880—the first white child born in the area—he named her Minnedosa, too.

Tanner was the grandson of John Tanner, at one time known throughout North America after being taken captive near his home in Kentucky. Tanner was abducted by the Shawnee there in 1789, when he was nine years old. The Shawnee sold the child to a band of Ojibwa and the boy was adopted by a woman named Netnowka. Tanner learned the ways of the Ojibwa, around Sault Ste. Marie, but as he grew up the band moved steadily west, so that by the early part of the nineteenth century he was already occasionally living on the Manitoba prairie.

By the time the Selkirk settlers arrived in Manitoba, Tanner (who was called Falcon, by his Ojibwa family) had a reputation for his prowess as a warrior against the tribe's traditional enemy, the Sioux. Active in Métis politics, Tanner's son James was murdered near High Bluff, while campaigning during Manitoba's first election after becoming a province of Canada. The younger John Tanner, after returning from service in the Union Army during the American Civil War, had already established his ferry at Minnedosa at the time of his father's death.

Minto

Settlement approximately 40 kilometers south of Brandon on Highway 10

Minto was named in 1899 after the governor general of Canada at that time, the 4TH Earl of Minto, Sir Gilbert Elliot. The earl served under General Middleton during the 1885 Riel Rebellion, so unlike most early governors general he actually had a connection to Canada.

The Canadian Northern Railway established Minto in 1898. Local legend has it that an intense animosity developed between merchants on the north side of town with those on the south side. According to the story, Conservatives were on the north side of the street and Liberals were on the south side. At one point, tensions ran so high during the early part of the twentieth century that a barbed wire fence was put up briefly to separate the two sides.

Molson

Settlement approximately 70 kilometers northeast of Winnipeg off Highway 44 south of Seddons Corner

This Canadian Pacific Railway stop was originally called Monmouth. Later, the name changed to Molson, after a member of the prominent Molson family and one of the railroad's directors.

Moore Park

Settlement approximately 20 kilometers northeast of Brandon just off Provincial Road 353

The name Moore Park came about when the Canadian Pacific Railway arrived and the son of an early homesteader, who lived in Toronto, donated five acres of land to be used as a park. The townsite chosen by the CPR was on land once homesteaded by Colonel W. P. Moore. The younger Moore donated land for the park and sold lots at the new rail stop.

But even with a park the town failed to flourish. The post office closed at Moore Park in 1970 and, with the further decline of the town, the park was even abandoned after the railroad branch line was torn up in 1979.

Moosehorn

Settlement approximately 180 kilometers northwest of Winnipeg on Highway 6

Canadian Northern Railway officials named Moosehorn when the CNR branch line reached the area in 1911. According to a local legend railroad crews deduced that a great many moose and elk lived in the area because of the number of antlers they found nearby. Moose antlers were particularly numerous. Presumably one particular set of moose horns stood out enough to prompt railroad officials to name the new town after it.

Moose Lake

Settlement approximately 100 kilometers east of The Pas at the end of Provincial Road 384 on South Moose Lake

Deriving the name from the nearby lake, settlements and trading posts here have been known as Moose Lake, or some form of similar designation, since the first French traders reached the area in the mid-1700s. The continuity of the name suggests its use in aboriginal languages long before Europeans arrived. The Cree call the lake *Mosakahiken* and the Mosakahiken Cree Nation land surrounds Moose Lake today.

The word moose, itself, was derived from the Cree, or perhaps some other Algonquian language.

Moose Lake in 1925. By permission of Manitoba Archives. Campbell, John A. Collection, 115, Moose Lake, c. 1925.

Morden

Town approximately 10 kilometers from Winkler on Highway 3

Morden developed from two former settlements, Mountain City and Nelson, when the railroad arrived in 1882. At first the new rail point was called Cheval, after the nearby creek Le Cheval Mort, or Deadhorse Creek, that flows nearby. The name changed to Morden a year later.

Alvey Morden was an early settler who had homesteaded land where the railroad established its station. Many residents of Nelson and Mountain City moved their respective communities, buildings included, to the railroad at Morden about this time.

A train of covered wagons at Dead Horse Creek near Morden on the Boundary Commission Trail in 1872. BY PERMISSION OF MANITOBA ARCHIVES, BOUNDARY COMMISSION (1872 – 1874) 108, N11953.

Morris

Town approximately 50 kilometers south of Winnipeg on Highway 75

The original settlement at what is now Morris was initially called Scratching River, after the nearby Scratching River. The name is said to have originated after Lord Selkirk traveled through the area on his way to the Red River Settlement. Various prickly plants scratched human beings and horses passing by the river on the journey north.

However, the name predates Selkirk's visit by some time. References noted the stream as Rivière aux Gratias (River of Burrs) long before the Selkirk settlement. David Thompson called the river Burr Brook in 1798.

Both Scratching Rivers, the new town and the stream, were renamed Morris in 1882. The new names honored Alexander Morris, the province's first chief justice and the Lieutenant Governor of both Manitoba and the North West Territories from 1872 to 1877.

In its early days Morris, or Scratching River, was a frequent stopping point on one of the trails between Winnipeg and St. Paul, Minnesota.

A mural on side of the museum at Morris depicts early history of the area. Photo by Ted Stone.

Mountain Road

Settlement approximately 90 kilometers northwest of Portage la Prairie on Provincial Road 357

The name is descriptive. To get to this spot, just south of Riding Mountain National Park, you have to drive up a steep mountain road.

Mulvihill

Settlement approximately 135 kilometers north of Winnipeg on Highway 6

A post office opened in 1912 as Mona, but postal officials changed the name to Mulvihill the following year. Officials with the Canadian Northern Railway had named the rail stop here Mulvihill, so the post office followed suit.

The new name recognized a Roman Catholic brother, J.M.J. Mulvihill, who worked with Father Joseph Charles Camper to establish a mission at St. Laurent. Camper is the next stop to the north on the rail line.

Munk

Rail point approximately 115 kilometers northeast of Thompson on the Hudson Bay Railway

The rail point here commemorates the Danish explorer Jens Munk, who sailed into Hudson Bay in 1619. Unfortunately for Munk, and even more unfortunately for most of his crew, an early freeze trapped his two ships and forced Munk and his men to spend the following winter at the mouth of the Churchill River.

Before spring, all of Munk's crew with the exception of two seamen died. Munk had come to the bay with 63 men in two ships. As the winter bore on there was no doubt some of the men suffered from scurvy, but historians have questioned whether that disease is solely responsible for so many deaths. The men started the winter with lots of wild berries, ptarmigan and beluga whale meat. During the winter they also had polar bears to eat.

According to Munk's journal, however, he preferred to cook his meat until it was well done, while his crew preferred to eat theirs cooked rare. Some have suggested that under-cooking the polar bear meat left crewmembers vulnerable to the parasites that cause trichinosis.

By spring, Munk and the two crewmembers who survived were so weak they were no longer able to dispose of the bodies of the men who had perished. Rather miraculously, the three men were able to sail home to Europe in the smaller of the two ships. For years afterwards what we call the Churchill River today was known as Munk's River.

Myrtle

Settlement approximately 25 kilometers northeast of Winkler on Highway 23

An early settler, Alexander McDonald, owned the townsite. He named it Myrtle after his young niece, Myrtle Berry, in 1889 when Canadian Northern Railway established a stop here. Young Myrtle lived in Ontario at the time, but later moved with her family to the new town.

Napinka

Settlement approximately 210 kilometers southwest of Brandon on Provincial Road 452

The name Napinka is taken from the Sioux word for "two," "equal to two" or "double." The significance of the name to the community is no longer known, but its use here dates to almost immediately after settlers arrived in the area in the early 1880s.

Narcisse

Settlement approximately 90 kilometers northwest of Winnipeg on Highway 17

The rail point here was named in 1914 after Narcisse Leven, the president of the Jewish Colonization Association. Bender Hamlet, the first Jewish farm colony in Manitoba, had been founded a short distance away in 1903.

The founding of that settlement was largely the result of work by Jacob Bender who first saw the heavily wooded area as suitable for Jewish immigrants. Bender obtained a quarter section of land for a townsite in the Manitoba Interlake from the Canadian government. He then went to Europe to recruit immigrants for his proposed settlement.

In the end, nineteen families came to Bender Hamlet, mostly from England and Russia, but a few families came from Winnipeg and one family came from Boston. The community was based on a European model, with the initial quarter section divided into long individual lots for each family, who, in turn, farmed nearby quarter sections obtained under the Homestead Act. There was also a lot set aside for a school and synagogue.

But the rocky land, although suitable for livestock, for the most part could not support cereal crops. And most of the new immigrants had no experience in agriculture. Combined with the harsh Manitoba climate these factors insured the settlers faced more than the usual number of obstacles to making a living on the land. Despite the situation, however, Bender Hamlet got underway successfully and was firmly established by the time the railroad arrived in 1914.

Unfortunately, however, the railroad passed a short distance from the settlement site. Even if it could survive, that meant Bender would never become a commercial center.

By the time the railroad arrived World War I was already underway in Europe and prices for cattle and other agricultural commodities were high. The settlement, despite its distance from the rail line, began to thrive. There was, after all, a nearby railroad and a new town called Narcisse, and cattle were bringing the best prices anyone could remember.

With the end of the war came several years of bad weather and depressed cattle prices, which put an end to the Jewish colony. Family after family left the farm to start businesses in nearby towns or to find work in Winnipeg. By the end of the 1920s, the old settlement at Bender Hamlet had been abandoned.

Today, Narcisse is known primarily for the migration of garter snakes every fall to the limestone caves, crevices and sink holes that helped make the land so unattractive to agricultural settlement. The snakes come to the area to hibernate in underground caves through the winter. Each spring tens of thousands of them emerge in the Narcisse Wildlife Management Area. The site boasts the largest concentration of red-sided garter snakes in the world.

Bender Hamlet near today's Narcisse. By permission of Manitoba Archives, Bender Hamlet 2, N9615.

National Mills

Settlement approximately 190 kilometers south of The Pas on Highway 77

National Mills was established as a rail point on the Canadian Northern Railway. It was named after nearby lumber mills at the request of the National Timber and Fencing Company.

Neelin

Settlement approximately 120 kilometers southeast of Brandon on Highway 5

The Canadian Northern Railway built a branch line here and laid out a townsite on land homesteaded by Joseph Neelin in 1881. The post office, which opened in 1906, closed in 1970, after the railroad and most of the town's former residents and businesses had already departed.

Neepawa

Town approximately 75 kilometers northeast of Brandon on Highway 16

The name Neepawa is from aboriginal words selected by early town promoters to signify the rich agricultural productivity of the area. The name is apparently from the Ojibwa word *nibiwa,* which means "plenty of." At the time of its naming, there was plenty of free land available for homesteading, where plenty of good crops could be grown for market, so *nibiwa* appeared to be a good name. There is also a similar Cree word that means the same thing.

Nelson House

Settlement approximately 75 kilometers west of Thompson about 10 kilometers off Provincial Road 391 on Footprint Lake

The Hudson's Bay Company first established a post called Nelson House, sometimes known as Nelson River House, between 1740 and 1760. It was one of the earliest posts in Western Canada, and one of the first HBC posts built inland from Hudson Bay.

Over the years it changed its location several times, with some early maps placing it west of the present location, between Nelson Lake and Highrock Lake. The post moved to its present location in 1878.

The early name Nelson River House suggests a post on that river which kept the Nelson name when it moved to other locations: first to Nelson Lake, where the name of the post was given to the lake, and then on to Nelson House, where the community took the name of the trading post. Nelson River was named after one of Thomas Button's crewmembers, a man who lost his life on the river during the winter of 1613.

Nesbitt
Settlement approximately 35 kilometers south of Brandon on Highway 2

Politicians were no more likely to keep their promises in the early days of Manitoba than they are today. Nesbitt was named for John Nesbitt Kirchhoffer, an early MLA for Brandon West.

Kirchhoffer was a member of the Sowden Land Syndicate when he moved from Ontario to Manitoba in the 1880s and was one of the founders of the nearby town of Souris. Kirchhoffer missed the chance to have his name grace a town when Souris was named after the river where it is located, but the idea of having one of Manitoba's new communities named in his honor appealed to him.

Kirchhoffer let the Canadian Pacific Railway know that if the CPR named a nearby rail point after him he'd give the new town a bell for the town hall. The CPR came through with the name, but Kirchhoffer never came through with a bell. Some reports indicate that he died the next year and was unable to make good on his promise, but the truth is he didn't die for some time afterwards. He was only appointed to the Canadian Senate.

Kirchhoffer lived in Ottawa until his death in 1914, so there was never a need for the senator to fight another election or furnish the residents of Nesbitt with a town bell.

Netley
Settlement approximately 40 kilometers north of Winnipeg on Highway 9

The community and nearby lake take their names from the river. It in turn was historically known as Nebowesebe or Rivière aux Morts, the River of the Dead. Two stories survive about the origin of those names. One has it that a party of Cree on the way to Hudson Bay to trade at York Factory left many of its older members along the banks of the river for the summer, where they were to wait until the rest of the group returned. Before that could happen, however, the Sioux attacked the camp of elderly people. The raid left no survivors.

A somewhat more plausible version of the story claims that when the Saulteaux first came to the area at the south end of Lake Winnipeg they found a large camp along the river where almost all of the people had died from smallpox. Only one small boy, Pocwanow, remained alive and the Saulteaux adopted him.

No one seems to know how the name Nebowesebe became Netley, but Pocwanow was still alive at the time the Selkirk Settlers arrived in the area in 1812.

Neubergthal

Settlement approximately 55 kilometers southeast of Winkler on Provincial Road 421

Mennonite settlers named Neubergthal. The name means "new mountain valley" in German. Since the settlement lies in the wide, mountain-less Red River Valley, one can only surmise they were smitten with wishful thinking or else picked the name before laying eyes on the geography. It's also possible the community was named after another location.

Neuhorst

Settlement approximately 30 kilometers southeast of Winkler near the American border

In German, *Neuhorst* means "new grove." The grove in question was new for Mennonite settlers when they established the settlement in 1876.

New Bothwell

Settlement approximately 30 kilometers southeast of Winnipeg on Provincial Road 216

A post office using the name New Bothwell was first noted on a map in 1947. At one time there was also a school district in the area known as Bothwell. Since the community is named New Bothwell it seems reasonable to assume there is an old one somewhere else. There are two Bothwells in Eastern Canada, one in Ontario and one in Prince Edward Island, but no evidence exists to support either as the source for the Manitoba name.

Newdale

Settlement approximately 75 kilometers northwest of Brandon on Highway 16

In about 1881 brothers John and Edward Cook opened a trading post near here. Not long after starting business they provided the descriptive name Newdale to the community and the district around the store because of the availability of new land for homesteading.

At the time Newdale was in an area south of what was known then as Mosquito Hill and a few kilometers from the present site of the town. Even at the time the Cooks admitted that the name scarcely resembled what is thought of as typical terrain of mountain and dale. Mosquito Hill, in fact, is little more than a rise on the surrounding prairie.

After the Canadian Pacific Railway arrived in 1885 the Cooks moved their operation to the railroad on the town's present site, taking the name and the post office with them.

Newton

Settlement approximately 15 kilometers southeast of Portage la Prairie on Provincial Road 331

Newton was established as a rail point in 1888. At first known as Newton Siding, the name was apparently to honor an early settler, although there is also a theory that it was simply a "new town" that became Newton.

Ninette

Settlement approximately 70 kilometers southeast of Brandon on Highway 23

When it came time to pick a name for a post office in the new settlement of Ninette residents had a hard time agreeing. The district had originally been known as Elkhorn, but another Manitoba town had already taken that name.

According to a local legend, residents hadn't decided on a new name before one of the settlers, J. H. McLean, had to leave on a trip to Winnipeg to meet with the postal inspector to ask for a post office. On his journey McLean met a French Canadian homesteader a few kilometers away who asked that the town be named after his daughter,

Antoinette, whom they called "Ninette." Ninette had recently succumbed to illness and McLean agreed to name the town after her.

Another version of the story is that McLean simply named the town after a heroine in a novel. Still another story, somewhat less touching, is that Ninette was a waitress in a saloon where MacLean had stopped on his trip to Winnipeg. Although no one story seems more likely than the others, and none can be documented, the tale of the deceased daughter seems most appealing.

Waiting for the train at Ninette in 1910. BY PERMISSION OF MANITOBA ARCHIVES, NINETTE 4.

Ninga

Settlement approximately 80 kilometers south of Brandon on Provincial Road 443

Charles W. Seefield named the town of Ninga in 1889 after postal inspectors had rejected the community's first choice. The settlement had originally been known as Stanley, but the post office balked because of a similar name already in use.

Seefield chose Ninga from the Ojibwa word for mother. He had learned the word from his Ojibwa neighbors back in Minnesota before coming to Manitoba in 1888. Seefield came to the new railroad town here with two cousins, Emma and Minnie Zickrick, and he went on to build many of the community's first commercial buildings.

Seefield started the first dry goods store in town and built the community's first lodging house, the Turtle Mountain Hotel. He also built a sugar beet refinery, but later converted it to a skating rink. According to neighbors, Seefield's wife had originally intended to join her husband at Ninga, but changed her mind and refused to leave Minnesota. Eventually, Seefield, too, returned to the United States.

Niverville

Town approximately 25 kilometers south of Winnipeg on Provincial Road 311

Memorial to early settlers in Niverville area. PHOTO BY TED STONE.

Niverville was named by Bishop Taché after Chevalier Joseph Claude Boucher de Niverville, an officer of the company of Legardeur de St. Pierre, and La Verendrye's successor as the French commander of the fur trade in Western Canada. Despite these French roots, German-speaking Mennonites from Russia were the predominant settlers in the area.

In the 1870s, many Manitobans hoped that French-speaking people would settle the southeastern part of Manitoba. In 1874 a large grant of land north and east of the Rat River to Mennonite immigrants from Russia dashed those hopes. Hundreds of Mennonite settlers came in 1875. After the success of the first land grant, the following year a second block of land was reserved for Mennonite settlement on the west side of the Red River.

Near the Red River where the first settlers disembarked after arriving in Manitoba by steamboat, Niverville is touted as the first Mennonite community in the province.

Nonsuch

Rail point approximately 345 kilometers southwest of Churchill on the Hudson Bay Railway

The Nonsuch was the name of the sailing vessel that brought explorers from England to North America in 1668 to investigate the possibility of trading furs through posts on Hudson Bay. A Frenchman, Médard Chouart Sieur Des Groseilliers, along with his brother-in-law, Pierre-Esprit Radisson, brought the idea to the English after the pair had traveled through the Great Lakes, at least as far as the western reaches of Lake Superior.

Des Groseilliers and Radisson came up with the notion of trading through the northern bay, and its water routes south to the great prairies west of Lake Superior, after learning some of the geography of the interior of the continent from the aboriginal peoples. After failing to find interest in their plan from officials in New France the pair found English supporters for their ideas instead.

Des Groseilliers traveled on the Nonsuch, under Captain Gillam, on a voyage meant to test the possibility of the trade route. After spending the winter on the shores of James Bay, at the south end of Hudson's discovery, the Nonsuch returned to England with too few beaver pelts to have actually made money, but enough pelts to show there was profit to be made through the northern bay.

The following year a charter was granted to the Governor and Company of Adventurers Trading into Hudson's Bay, giving the new company exclusive rights to trade anywhere in the Hudson Bay watershed. Today, the Manitoba Museum has a replica of *The Nonsuch* on permanent display. The vessel actually sailed the British Isles and between a number of Canadian ports on the St. Lawrence before being trucked to Manitoba in the early 1970s.

Norgate

Settlement 145 kilometers northwest of Portage la Prairie on Highway 5

Early settler Malcolm McGillivray named Norgate because he said the locality provided a "northern gate" through a narrow strip of land between Riding Mountain and the swampy land farther east. The Canadian Northern Railway evidently agreed that the locality provided a gateway to the north when it made Norgate a rail point. A post office opened in the community in 1895, but closed in 1911.

North Knife Lake

Settlement approximately 200 kilometers southwest of Churchill on North Knife Lake

North Knife Lake takes its name from the lake and the lake apparently takes its name from the North Knife River, which flows from the lake north to Hudson Bay. There's also a South Knife Lake, but it lies east of North Knife Lake on the South Knife River, which flows into Hudson Bay on the south side of a delta where it joins its sister stream before entering the great bay. It's fair to speculate both Knife rivers received their names as translations from the aboriginal designation for the stream where the two rivers merged.

To complicate matters even further, Etawney Lake, which lies upstream and south of South Knife Lake, was known to aboriginal speakers as Knife Lake.

North River

Settlement on the Knife Delta approximately 30 kilometers northwest of Churchill

North River is the site of a former Chipewyan trading post and probably takes its name from the nearby North Knife River.

Norway House

Settlement approximately 200 kilometers south of Thompson on Provincial Road 373

The name Norway House originated when a group of Norwegians lived temporarily on Big Mossy Point, across Playgreen Lake from the present community. The Norwegians came to the area in 1814 because of their prowess at cutting trees. The Hudson's Bay Company wanted them to cut a path through the northern forest, all the way from Lake Winnipeg to Hudson Bay. The HBC thought they could move more goods by horses and sleighs in winter than boats in summer.

The idea was sound, as the suitability of winter roads in the north demonstrates today, but the practical application was found wanting at the time. Although the Norwegians reached York Factory nothing came of the overland trade route. The peninsula where the Norwegians built their shelter, however, took the name Norway Point and the following year when the Hudson's Bay Company moved a trading post there it was only natural for the new post to take the name Norway House. Ten years later when the fur post moved across Playgreen Lake to the community's present location it kept the original name.

In 1815, after the Selkirk Settlers fled to the northern end of Lake Winnipeg following the Battle of Seven Oaks, Norwegian axe-men returned to the Red River with the settlers to help them rebuild their homes and harvest their crops.

Notre Dame de Lourdes

Village approximately 100 kilometers southwest of Winnipeg on Provincial Road 244

Notre Dame de Lourdes takes its name from a city in France. A Canadian post office using the name opened here in 1892, but the community and surrounding parish was apparently named by Bishop Taché nearly ten years earlier. A seminary operated here in the early years of the community.

Novra

Settlement approximately 50 kilometers north of Swan River on Highway 10

Novra began its life as a rail point. The name was created by combining part of the word *nova,* meaning "new" in Latin, with the first two letters of railroad.

Oakbank

Town approximately 15 kilometers east of Winnipeg on Provincial Road 206

The original Oakbank post office was located near Moose Nose Hill. The hill had a number of Oak trees growing along one side, which contributed to the town's name. Later, the post office moved to a more advantageous location near the Canadian Pacific Railway at the town's present site.

Moose Nose Hill is still there. The hill, which is actually part of a long gravel ridge, at one time had vegetation growing in a way that caused the spot to resemble the head of a moose with a large nose.

Oak Bluff

Settlement on the southwestern edge of Winnipeg

The name describes a bluff of nearby oaks. The post office opened using the name in 1890, but locals were evidently already using it. The word "bluff" here reflects a western Canadian usage meaning a stand of trees, not a landform.

Oakburn

Settlement approximately 145 kilometers northwest of Brandon on Highway 45

Oakburn didn't get its name from any nearby charred oak trees. Oaks, in fact, aren't all that common in the area. The Oak River flows close by, however, and the Scottish settlers evidently bestowed the name. Scots used the word "burn" for "creek," and began to call the stream Oakburn.

Oak Lake

Town approximately 50 kilometers west of Brandon on Highway 1

When the Canadian Pacific Railway first built a station in the community in 1881, they called it Flat Creek. The name came from a creek a couple of kilometers up the line from the town. Community members were not happy with the name, however, and they lobbied to change it to that of nearby Oak Lake. That name had been used since fur trade days, first as Lac des Chênes then in the English translation. Large oak trees grow along the shore.

Oakner

Settlement approximately 80 kilometers northwest of Brandon on Highway 21

At first called Eden, the pioneer district here changed its name to Oakner when the railroad arrived. Officials of the Grand Trunk Pacific were naming stops in alphabetical sequence at the time and when the tracks reached Eden they needed a town that began with the letter *O*.

Overnight, Eden became Oakner. There is no record of it, but early residents have suggested that the name may have originated with nearby oak trees.

Oak Point

Settlement approximately 45 kilometers northwest of Winnipeg on Highway 6

Oak Point was named for the point of land covered in oak trees jutting into nearby Lake Manitoba. The site was a Hudson's Bay Company trading post and ranch used by the company to winter cattle. A post office opened at Oak Point in 1872. The railroad reached the district in 1910.

A group of Lake Manitoba picnic-goers near Oak Point in 1917. By permission of Manitoba Archives, Oak Point 1, N21712.

Oak River

Settlement approximately 65 kilometers northwest of Brandon on Highway 24

A post office named Oak River served the district near the river of that name for more than a decade before the railroad arrived. Once the track was laid the post office moved away from the stream to become part of the new community on the rail line.

The river was descriptively named for the oak trees found along its banks.

Oakville

Settlement approximately 20 kilometers southeast of Portage la Prairie on Highway 13

Residents of Oakville seemed to have had some trouble deciding on a name. The community originally was Elm River and when the post office opened in 1891 it went by that name. The next year the name changed to Oakville. Eight years later it changed again, this time to Kawende. Then in 1939 it reverted to Oakville.

Postal officials were responsible for changing the name to Kawende after they revoked the name of Oakville in an effort to halt the mix-ups with other similarly named communities, particularly the larger Oakville in Ontario. *Kawande* is an Ojibwa word meaning "no name."

Losing the name Oakville was perhaps fitting since there weren't an abundance of local oak trees anyway. The name originated because many of the early residents in the district came from the Oakville area of Ontario. Despite the new non-name, residents of the Kawande still preferred the name Oakville. It took nearly forty years, but eventually that name was restored.

Ochre River
Settlement approximately 25 kilometers southeast of Dauphin on Highway 20

Ochre River was named after the nearby river. The river was named because of its color, caused by yellowish-red marl in the riverbed. Peter Fidler referred to the stream as the Red Paint River in 1820.

O'Day
Rail point approximately 130 kilometers south of Churchill on the Hudson Bay line

Canadian National Railways officials made O'Day a rail stop after construction of the railroad in 1929. J. E. O'Day was an engineer involved in the building of the final leg of the rail line.

Odhill
Rail point approximately 240 kilometers northeast of The Pas on the Hudson Bay line

The rail stop at Odhill went through a couple of names before landing its current one in 1928. Railway officials first named the stop Monty, after an engineer involved in the railroad's construction. The name Monty was dropped, however, in favor of Robson, after Joseph Robson, the first English writer to visit Fort Churchill and York Factory in the 1700s. Since there were places with similar names other places, however, the railroad changed the name again, this time to Odhill.

The new name had nothing to do with any odd hills in the area. O. D. Hill of Melfort, Saskatchewan, was a politician and railroad promoter.

Ogilvie

Settlement approximately 75 kilometers northwest of Portage la Prairie on Provincial Road 260

Originally called Blake when the post office opened here in 1879, the name was changed to Ogilvie Station by the Canadian Northern Railway when it made the community a stop on its new line in 1898. Ogilvie was the new Canadian Commissioner of the Yukon Territory at that time. He went north to assume his duties at the height of the Klondike Gold Rush.

Olha

Settlement approximately 140 kilometers northwest of Brandon on Provincial Road 577

This district was first known as Boseslav, but when a post office opened here in 1908 it took the name Olha, after a Kiev princess who reined in the Ukraine during the 10th Century.

Onanole

Settlement approximately 90 kilometers north of Brandon on Highway 10

Although Onanole might be described as situated "on a knoll," the community is actually named after the Onanole Hotel. The Onanole was once a well-known tourist stop in New York's Adirondacks. And the hotel was, in fact, on a knoll, and received its name because of its location.

Orok

Rail point approximately 20 kilometers northeast of The Pas on the Hudson Bay line

The Hudson Bay Railway's stopping place here was named in 1928 after the Canadian National Railways' medical officer in The Pas, Dr. R. D. Orok. The good doctor was also a member of the Manitoba Legislature for several years. Before acquiring the name Orok the railway stop here had been named Jeff, after railroad engineer Jeff Mowat.

Osborne

Settlement approximately 10 kilometers south of Winnipeg on Provincial Road 330

Canadian Pacific Railway officials named Osborne after Colonel W. Osborne-Smith, Commander of the Winnipeg Light Infantry during the North-West Rebellion in 1885. Osborne-Smith was also the first commander of the North West Mounted Police. He first came to Manitoba in 1871, commanding a second military expedition soon after the Red River Rebellion.

Osborne-Smith lived in Winnipeg where he ran for a seat in the House of Commons several times, but was never elected. He died in 1887 while visiting his birthplace in Wales.

Ostenfeld

Settlement approximately 50 kilometers southeast of Winnipeg on Provincial Road 302

Ostenfeld was a rail point on the Greater Winnipeg Water District Railway. Early Danish settlers named it after a bishop in Denmark. Apparently Reverend Nels Damskov suggested the name.

Osterwick

Settlement approximately 15 kilometers southwest of Winkler on Provincial Road 201

The name Osterwick, meaning Easter Vetch, is of German origin. Mennonite settlers named the community in 1876. It comes from the tradition of decorating at Easter with the vetch plant. In many places the decorative plant was one of the few to be found at a time of year when most showy plants and flowers were still unavailable. Because of this several species of vetch, particularly the Coronilla valentine found in Europe, have come to be associated with Easter.

A local legend has it that vetch was available for decoration at the first Easter service held at Osterwick. Easter comes early in the prairie spring, however, and it's probably just as likely the community received its name because of a local species of vetch found growing in the area or, simply, the European memory of Easter vetch among early settlers.

Otterburne

Settlement approximately 40 kilometers south of Winnipeg near Highway 59

Some have suggested that Otterburne's name is after the village of Otterburn in Northumberland, England. But the community almost certainly derived its name from an officer by the name of Otterburne who served under the Jacques Legardeur de Saint-Pierre in the French Troupes de la Marine. Legardeur served throughout New France and succeeded Joseph Claude Boucher de Niverville in command of the French fur trade in the North West.

Bishop Taché suggested Otterburne's name for the Manitoba village. Several nearby towns also bear the names of early French explorers in western Canada.

A group gathers around the pig display at Otterburne in 1920. BY PERMISSION OF MANITOBA ARCHIVES, OTTERBURNE 1, N10438.

Overflowing River

Settlement approximately 130 kilometers north of Swan River on Highway 10

The community takes its name from the river that flows from Saskatchewan southeast into Dawson Bay on Lake Winnipegosis. The name is descriptive, as the river is often overflowing along stretches of lowland near its mouth.

Oxford House

Settlement approximately 180 kilometers southeast of Thompson on Oxford Lake

The Hudson's Bay Company first built a post on Oxford Lake here in 1798. The site was approximately-half way between York Factory on Hudson Bay and the north end of Lake Winnipeg. The Cree name for the lake, *Poonapowwanippeeko,* means "lake with a hole in the bottom," which alludes to the lake's extreme depth at one end. David Thompson called it Deep Water Lake. Presumably William Sinclair, who built the first post here for the Hudson's Bay Company, named it after Oxford in England.

Paterson

Rail point approximately 120 kilometers northwest of The Pas on the Hudson Bay line

This stop on the railroad to Churchill is named after one of the prominent promoters during the 1920s of the line to Hudson Bay. At that time the railroad had been constructed part way to the bay, but then had been allowed to deteriorate during World War I.

General Paterson, the president of a lobby group called "On-to-the-Bay," led just one of the groups promoting the use of Hudson Bay as a transportation route for prairie grain.

Pawistik

Rail point approximately 115 kilometers northeast of Flin Flon on the Sherritt–Lynn Lake rail line where it crosses the Churchill River

Pawistik is taken from the Cree word for waterfall. It is a descriptive name that describes nearby rapids on the Churchill River. The rail point is named for the rapids.

Payuk

Rail point approximately 35 kilometers southeast of The Pas near Sherritt Junction

The rail point here takes its name from nearby Payuk Lake. *Payuk* is a Cree word meaning the number one and Payuk Lake is the first lake in a string of lakes designated in numerical order by Cree residents of the region at the time Europeans arrived.

Pelican Rapids

Settlement approximately 110 kilometers northeast of Swan River on Provincial Road 483 at the mouth of the Shoal River on Lake Winnipegosis

The name refers to the many pelicans in the area. The settlement took its name from the nearby rapids. Pelican Lake is southeast of the community; Pelican Bay is to the east.

Petersfield

Settlement approximately 35 kilometers north of Winnipeg on Highway 9

The post office here opened as St. Louis Station in 1908, but it became Petersfield in 1917. By some accounts the new name honors early settler Peter Sinclair. Another explanation claims that the town takes its name from the English home of another of the early settlers in the district whose name was Bowman.

Pierson

Settlement approximately 175 kilometers southwest of Brandon on Highway 3

The town of Pierson was named after a banker, although not a local banker. When the Canadian Pacific Railway constructed a branch line in 1890, railroad officials named the settlement after Jean Louis Pierson, an Amsterdam banker. In 1882 Pierson was the first to sell CPR shares in the European market. He was a partner in the Dutch banking firm of Adolf Boissevain and Company, which later became Pierson and Company.

The railroad also named the town of Boissevain, after Pierson's partner.

Pikwitonei

Rail point approximately 55 kilometers southeast of Thompson on the Hudson Bay line

The rail point here was named after the nearby Pikwitonei River. The Cree name for the river means "broken mouth." Apparently the name refers to the fact that the mouth of the river breaks up into several marshy lakes and streams.

Pilot Mound

Town approximately 75 kilometers west of Winkler on Highway 3

The nearby, mostly shale rounded hill earned the name Pilot Mound because of its noticeable height above the surrounding hills and prairie. The hill stood as a landmark for travelers in the days before pioneer trails turned into prairie roads.

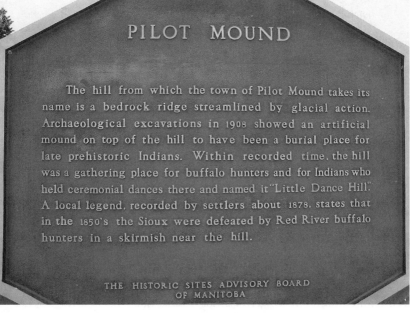

Plaque at foot of Pilot Mound, the original site of the town where an Indian battle in the 1850s left nearly 600 Sioux dead. PHOTO BY TED STONE.

According to some stories, aboriginal people in the region called the mound Dancing Hill at the time Europeans arrived. Using the name Pilot Mound, a post office opened on the east slope of the hill in 1880, but it moved two kilometers south of its original location when the railroad arrived in the area four years later.

Dancing Hill, or Pilot Mound, is also famous for an battle that took place there in the mid 1850s. A fight broke out near the hill between a large group of Red River hunters and a band of Sioux. Both groups were hunting buffalo when the fighting started. Reports claim that as many as six hundred Sioux were killed in the battle. Only two of the Sioux survived. It is said the Red River buffalo hunters purposely let the two live so they would warn other Sioux not to bother hunters from Red River.

Some have described the battle as the last armed conflict with the Sioux in the Canadian west.

Pinawa

Town approximately 100 kilometers northeast of Winnipeg on Provincial Road 211

The name Pinawa evidently derives from aboriginal words that mean "calm" or "sheltered waters." The Lee River was once known as the Pinawa, although today the name refers only to one portion of the river known as the Pinawa Channel.

No one knows how long aboriginal people in the area called it the Pinawa, but Alexander Henry, the elder, noted the name as far back as 1775.

Pine Falls

Village approximately 110 kilometers northeast of Winnipeg on Highway 11

The village here was named after the falls two kilometers upstream on the Winnipeg River. Today the falls have disappeared under a hydroelectric dam, as have the jack pines that provided the inspiration for the name when the Winnipeg River was a major leg of the fur trade route from Montreal to Western Canada. At that time Pine Falls was just one of the many portages that had to be made along the river's course.

Today Pine Falls has amalgamated with the neighboring community of Powerview.

Pine River

Settlement approximately 90 kilometers northwest of Dauphin on Highway 10

The community stands part way between the north and south branches of the Pine River. The two branches join before emptying into Lake Winnipegosis. The community takes its name from the river.

The river name is descriptive of local evergreen trees, but seems to have been imprecisely used on early maps.

Piney

Settlement approximately 80 kilometers southeast of Steinbach on Highway 89

The post office opened here in 1901 as Pine Valley, but the name changed to Piney in 1913. The community had, at first, been called Pine Creek after the nearby stream when the area was first settled in the late 1890s. Evidently, the name Piney came into common use as a shortened form of Pine Valley before the official change of names.

Nearby Piney Hill and Piney Bog were named after the community in the mid-1900s.

After a hunt near Pipestone. By permission of Manitoba Archives: Pipestone 2, c.1910.

Pipestone

Settlement approximately 100 kilometers southwest of Brandon on Highway 2

The community derived its name from nearby Pipestone Creek. The original settlement was closer to the creek than the town's current location, which was established in 1892 as a rail point.

Although records are unclear, the creek was recorded with variations of the name Pipestone from early in the nineteenth century. This seems to indicate that the name stems from aboriginal sources.

Pipun

Rail point approximately 115 kilometers southwest of Thompson on the Hudson Bay line and Highway 6

Pipun was established as a rail point on the Hudson Bay line in 1928, but the area may have been called Pipoon as early as 1915. The name is from the Cree word for winter.

Pit Siding

Rail point approximately 100 kilometers east of Thompson on the Hudson Bay line

The rail point at Pit Siding sits at the junction of a branch rail line to Kelsey and the main line of the Hudson Bay Railway. The name came about because of gravel pits established in the area. During the building of the railroad, these pits supplied material used for construction of the rail bed.

Plumas

Settlement approximately 95 kilometers northwest of Portage la Prairie on Provincial Road 260

A local postmaster gave the community its Spanish name in 1888. James Anderson had either visited or lived in Plumas County, California before arriving in frontier Manitoba sometime in the late 1870s. After postal officials gave him the opportunity to change the name of the local post office—Quaker settlers originally called the district Jordon, and then those who followed called it Richmond—Anderson chose the Spanish word for feathers, in memory of the time he had spent in northern California.

Plum Coulee
Village approximately 10 kilometers east of Winkler on Highway 14

Plum Coulee was established as a rail point near the Plum River. A short distance away the river valley opened into a wide coulee. A number of wild plum trees grew in the coulee. Supposedly, surveyors working in the area picked plums in the coulee, and then gave the coulee and the river its name. The rail point was named after the coulee.

Point du Bois
Settlement approximately 150 kilometers northeast of Winnipeg at the end of Provincial Road 313 in Whiteshell Provincial Park

The point in the woods that gave the community its name was on the Winnipeg River. A series of waterfalls began here, and the spot has been known at least since the early 19th Century as Point du Bois.

The falls were submerged by a hydroelectric dam built in the early years of the 20TH century by the Winnipeg Electric Company.

Polonia
Settlement approximately 125 kilometers northwest of Portage la Prairie on Provincial Road 265

Known as Huns Valley until the 1920s,. Polonia's original name came from the community's earliest immigrants. The first settlers in the area came from Hungary in 1885, under the leadership of the agriculturalist Geja St. de Dory. The settlers called their new home Hungarian Valley, but the name was shortened to Huns Valley by the time the first post office opened in 1886.

Then, in 1921, the post office changed its name to Polonia, the Latinized word for Poland. The name change recognized the large number of Polish settlers in the area by that time.

Ponemah

Settlement approximately 25 kilometers south of Gimli on the west shore of Lake Winnipeg

The name Ponemah was taken from *Hiawatha,* a poem by Henry Wadsworth Longfellow. The resort community here is now part the amalgamated village of Dunnottar, which includes the nearby communities of Matlock and Whytewold.

Ponton

Rail point approximately 150 kilometers southwest of Thompson on the Hudson Bay line near the junction of Highway 6 and Highway 39

Archibald W. Ponton was an early surveyor in Manitoba. He is credited with surveying the extension of the Principal Meridian in the province across Lake Winnipeg into Manitoba's north. Ponton died two years after the rail point here received his name in 1913.

Poplarfield

Settlement approximately 105 kilometers northwest of Winnipeg on Highway 17

The name describes the fields of poplar trees around this Interlake community. The name came into use as a post office and rail point in 1913.

Poplar Point

Settlement approximately 20 kilometers northeast of Portage la Prairie on Highway 26

The community here received its name because of a nearby prominent stand of poplar trees that once jutted into the surrounding prairie. The trees formed a ragged dagger onto the open plains. The name was first noted as a Roman Catholic parish and then a post office and rail point.

Portage la Prairie

City approximately 65 kilometers west of Winnipeg on Highway 1

The name Portage la Prairie dates to early in the fur trade, and describes the portage across the prairie near here between the Assiniboine River, Rat Creek and the delta at the south end of Lake Manitoba. Other early names for the portage included "Plain Portage" and "Meadow Portage." According to La Verendrye's 1739 journal the Assiniboine used the route to travel north to Hudson Bay where they traded furs to the English Hudson's Bay Company.

Apparently, the portage was usually about nine kilometers, but at times of high water could be much shorter.

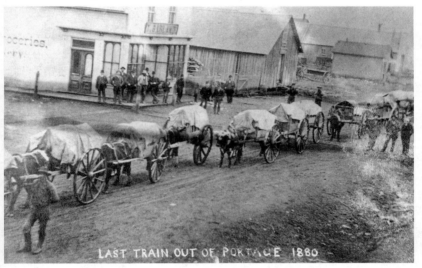

The last ox train to leave Portage La Prairie in 1880 By PERMISSION OF MANITOBA ARCHIVES: PORTAGE LA PRAIRIE 2 – 4, C. 1880.

Powell

Settlement approximately 100 kilometers north of Swan River on Highway 77

Sir Robert Stephenson Smyth Baden-Powell became famous all over the world during the Boer War in South Africa from 1899 to 1900 for his defense of the town of Mafeking. During the siege he successfully defended the town with 1,200 men against a Boer force of 9,000.

Three Manitoba rail points—Baden, Powell and Mafeking—were named during the war, which lasted until 1902. Baden-Powell went on to found the Boy Scouts. The book he wrote to help train young soldiers began to be used to help teach boys. He wrote *Scouting for Boys* in 1908 and soon afterward boys in England, and then around the world, spontaneously began organizing themselves into scout patrols. The book was translated into several languages and in 1920, at the first International Scout Jamboree, Baden-Powell was acclaimed the "Chief Scout of the World."

Powerview
Village approximately 110 kilometers northeast of Winnipeg on Highway 11

Powerview came about as a result of the hydroelectric damn built on the nearby Winnipeg River in 1951. The name is descriptive of the view of the power plant as seen from the community and was chosen in a contest.

Today the village of Powerview has been amalgamated with the neighboring town of Pine Falls.

Prawda
Settlement approximately 90 kilometers west of Winnipeg on Highway 1

The community's first postmaster, Evangeline Andrusko, named Prawda. Some have suggested it comes from a similarly named community in Poland or Ukraine.

The name is actually derived from the word *Pravda,* meaning truth. It could also have come from the prominent Ukrainian literary magazine, *Pravda,* which was popular at that time.

Princess Harbour
Settlement approximately 210 kilometers north of Winnipeg on the east shore of Lake Winnipeg

Apparently when a post office opened here it dropped the traditional name of Rabbit Harbour and adopted the new name of Princess Harbour. No one knows if the new name is derived from a real princess—perhaps Princess Elizabeth, who went on to become a queen—or if the name is in recognition of the commercial boat named the *Princess* that plied the waters of Lake Winnipeg for a quarter of a century, supplying small communities such as Rabbit Harbour. It's also possible the name change came about because someone thought Princess Harbour sounded more impressive than Rabbit Harbour.

Pukatawagan

Settlement approximately 120 kilometers northeast of Flin Flon on Pukatawagan Lake

The community here takes its name from the nearby lake. The name is from the Cree language and signifies a fishing place. This particular fishing place has been used by aboriginal people of the region, and later by Hudson Bay traders, for generations.

Purves

Settlement approximately 70 kilometers southwest of Winkler on Provincial Road 423

When the railroad arrived here in 1899 it crossed a ranch belonging to Purves Thompson. The Canadian Pacific Railway recognized Thompson by naming the rail point after him. A post office, using the same name, opened here in 1903.

Rackham

Settlement approximately 85 kilometers north of Brandon on Provincial Road 270

The Canadian Northern Railway named the stop here Rackam in 1921, after the man who ran the station for them. Two years later when the post office opened it took the same name. The post office closed in 1971.

Randolph

Settlement approximately 10 kilometers west of Steinbach on Provincial Road 206

Reportedly named after an early settler, the community had been known as Chortitz until the 1960s, when the name was apparently changed to avoid confusion with another Manitoba settlement called Chortitz located near Morden. Randolph was also once the name of a school district in the area.

Rapid City

Town approximately 35 kilometers north of Brandon on Highway 24

When the first settlers came to the Rapid City district they called the place Ralston's Colony, after John Ralston who helped bring several families here from Ontario. In 1877, however, the settlers got together and named the new town Rapid City, because of the nearby fast moving waters of the Little Saskatchewan River.

Evidently, there had been some talk of naming the town Saskatchewan City, but most people felt that the name would be just too long. Saskatchewan, though, is an anglicized version of Cree words that mean "rapid river." Thus, Rapid City was born. The post office opened here in 1879.

Main Street Rapid City. By permission of Manitoba Archives: Rapid City 19, c. 1880s.

Rathwell

Village approximately 45 kilometers southwest of Portage la Prairie on Highway 2

Early homesteader John Rathwell came to the area from Innisville, Ontario in the early 1880s. The Canadian Pacific Railway bought 80 acres of land from Rathwell on the condition that its new rail line would be able to cross his homestead. To sweeten the deal, the railroad named the station Rathwell.

But Rathwell reportedly soon regretted his decision. He abandoned his homestead and another settler took it up. Meanwhile the CPR established the siding intended for Rathwell's homestead on another property nearby. Despite the fracas, the CPR forgot to change the new station's name, so it remained Rathwell.

A nearby post office also took that name when it moved to the rail line.

Rawebb

Rail point approximately 115 kilometers northeast of The Pas on the Hudson Bay line

Named for the mayor of Winnipeg, Ralph Webb, Rawebb uses the first two letters of his first name, along with his entire last name. Born on an English steamer sailing between England and India in 1887, Webb came to Manitoba in 1902 and operated a lumber business before joining the military during World War I. He rose to the rank of lieutenant-colonel before returning to Winnipeg where he operated a hotel and served seven terms as mayor.

Webb also served two terms in the Manitoba legislature before moving to Ottawa to work in the quartermaster-general's department during World War II.

Red Deer Lake

Settlement approximately 100 kilometers north of Swan River on Red Deer Lake

Early Europeans in the area seem to have called the lake here Red Deer, or elk, at least as far back as the 1790s. The aboriginal people of the area probably called it by that name long before that. The settlement took its name from the lake. A post office opened here in 1904.

Red Rose

Settlement approximately 180 kilometers north of Winnipeg near Peguis First Nation

With an attractive name like Red Rose, a prominent town should have developed here after the post office opened in 1921. Early resident John Grabowski chose the name because of the profusion of wild roses in the area.

Despite the inviting name not many people ever came to Red Rose. It failed to grow and the post office finally closed in 1969.

Red Sucker Lake

Settlement approximately 900 kilometers northeast of Winnipeg on Red Sucker Lake

Cree people called this area *Okao-pukatawagan,* meaning "a good place to fish for walleye," but when fur traders moved into the area it somehow became Red Sucker River and Red Sucker Lake. Peter Fidler showed a fur post here as early as 1807.

Apparently the name came about because aboriginal people called the river *Mohkamipin,* or Red Sucker, after a species of fish that could be caught there.

Regent

Settlement approximately 80 kilometers southwest of Brandon near Provincial Road 448

In 1915 the post office serving this district moved to a spot along the railroad and renamed itself Regent. Until then the postal address here had been Wapaha, a Sioux word meaning "war bonnet." No records remain for the reason for giving the settlement either name.

Rennie

Settlement approximately 110 kilometers east of Winnipeg on Highway 44

The Canadian Pacific Railway established the settlement of Rennie as a stopping point on the mainline in eastern Manitoba about where the railroad leaves the Canadian Shield and begins its route across the prairies. Railroad officials named the rail point after British engineer John Rennie. The post office here opened in 1901. The nearby Rennie River was named after the settlement.

Renwer

Settlement approximately 35 kilometers east of Swan River on Highway 10

Named 1904, the community came into existence a few years earlier as a rail siding on the Canadian Northern Railway. Some judged its original name, Fisher's Siding, as too common, so the railroad made up a new name for its station here.

The first three letters, "Ren," derive from the last three letters of A. E. Warren, the railroad's chief clerk and a later vice president. The last three letters in the name, "wer," derive from the first three letters of W. E. Roberts, the company's superintendent at Brandon.

Reston

Settlement approximately 110 kilometers southeast of Brandon on Highway 2

Horses and wagons at Reston fair in 1909. By permission of Manitoba Archives, Reston – fair 2, N4145.

Many of the first settlers in this area came from a place called Reston Junction in Berwickshire, Scotland. First applied to an early school here, the name later graced the rail siding and post office.

Reykjavik

Settlement approximately 115 kilometers east of Dauphin just northwest of the Narrows on Lake Manitoba

Named for the capital city of Iceland, Reykjavik was one of several Icelandic settlements on Lake Manitoba. The word itself comes from a Scandinavian word for smoke, first applied by Norse sailors coming upon Iceland's steaming hot springs. A post office opened at Manitoba's Reykjavik in 1911, but closed in 1970.

Ridgeville

Settlement approximately 85 kilometers south of Winnipeg on Provincial Road 218

Ridgeville is a descriptive name, taken from a long, north-south ridge, prominent here. Running sometimes almost imperceptibly through Manitoba and Minnesota east of the Red River, the ridge marks one of the ancient beaches left by glacial Lake Agassiz before it disappeared from the area several thousand years ago. (See entry for Green Ridge.)

Riding Mountain

Settlement approximately 100 kilometers southeast of Dauphin on Highway 5 east of Riding Mountain National Park

The Riding Mountain post office opened in 1892 and later moved closer to the rail line after it was built. Riding Mountain is part of the Manitoba Escarpment just to the northwest. Early fur traders used the name to describe the high plateau. The aboriginal name apparently referred to horses being ridden there.

One Ojibwa story that may explain the origin for the name tells of an extended period riding after buffalo there, thus becoming the Riding Mountain.

Rivers

Town approximately 45 kilometers northwest of Brandon on Highway 25

The Little Saskatchewan River runs through the town, but Rivers could have been river-less and still ended up with the same name. The town evidently gets its name from Sir Charles Rivers-Wilson, the chairman of the board of directors for the Grand Trunk Pacific Railway when the railroad arrived here in 1907.

Riverside

Settlement approximately 50 kilometers south of Winnipeg near Morris

The name for this village along the Morris River bank is purely descriptive.

Riverton

Village approximately 40 kilometers north of Gimli on Highway 8

A post office opened here on the Icelandic River using the name Gimli in 1877. The postal address changed to Icelandic River in 1886 and then to Riverton in 1924. Despite the post office name, the community itself initially went by the name Lundi, an Icelandic word for meadow.

Later, the settlement was generally known as Icelandic River. Then, in 1914, the village officially changed its name to Riverton, presumably because, through all the confusion surrounding its name and post office address, it had always remained a river town.

Roblin

Town approximately 95 kilometers west of Dauphin on Highway 5

Named after a nearby body of water, the settlement here was called Goose Lake when the post office opened in 1904. But postal officials, the railroad and community boosters lost no time changing the name to Roblin, after Rodmond P. Roblin, the premier of Manitoba at the time.

Whether or not extra-provincial aid was subsequently forthcoming has not been documented.

Rock Ridge

Settlement approximately 150 kilometers northeast of Dauphin on Provincial Road 276

Rock Ridge sits on a slightly elevated point of rocky land surrounded by the lowlands between Lake Manitoba and Lake Winnipegosis.

Roland

Village approximately 20 kilometers north of Winkler on Highway 23

Railroad officials named the stopping point here after an early settler, Roland McDonald, when the townsite was laid out in 1890. According to one account, surveyors scouting a possible railroad route named the site after boarding with the McDonald family.

Roland organized the first 4-H Club in Canada. In the photo members display steers in 1962.
By permission of Manitoba Archives, 4-H Clubs 121, N4306.

Root Lake

Settlement approximately 35 kilometers north of The Pas on Highway 10

Canadian National Railways officials established Root Lake as a rail point and named it after the nearby lake. The lake name is an English translation of the Cree name in use when Europeans arrived in the area. Presumably, there were once a lot of roots visible in the lake's waters.

Rosa

Settlement approximately 70 kilometers south of Winnipeg on Highway 59

Despite adopting a variant spelling, early Ukrainian settlers named Rosa after the nearby Roseau River. Roseau is the French word for "reed." La Verendrye translated the river's name to the French from the aboriginal name. It describes the water reeds that grow along the river's upper reaches near Lake of the Woods. Aboriginal people once made flute-like instruments from one of the species of reed that grows here. (See next entry.)

Roseau River

Settlement approximately 75 kilometers south of Winnipeg on Highway 59

Built on the banks of the Roseau River, the village takes its name from a French translation of the Ojibwa *Pipigwewanashk Sibi,* or Flute-Reed-Grass River. Aboriginal people knew a trail along the river to Lake of the Woods as the War Road, because Sioux and Ojibwa warriors used the route to travel back and forth as they battled against each other.

Rosebank

Settlement approximately 30 kilometers northwest of Winkler on Highway 23

The community here was established with the coming of the Northern Pacific and Manitoba Railway. An early settler, Alice York Thompson, reportedly suggested the name because of the surrounding banks of wild roses.

Roseisle

Settlement approximately 65 kilometers northwest of Winkler on Provincial Road 245

Presumably, this spot was an isle of wild roses at the time settlers began coming to the area. The first post office using the name opened here in 1886. The settlement's first postmaster, Alex Begg, chose the name.

Rosenfeld

Settlement approximately 30 kilometers east of Winkler on Highway 14

The Canadian Pacific Railway named Rosenfeld when it established a rail point here in 1882. Mennonites had used the name for a settlement located in the vicinity of the railroad when it was built through the area. *Rosenfeld* is German for "rose field."

Rosenort

Settlement approximately 50 kilometers southwest of Winnipeg on Provincial Road 205

The post office in Rosenort opened in 1899, but a Mennonite settlement had existed near here for nearly 25 years by that time. The settlement was apparently named after a Mennonite village in Russia. In German the compound word means "a place of roses."

Rosetown

Settlement approximately 30 kilometers southeast of Winkler

Rosetown was once known as Rosenort, but Manitoba has another Rosenort. To avoid the confusion residents of this Rosenort decided to change the name of their village to Rosetown. The two words that make the name are an approximate translation from the German to English. The name describes the wild roses found in the area.

Ross

Settlement approximately 35 kilometers northeast of Steinbach on Provincial Road 501

The rail point here on the Greater Winnipeg Water District Railway was first called Ste. Genevieve, apparently after the Parish of Ste. Genevieve in Paris. When a post office opened in 1923, though, it took the name Ross, after a prominent local family, and that's the name that stuck. Nearly thirty years later a nearby community took the old post office name of Ste. Genevieve.

Rossburn

Town approximately 135 kilometers northwest of Brandon on Highway 45

One of the area's first settlers, R. R. Ross was an early postmaster in the community who later became a reeve in the municipality. He became the postmaster of the town named for him in 1882, after moving to the district from Ontario. *Burn,* Gaelic for "creek," was presumably added to the name because of nearby Ross Creek.

Rossendale

Settlement approximately 45 kilometers southwest of Portage la Prairie on Provincial Road 242

Rossendale first went by Loveville, and then Elmwood, but when the post office opened in 1896 the official name became Rossendale. Apparently an early resident named Sager who hailed from Ontario wanted the new town named Ross-in-Dale, after a community in his former province. By the time postal officials were through with that name, though, the community had become Rossendale.

Rossville

Settlement at the edge of Norway House approximately 200 kilometers south of Thompson on Provincial Road 373

The Methodist missionary James Evans named Rossville in 1840 after the chief factor at the nearby Hudson's Bay Company post, Donald Ross. Evans established Rossville around his mission.

Missionary Evans was also the inventor of a Cree syllabic, into which he translated hymns and Bible passages. His *Cree Syllabic Hymnbook*, printed in 1841, was the first book published in the Canadian West.

Rounthwaite

Settlement approximately 30 kilometers south of Brandon on Provincial Road 453

Irish settler Samuel Rounthwaite named the first post office in this locality after himself when he opened it here in 1881. A new Canadian Northern Railway point also took the name when it arrived in the area, as did a local school district.

Government officials asked Rounthwaite to supply a aboriginal name for his new post office when it opened. He wrote back that he "didn't know any Indians." It is said that someone in the postal department replied that Rounthwaite "was Indian enough," and so that became the community's official address until the post office closed in 1971.

Ruddock

Rail point approximately 80 kilometers northeast of Flin Flon on the Sherritt–Lynn Lake line

Ruddock was first called Gallie when the rail point was established here in 1954. The stop was named for Alan E. Gallie, the Superintendent of Sherritt-Gordon Mines at Lynn Lake at that time. Later that year, however, Canadian National Railways officials decided to choose a new name to avoid confusion with a place in Saskatchewan called Galilee. The name Ruddock was chosen, after Ruddock Neely, the resident administrator of the Local Government District of Lynn Lake. Neely was also once the mayor of The Pas.

Russell

Town approximately 170 kilometers northwest of Brandon on Highway 83

The first post office serving settlers here was called Shell River, after the nearby stream of that name. Within a year of being named, however, Charles Boulton, who owned land where the Canadian Pacific Railway intended to establish a rail point, and who later would be appointed to the Canadian Senate, laid out a townsite on his property.

He named the proposed town Russell. No one can be sure of his motives today, but it's probable that Boulton, who had been a member of the Canadian survey party that came to Red River in 1869, chose the name in honor of Lindsay Russell, the Surveyor General of Canada in that year.

The Russell Ladies Band in 1912. By permission of Manitoba Archives, Russell 6, N19905.

When Louis Riel's Red River Rebellion started—at least partly sparked by Boulton's survey party—Boulton attempted to organize military support for Governor William McDougall. He led an armed group of men from Portage la Prairie to Fort Garry, intending to free prisoners being held by Riel, but he was captured himself instead. Boulton was sentenced to be executed by Riel's forces, but Donald Smith of the Hudson's Bay Company intervened and convinced Riel to set Boulton free.

After the rebellion Boulton returned to Ontario, but he failed in business there. In 1880, ten years after he had left the province, Boulton returned to Manitoba with his family. Once here he obtained land the CPR intended to use for a rail point at Russell and nearby Shellmouth, where he also had the townsite surveyed so he could sell lots.

In 1885, Boulton raised a militia unit called Boulton's Scouts for service in the North-West Rebellion. After the Métis were suppressed, he wrote an account of his experiences called *Reminiscences of the North-West Rebellion.* The book became an almost instant bestseller, and also led directly to Boulton's appointment in 1889 to the Canadian Senate.

There are more than two-dozen Manitoba communities named for religious saints. These include: St. Adolphe, St. Alphonse, St. Ambroise, St. Eustache, St. Jean Baptiste, St. Joseph, St. Labre, St. Laurent, St-Lazare, St. Lupicin, Ste. Theresa Point, Ste. Agathe, Ste. Elizabeth, Ste. Genevieve and Ste. Rita. A few of the stories behind some of the names include:

Ste. Agathe

Settlement approximately 25 kilometers south of Winnipeg on Highway 75

Father Richot named the parish of Ste. Agathe after Ste. Agathe des Monts, a church in Quebec where he had been a priest before coming to Manitoba. First settled by Métis families in the 1870s, the community was originally known as Pointe de Grouette. A post office opened here under that name in 1873. In 1878 the name was changed to Ste. Agathe to correspond with the name of the parish.

Ste. Amelie

Settlement approximately 70 kilometers southeast of Dauphin on Provincial Road 360

Ste. Amelie was evidently named after Princess Amelie of Belgium. Unfortunately, there have been a couple of Belgium Princess Amelies, so it's impossible to know today which one residents had in mind in the early years of the twentieth century when the first post office opened here.

St. Claude

Village approximately 35 kilometers south of Portage la Prairie on Highway 2

The Canadian Pacific Railway established St. Claude as a station in 1892 and named it after the village of St. Claude in France. Colonists from that area of Europe, led by Dom Paul Benoit, arrived in the district the same year as the railroad.

St. François Xavier

Settlement approximately 15 kilometers west of Winnipeg on Highway 26

The Catholic parish here was named St. François Xavier in 1824, but the community was known as Grantown, after its founder Cuthbert Grant, until well after Grant's death in 1854. Grant led the Métis in the Battle of Seven Oaks in 1816. The battle was the culmination of the resentment that developed between Lord Selkirk's Scottish settlers, who began arriving on the Red River in 1812, and Métis employees of the North West Company who had already settled in the region and considered the junction of the Red and Assiniboine rivers strategically important to their supply route to the northwest.

After the Hudson's Bay Company absorbed the North West Company in 1821, Grant became an employee. One of his initial roles with the company was to encourage Métis living south of the 49th parallel on the Pembina River to move north, where they would be less likely to work for American fur companies. Grant led the repatriation of about 50 Métis families to what was then known as the White Horse Plains.

According to an aboriginal legend, the area called White Horse Plains got its name after the death of a Cree warrior who gave an Assiniboine chief a superb white horse in exchange for the hand of his daughter in marriage. This was not a popular decision among the Assiniboine, who were relatives of the Sioux, the traditional enemies of the Cree. The decision was particularly galling to a rejected Sioux warrior who had already asked for the daughter's hand.

The young warrior vowed to kill his Cree rival, but news of the threat reached the Assiniboine chief in the middle of a night. He saddled the white horse and urged his daughter and new son-in-law to escape. In the morning they were gone, but the Sioux warrior went after them as soon as he discovered them missing. Somewhere along the Assiniboine River, near present day St. François Xavier, he caught up with the couple where they camped. He shot arrows through them both as they tried to flee on their beautiful white horse.

The new bride and groom were both killed, but the white horse escaped. For years afterward, it was often seen running across prairie. At first, people tried to capture the horse when they saw it, but the great white horse was always too fast and remained free.

St-Georges

Settlement approximately 100 kilometers northeast of Winnipeg on Highway 11

Bishop Langevin chose the name St-Georges to honor Georges Chevrefils, the oldest of the community's early settlers at that time. Some say it commemorates Georges Vincent, the first child born in the new settlement.

For a time the community was known as St-Georges Chateauguay, in recognition of the county in Quebec where most of the original settlers came from, but the Chateauguay soon dropped from use.

St. Leon

Settlement approximately 65 kilometers northwest of Winkler just off Highway 23

St. Leon is said to have been named after Pope Leo XIII because the first settlers arrived here in 1877, the year he became pope. Today, St. Leon is primarily known for the large number of electricity-producing windmills in the area.

St. Martin / St. Martin Junction

Settlements approximately 240 kilometers northwest of Winnipeg on and near Highway 6

St. Martin is named after the nearby lake. St. Martin Junction is named because of its location at the highway where traffic turns to go to the community of St. Martin. No one really knows where the name of the lake comes from anymore, but it has been used for several locations in the region from the earliest days of the fur trade.

References to the St. Martin Islands in Lake Winnipeg go back as far as 1760 and documentation of the name Lake St. Martin goes back nearly as far. Lake St. Martin was an important link in the fur trade on the canoe route between Lake Winnipegosis, Lake Manitoba and Lake

Winnipeg, as well as Lake Dauphin. It's possible, and even likely, that the name dates as far back as La Verendrye's first exploration in the area before 1740.

Ste. Anne

Town approximately 30 kilometers southeast of Winnipeg on Highway 1

Ste. Anne was originally known as Grande Pointe Des Chênes, or the big point of oak trees, along the Seine River. An early priest, Father LaFloch built the community's first chapel and called the settlement Ste. Anne des Chênes, after the patron saint of Brittany, where he had grown up in France.

Today, the town and surrounding municipality are officially named simply St. Anne. Only the post office, officially Ste. Anne des Chênes, retains the entire name. The original oaks along the river here are mostly gone as well.

St. Malo

Town on Highway 59 approximately 50 kilometers south of Winnipeg

Some people say St. Malo took its name from the seaport in France, but the local story is that it was named after one of the town's first residents, Louis Malo and his family. According to the tale, Malo, who came to the district in 1870, made the fifteen kilometer trip to church in St. Pierre every Sunday, a practice that was often publicly noted by the parish priest at the time, Father J-M Jolys.

As a result, Malo was sometimes referred to in jest as St. Malo. Eventually, the name St. Malo began to be used to denote the area where the Malo family lived. The name first appeared on a map in 1885.

St. Pierre-Jolys

Village on Highway 59 approximately 40 kilometers south of Winnipeg

The name combination of St. Pierre-Jolys derives from the Catholic saint and the area's first priest, Father J-M Jolys. Father Jolys was a community leader when the town was founded.

St. Malo Catholic Church. PHOTO BY TED STONE.

Father Jolys originally suggested the name St. Pierre. It was in common use almost from the town's beginning, although the post office was briefly known as Rat River, and then Laurier for a number of years after that. In 1922 the combined name of St. Pierre-Jolys was officially adopted for the village.

Ste. Rose du Lac

Town approximately 50 kilometers east of Dauphin on Highway 10

Métis families first settled the Ste. Rose area in the late 1880s. An early priest, Father Lacoq, gave the community the name Ste. Rose du Lac. He evidently chose the name because of the town's proximity to Dauphin Lake.

While the town is called Ste. Rose du Lac, the parish here is officially Ste. Rose de Lima. The post office and surrounding municipality simply use the name St. Rose.

San Clara

Settlement approximately 85 kilometers south of Swan River on Provincial Road 367

Apparently San Clara was to have been St. Claire, except the post office already had a mail point with that name. To avoid confusion, the new settlement's first post office adopted the Spanish San Clara rather than the French St. Claire.

Sanford

Settlement approximately 25 kilometers southwest of Winnipeg on Highway 3

The post office here was known as Mandan when it opened in 1900. It was named after the First Nation that lived along the Missouri River in North Dakota, but came north to trade with Manitoba aboriginal groups up until about the time the post office opened here at the turn of the 20th century. The name of the Mandan post office changed to Sanford in 1906.

Apparently the new name originated with a sandy ford on the nearby LaSalle River, although Robert Douglas, in *Place-Names of Manitoba,* claims railroad officials named the town after a Canadian Senator. Some have suggested the railroad chose the name for Sanford Fleming who had been in charge of the initial survey for the Canadian Pacific Railway twenty-five years earlier. Fleming also designed the first Canadian postage stamp and developed the concept of time zones.

Sandy Hook

Settlement approximately 10 kilometers south of Gimli on Highway 9

The community took its name from the sandy spit of land on nearby Lake Winnipeg. Sandy Hook became a Canadian Pacific Railway stopping point in 1912. A post office opened here the same year.

Sarto

Settlement approximately 15 kilometers southwest of Steinbach on Provincial Road 205

The earliest settlement here was called New York, but the post office opened in 1904 with the name of Sarto. Two versions describe how the name came about. One story has the town named after Andrea del Sarto, a sixteenth-century Italian painter. The other story ascribes the name to Pope Pius X, whose family name was Sarto.

If the community had just stuck with the name New York, it could have been known today as the Little Apple.

Scarth

Settlement approximately 75 kilometers west of Brandon on Highway 85

The railroad station here took the name Scarth in 1905, after William Bain Scarth, who had died three years before. He had owned land where the railroad passed through near here. Born in Scotland, Scarth immigrated to Ontario in 1855. He made a fortune in the lumber and shipbuilding business before coming to Manitoba where he prospered even more during the land boom of the 1880s. A few of Scarth's real estate deals were thought by some to be on the shady side of the street, but nothing against him was ever proven in court.

Although Scarth ran into financial trouble when the Manitoba land boom collapsed, he managed to carry on a political career after that in the Conservative Party. In 1895 he was appointed the federal deputy minister of agriculture.

He died in Ottawa in 1902. Binscarth, where Scarth owned a cattle ranch, is another Manitoba town that took Scarth's name.

Schanzenfeld

Settlement just south of Winkler off Highway 32

Schanzenfeld was named for Jacob Shantz, an Ontario immigrant who in 1873 helped Mennonite emissaries from Russia look into the possibility of new settlements in Manitoba. After a deal was made with the Canadian government, the first Mennonite reserve in the province, north and east of Rat River, was established in 1874. The original colony turned out to be so successful a second Mennonite reserve was established in 1876, in southern Manitoba west of the Red River. Schanzenfeld became one of the new settlements in the West Reserve.

The name, with some spelling liberties, is German for "Shantz's field."

Schist Lake

Rail point approximately 10 kilometers south of Flin Flon on the Hudson Bay Railway's Flin Flon–The Pas branch line

Canadian National Railways named this station stop in 1928 after nearby Schist Lake. Schist is a type of rock presumably found in abundance at Schist Lake.

Schoenwiese

Settlement approximately 20 kilometers southeast of Winkler on Provincial Road 421

Mennonite settlers named Schoenwiese in 1876 with the German words for "fair meadow." The community was established in the new West Reserve in 1876.

Sclater

Settlement approximately 110 kilometers northwest of Dauphin just off Highway 10

Sclater is a former rail point named by the Canadian Northern Railway in 1904 after one of its construction contractors. A post office opened here in 1911, but closed for good in 1976. The nearby Sclater River is named for the settlement.

Seddons Corner

Settlement approximately 65 kilometers northeast of Winnipeg on Highway 44

When the post office first opened here in 1931 it was called Buchan after a nearby rail point. The rail point had been named after Colonel Lawrence Buchan, who had fought against the Métis in the North West Rebellion of 1885. But the post office and settlement are not on the rail line.

Local residents called the community Seddons Corner for years. The name came about because Jack Seddon owned property at what is still a prominent intersection, at the corner of today's Highway 44 and Provincial Road 214. Seddon owned the land on the northeast corner of the intersection, where Seddons Corner Store is today.

At one time Highway 44 was the primary east-west route between Winnipeg and the Ontario border and Seddons Corner was a place to catch one of the main routes north. In 1967, the post office finally adopted the name commonly used for the settlement, making Seddons Corner official. Jack Seddon's parents, William and Rose, came to Manitoba from England in 1897.

Seddons Corner Store on property once owned by Jack Seddon. Photo by Ted Stone.

Selkirk

City approximately 20 kilometers northeast of Winnipeg on Highway 9

The city of Selkirk was named after Thomas Douglas, the 5TH Earl of Selkirk and the founder of the Red River Settlement.

Selkirk was the seventh son in the family, and would normally have been an unlikely prospect to inherit the earldom. But one by one older brothers died off and he inherited the title at the relatively young age of twenty-eight. After his peerage Selkirk became something of a philanthropist and he developed a particular interest in the plight of Scottish crofters, tenant farmers from the Scottish Highlands, many of whom were evicted from their farms beginning in the late eighteenth century in order to allow wealthy landowners to raise sheep.

It was Selkirk's idea that the displaced crofters would be better off in the new world than in the slums of England and Scotland where most would otherwise end up. To this end he organized a couple of small colonies in eastern Canada, but his biggest effort came in 1811 when he began sending emigrants from Scotland to the Red River.

Selkirk's interest in colonizing Manitoba's Red River was more than just philanthropy, however. Selkirk had become a shareholder in the Hudson's Bay Company. He was one of several new shareholders who pushed for a more aggressive stance against the North West Company in the competition for North American furs. Selkirk convinced the other HBC directors of the need for an agricultural settlement in the heart of the fur country. With farmers at Red River, Selkirk said, the company would obtain provisions "in country" instead of shipping more expensive goods from Europe through Hudson Bay. With this advantage, the company could compete more effectively in the Athabasca region of the far northwest.

The HBC granted Selkirk a huge tract of land along the Red and Assiniboine rivers, as far east as Lake of the Woods and as far south as today's South Dakota. The first settlers arrived at Red River in 1812, but life wasn't easy in the new colony. In addition to the challenges of isolation and climate, pioneering at Red River also roused the resentment of the mostly Métis employees of the North West Company there.

Individual settlers came to make a new home for themselves, but it was not lost on the Métis that the HBC had brought in the settlers to gain the upper hand in the fur trade. Tension between the two groups mounted until the summer of 1816 when an armed confrontation between settlers and Métis left nineteen settlers and Governor Semple dead after a skirmish at Seven Oaks. It was a battle neither side had intended, but the settlers clearly got the worst of it. The Métis may have lost one of their number in the fighting.

Despite the Métis victory, the Red River Settlement continued to grow in the years after Seven Oaks. A large part of the settlement's growth came about because the community provided a place for retired employees of both fur companies, and for the Métis themselves.

Selkirk, however, fell on hard times. In the aftermath of Seven Oaks he was forced to fight legal charges brought against him by North West Company interests. Never robust, his health worsened after a visit to Red River in 1817. By 1819, when the government in London finally obtained papers detailing the Red River troubles with the North West Company that essentially exonerated Selkirk, his health had deteriorated so badly he retired to the south of France where he died the following spring.

"I feel confident if we are patient," his sister Katherine wrote to Lady Selkirk, "he will have ample justice, and when the North West Company are forgotten his name and character will be revered. . . ."

Seven Sisters Falls

Settlement approximately 90 kilometers northeast of Winnipeg on Provincial Road 307

Voyageurs called the series of falls on the Winnipeg River near here "the seven sisters." The community of Seven Sisters Falls developed after the Winnipeg Electric Company built a dam in 1931. The dam flooded the first four of the seven falls and diminished the flow over the other three, so that today the water shows little of the ferocity that worried the coureurs de bois in the fur trade era.

Of course, the coureurs de bois of the fur trade had a lot to worry about on the river. One of the qualifications looked on favorably by the North West Company when hiring voyageurs was an inability to swim. Non-swimmers, it was felt, would be a lot more careful with company canoes on the water-route west, including the series of seven falls that would one day name a community.

Seymourville

Settlement approximately 200 kilometers northeast of Winnipeg at the edge of Hollow Water First Nation

Seymourville was named for members of an early Métis family in the community. Reports differ on whether the source was Wilfred Seymour or Bill Seymour. It's just as likely that the name Seymourville developed because several people from the Seymour family lived there.

Shamattawa

Settlement approximately 350 kilometers east of Thompson at the junction of Gods and Echoing rivers

In the Cree language *Shamattawa* means the joining of two rivers. The village where the Gods and Echoing rivers meet is also the site of the Shamattawa First Nation. At one time the river, after the confluence of the Gods and Echoing rivers, was known as the Shamattawa River.

Today most maps show the Gods River flowing north past Shamattawa until it joins the Hayes River south of York Factory.

Shellmouth

Settlement approximately 200 kilometers northwest of Brandon near Provincial Road 482

This settlement is on the Shell River, about five kilometers above its mouth on the Assiniboine. Charles Boulton, who owned the land where the post office opened, named the community. When the Canadian Pacific Railway arrived he had a town site surveyed and began selling lots in the new town.

Boulton also owned the land where the nearby town of Russell was established. (See entry for Russell.)

Shergrove

Settlement approximately 70 kilometers east of Dauphin on Highway 68

When the post office opened here in 1914 the new postmaster, David Henry, wanted to give it the name Sherwood, but the name was already taken. Henry, whose middle name was Sherwood, had homesteaded here the same year. The family had moved to Manitoba from Ontario in the late 1880s and Henry had operated a store southwest of Portage la Prairie before moving north.

Unfazed by a little red tape from the post office department, Henry figured Shergrove would be an acceptable alternative for using his middle name. This time postal officials accepted the name and it stuck. The post office, operated by members of the Henry family, lasted for more than fifty years, but finally closed in 1970.

Sherridon

Rail point approximately 65 kilometers northeast of Flin Flon on the Sherritt–Lynn Lake line

Sherridon grew up around the Sherritt-Gordon mine near here. The mine began operations in the early 1930s and was named after the prospector who discovered the mineral deposits, Carl Sherritt, and his backer, John P. Gordon, who provided the grubstake.

The mining community of Sherridon also took its name from the two men, manufacturing the first half of the name from the first letters of Sherritt and the final letters of the name from the ending of Gordon. By the 1950s the mine here had mostly played out and the operation, including buildings and homes, was taken north to Lynn Lake where more nickel and copper had been discovered.

Sherritt Junction

Rail point approximately 25 kilometers southeast of Flin Flon at the start of the Sherritt–Lynn Lake branch line

Sherritt Junction was named after Carl Sherritt (see above entry) about 1930, at the point where the railroad's branch line extended north to the Sherritt-Gordon Mine at Sherridon. Later, the railway extended more than two hundred kilometers farther north to Lynn Lake and new mining operations there.

Shilo

Settlement approximately 15 kilometers east of Brandon on Provincial Road 340

First noted as a rail point in 1905, Shilo didn't gain prominence in Manitoba until the 1930s when the federal government established a military base here. A post office using the name opened in 1934.

It's said the rail point took its name from a Jewish peddler who sold household goods in the area around the turn of the twentieth century.

Shoal Lake

Town approximately 100 kilometers northwest of Brandon on Highway 16

The community here takes its name from the nearby lake. The first post office using the name opened in 1877, but it was moved to the community's present location at the north end of the lake in 1886, in order to be on the new Manitoba and Northwest Railway. The name of the lake is apparently descriptive of visible shoals along the lake's shallow bottom.

Shorncliffe

Settlement approximately 60 kilometers north of Gimli, west of Highway 8 and Hecla/Grindstone Provincial Park

Shorncliffe was named after Shorncliffe, England, where Canadian soldiers trained during World War I. The post office opened here a few years after the war, in 1923, and closed in 1968.

Shortdale

Settlement approximately 70 kilometers west of Dauphin on Provincial Road 584

Shortdale was established as a rail point in 1904. The manufactured name was partly taken from nearby Short Creek, with the ending descriptive of the surrounding countryside.

Sidney

Settlement approximately 60 kilometers west of Portage la Prairie on Highway 1

The twin railroad sidings of Sidney and nearby Austin were named by the Marquis of Lorne, who was then Canada's Governor General. Canadian Pacific Railway officials gave the Marquis the chance to name six rail stops between Portage la Prairie and Brandon while he was on an official visit to Western Canada in 1881. He named Sidney and Austin after Sidney Austin, a newspaper reporter who accompanied the Marquis and his wife, Princess Louise, on the journey.

The Governor General also named Bagot, MacGregor, Douglas and Chater.

Sifton

Settlement approximately 30 kilometers north of Dauphin on Provincial Road 267

Most folks assume that Sifton was named after Clifford Sifton, a Member of Parliament from Manitoba who became the Minister of Interior and encouraged European immigration to Western Canada in the late nineteenth and early twentieth centuries. After all it seems logical to name a town somewhere in the West after a politician whose policies contributed to the settlement of the prairies.

The only problem with this theory is that Sifton wasn't named after the prominent cabinet minister at all. The town's name derives from a railroad contractor, William Sifton, who was responsible for this section of the railroad track.

In fact, Sifton, the Minister of Interior, preferred not to have any rail stop named after him. When he heard there was a Sifton, Manitoba in the works, he tried to get the railroad to change the name to something else. Nothing came of his efforts, however, and when the post office opened in 1898 it, too, was called Sifton.

Silver

Settlement approximately 30 kilometers northwest of Gimli on Highway 7

Businessman N. T. Silver gave this rail point its name when the Canadian Pacific branch line reached here in 1911. Mr. Silver bought large quantities of firewood and lumber in the area, most of which was shipped south to Winnipeg.

Silverton was named after a nearby country store. The store, owned by Robert Anderson, was named after Silver Creek, which flows through the area. Because of the store, the community was first known as Silverton Station when the Canadian Pacific branch line arrived here in 1911. The name of the community was later shortened.

Simonhouse

Settlement approximately 65 kilometers south of Flin Flon on Highway 10

The settlement of Simonhouse was established as a rail point, but the name comes from the nearby lake. The lake was named much earlier, after a trading post operated Bill Simon for the Revillon Freres Trading Company.

Sinclair

Settlement approximately 125 kilometers southwest of Brandon on Highway 2

Named for its postmaster, Peter Sinclair, the first Sinclair post office opened in 1893, but it wasn't until the Canadian Pacific Railway arrived that the name was used at its present location. In 1900, the CPR established Sinclair Station as a rail point and post office, and named it in deference to the Sinclair post office located ten kilometers to the south.

Later, the Sinclair post office changed its name, and then closed. In 1952, since there was no longer any other "Sinclair," Sinclair Station dropped the "station."

Sipiwesk

Rail point approximately 45 kilometers southeast of Thompson on the Hudson Bay line

The rail point here was named after nearby Sipiwesk Lake in 1933. The name is from the Cree language and denotes a lake with a winding channel.

Skownan

Settlement on Waterhen Lake approximately 135 kilometers northeast of Dauphin on Provincial Road 276

A post office opened here in 1925 named after the neighboring Skownan First Nation. The origin of the word is Ojibwa and refers to a turning point or turn-around point in a road.

Snowflake

Settlement approximately 100 kilometers southwest of Winkler on Provincial Road 201

Snowflake takes its name from nearby Snowflake Creek. There's some question whether early settler James D'Avignon named the creek, or if, as is more commonly supposed, the name comes from aboriginal origins.

According to the first version of the story, D'Avignon, who was a land locater, brought two friends, Sam Oakes and James Blake, out from Ontario to homestead in Manitoba. It was late October when they camped along a creek close to the American border. That night there was a light snow and in the morning D'Avignon named the stream Snowflake Creek.

Another version of the name's origins holds that aboriginal inhabitants already called the creek "Snowflake" when the first settlers, including D'Avignon, arrived in the area.

Snow Lake

Town approximately 200 kilometers east of Flin Flon on Provincial Road 392

The Town of Snow Lake takes its name from the nearby lake. The lake is supposed to have been named by Lew Parres, whose father,

Chris Parres, staked the first mineral claim in the area in 1927. This claim eventually led to the establishment of a mine and the community followed.

The story goes that Lew named the lake because its naturally soft water was like melted snow. The first permanent residents in Snow Lake came in 1947 when Bill and Margaret English moved their house here from Herb Lake in order to open a general store in advance of the expected mining activity.

Solsgirth

Settlement approximately 125 kilometers northwest of Brandon on Highway 16

Early residents called their community Allendale, apparently after an early settler, but when the Manitoba and Northwestern Railway arrived in 1885 the company's general manager, W. A. Barker, announced that the town would henceforth be named Solsgirth, after a place he knew of in Scotland.

The name apparently comes from the Gaelic for "surrounded by the sun."

Somerset

Village approximately 70 kilometers northwest of Winkler just off Highway 23

The post office opened here in 1881 and Charles Clark, the first postmaster, gave the community the name of his hometown in England. At least one other settler in the area was also from that English village.

A local legend has an alternate version for the name, however. According to this explanation the community was named after the nearby creek. The creek got its name when a local settler, Tom Stevenson, was thrown from a wagon when the wagon came to a sudden stop in the middle of the stream. Stevenson did a somersault off the wagon into the water and so other residents of the area started to call the stream Somersault Creek. That name, so the story goes, was shortened by common usage to Somerset.

Sommerfeld

Settlement approximately 45 kilometers southeast of Winkler on Provincial Road 421

Mennonite settlers established this community in the late 1870s. The name is German for "summer field."

Souris

Town approximately 45 kilometers southwest of Brandon on Highway 2

This settlement was originally named Plum Creek, after the stream that flows into the Souris River at this point. When immigrants from Millbrook, Ontario arrived here in 1880 they attempted to give the new community the name of their old one in Ontario. In the end, though, both the post office and the railroad decided to use the name of the nearby Souris River, so both of the other names for the community were thrown out, and the town became Souris.

The Souris River begins in Saskatchewan and flows from there into North Dakota before entering Manitoba, where it eventually joins the Assiniboine River. Early French traders called the stream Rivière la Souris, which was probably the French translation of the aboriginal name. On the American side of the border the river is known by the English translation, Mouse River.

A scene at Beresford Stock Farm near Souris in 1889. By permission of Manitoba Archives, Souris – farms 2, N1147.

South Indian Lake

Settlement approximately 135 kilometers northwest of Thompson on Southern Indian Lake

South Indian Lake gets its name from the nearby lake. An early Hudson's Bay Company post was established here and a post office opened in 1952. Cree speakers referred to the community as "winter settlement" and called the lake *Missi Sakahigan* or "Big Lake." Early traders used the name Southern Indian Lake because the Cree, or southern Indians, lived there as opposed to the area north of the lake, which was largely inhabited by Chipewyans, or northern Indians.

South Junction

Settlement approximately 90 kilometers southeast of Steinbach on Highway 12

The community here was established where the southern parts of two rail lines in Manitoba once joined. This "south junction" is in the southeastern corner of the province, near the American border. A post office using the name South Junction opened in 1908, soon after the construction of the railroads.

South Knife Lake

Settlement approximately 150 kilometers southwest of Churchill on South Knife Lake

South Knife Lake, an area long used as a trappers' camp, takes its name from the lake. The lake probably takes its name from the South Knife River, which flows from the lake north to Hudson Bay. There's also a North Knife Lake, but it lies west of South Knife Lake on the North Knife River, which flows into Hudson Bay on the north side of a delta where the two streams join before entering the bay.

It's fair to speculate both Knife Rivers received their names as translations from the aboriginal designation for the stream where the two rivers merged, although it's also possible that it was the lakes who long ago gave their names to the rivers. To complicate matters, Etawney Lake, which lies upstream and south of South Knife Lake, was known to aboriginal speakers as Knife Lake.

Southport

Settlement on Provincial Road 331 just south of Portage la Prairie

A post office was established here in 1955 to serve what was then a Royal Canadian Air Force base. The name originated during World War II when there were two air bases in the Portage la Prairie area. Southport was the south airport.

Spearhill

Settlement approximately 180 kilometers north of Winnipeg on Provincial Road 237

J. R. Spear started a limestone quarry on the rise of ground here in the early eighteenth century. It was Spear's quarry that enticed the Canadian Northern Railway to build a spur line here. The post office opened in 1915 and closed in 1966.

Spence Lake

Settlement approximately 75 kilometers northeast of Dauphin on Provincial Road 276

The community of Spence Lake is named for the nearby lake. The lake was apparently named for an early cattle rancher in the area named John Spence.

Sperling

Settlement approximately 45 kilometers southwest of Winnipeg on Highway 3

Early residents here called their community Mariposa, after the place in Ontario from where many of them had immigrated. The post office opened here as Mariposa in 1901, but the same year the railroad arrived and chose the name Sperling instead. The post office changed to the new name the following year. As a result, instead of being named after a community in Ontario, Sperling is named after a British financial company, Sperling and Company. The company helped finance the railroad.

To add to the insult to the residents of Mariposa, the railroad's choice of the name was a mistake. Railroad officials had intended to name the community Brunkild, but got the section numbers mixed up and called the station Sperling, which had originally been designated for another stop on the line. (See entry for Brunkild.)

Split Lake

Both a settlement and a rail point approximately 120 kilometers northwest of Thompson

There are two community designations called Split Lake on Manitoba maps, one on Split Lake and the other a rail point a few kilometers south on the Hudson Bay Railway. The rail point was named in 1929 in recognition of the nearby lake. The community on the northwest side of the lake also took its name from the lake. It is the site of one of the first Hudson's Bay Company posts built inland from the bay, probably in the mid-1700s. Several other trading posts were built on the lake over the next two hundred years.

The name of the lake derives from its Cree name and may have been used because islands in the lake effectively split it into parts. During the fur-trading era aboriginal people also sometimes referred to the lake as the "lake of the forts" because of the many trading posts located there.

Sprague

Settlement approximately 110 kilometers southeast of Steinbach on Highway 12

Dan Sprague started a lumber company in southeastern Manitoba near Lake of the Woods in the 1880s. He cut huge white pine as well as other conifers, which he assembled into booms and floated south on Mud Creek into the United States, and then down the Roseau River to the Red where the logs made the rest of the trip to sawmills in Winnipeg.

Loggers would travel down the river with the booms, as would Sprague, although he traveled in a large riverboat named the Wanigan that he outfitted for the journey. At Roseau Rapids, south of present day St. Malo, Sprague had to negotiate with the local aboriginal community to remove rocks from the fish dam there so the logs could pass. It has been estimated that the fish dam, parts of which can still be seen in the river today, had been in use by aboriginal people for several hundred of years at this time.

Today, Mud Creek (also called the north branch of the Roseau) is known as Sprague Creek. The town that grew up around Sprague's company also took his name in 1900, after the site became the terminus for the Manitoba and South Eastern Railway. The first post office opened in 1901.

Low water where Dan Sprague paid Indians to open fish trap used for generations on Roseau River. The same spot was also used as a ford on the Roseau by ox trains traveling the Crow Wing Trail in the 19th Century. By permission of Manitoba Archives, Rosseau River.

Sprucewoods

Settlement approximately 15 kilometers east of Brandon on Provincial Road 340

The community of Sprucewoods was established as people moved to the region known as Shilo Siding School District in the years after World War II. In the 1950s an increasing number of residents just outside what was then known as the Sprucewood Forest Preserve formed an informal community club.

Initially, they built a dance platform in the open air inside the forest preserve, near the warden's residence and fire tower. Eventually, the group put together the money to put up a clubhouse for a community center. One of their members, a woman named Marg Haggarty, suggested the name at a meeting and Alice Gonbek, another club member, made a sign for the new Sprucewoods Community Center.

There was some discussion about whether the name should be Sprucewoods or Sprucewood, which was the name of the forest preserve at the time, but club members decided that the community was separate from the forest, so the name would be slightly different as well. The naming of the community club gave a name to what was still an unofficial hamlet.

By some accounts the settlement started when Tom and Marg Woods moved to what became Sprucewoods in 1954. The Woods, whose surname evidently played no part in the naming of the community, began to sell lots in the budding community soon after they arrived. They also started the town's first business, Woods Cartage. In the 1960s, several more businesses were established, including a store, restaurant and hairdresser. No post office was ever opened in Sprucewoods, but the forest preserve eventually became Spruce Woods Provincial Forest. Spruce Woods Provincial Park was also established nearby.

Starbuck

Settlement approximately 20 kilometers southwest of Winnipeg on Highway 2

Starbuck was established as a rail point on the Canadian Pacific Railway in 1885 and, according to Robert Douglas in *Place-Names of Manitoba*, was named after a community in Minnesota with that name.

But there are several other stories about how the name originated. One maintains the town was named after a pair of oxen that had been put to work building the rail bed during railroad construction. According to this version of the story, Starbuck commemorates the oxen, named Star and Buck, who drowned during a spring flood on the nearby La Salle River. The railroad construction contractor on that section of line, a man named Vanderslie, who Douglas said was responsible for naming the town after the Minnesota village, actually named the community to honor the fallen animals.

Steep Rock

Settlement approximately 220 kilometers northwest of Winnipeg on Provincial road 239

Steep Rock is an appropriately descriptive name. Steep limestone cliffs line the Lake Manitoba shore here. A limestone quarry was established here in 1913 and the railroad arrived soon afterward.

Steinbach

City approximately 50 kilometers southeast of Winnipeg on Highway 12

Early Mennonite settlers who came to the district from a community with the same name in Russia established Steinbach in 1874. That community, in turn, had been named after an earlier Mennonite community in Germany. The name means "stone brook" in German.

Stockton

Settlement approximately 60 kilometers southeast of Brandon near Highway 2

Stockton was named for the hometown of an early homesteader who came from Stockton-on-Tees in England. Two Stocktons have existed in Manitoba. The original moved to the present site on the Canadian Pacific Railway branch line when the railroad came through the area in 1890. At first known as New Stockton, the railroad town became simply Stockton after the complete demise of the former community, which had become known by that time as Old Stockton.

Like the original Stockton, the new one too experienced a period of steep decline after the homestead era, leaving little except its name on the map today.

Stonewall

Town approximately 20 kilometers north of Winnipeg on Highway 67

The first postmaster, O. P. Jackson, named Stonewall. The name originated with the American Civil War general, Stonewall Jackson. Because of the general's fame during the later part of the 19th century the name was often applied to any male Jackson on the continent.

Among the Manitoba Jacksons, though, the name was probably most often applied to O. P. Jackson's brother, Samuel, a prominent Winnipeg alderman. And the postmaster undoubtedly had Samuel in mind when he named the town.

In 1873 Samuel Jackson divided land he owned here into lots and began selling them. He eventually moved to the community himself, where he built a large house that's still standing today. Jackson represented the Stonewall riding in the Manitoba Legislature from 1883 until 1899. Later, he became a Member of Parliament.

Stony Mountain

Settlement approximately 10 kilometers north of Winnipeg on Highway 7

The hill rising above a gravel ridge here was known as Assinawa, or Stony Mountain, by aboriginals when Europeans arrived, and the name, in translation, continued to be used after that. The first post office here opened in 1873, using the name Rockwood. It wasn't until 1880 that it took the name of the nearby landmark.

Strathclair

Settlement approximately 90 kilometers northwest of Brandon on Highway 16

Strathclair can trace its history to an early settlement, first called The Bend, then Strathclair, at the big bend of the Little Saskatchewan River north of the present town. Duncan Sinclair surveyed the area in the mid-1870s. It was reportedly decided to name the settlement by using the last part of his name preceded by the Gaelic word *strath*, which means "valley."

Of course, the word *clair* means "clear," so the name could simply mean "clear valley," in which case the story about Sinclair materialized later. The possible existence of an earlier Hudson's Bay Company post called Strathclair nearby adds credence to this version of the story.

When the Manitoba and North Western Railway came through the area in 1885 it named the station closest to the river settlement Strathclair Station and the first post office on that site opened the following year. It wasn't long, of course, before the new town on the railroad eclipsed the old one on the river. The river town soon became known as Old Sinclair and eventually became a ghost town.

Stuartburn

Settlement approximately 85 kilometers south of Winnipeg on Provincial Road 201

Stuartburn was named after an early settler, probably Stuart Miller who lived along the Roseau River about 1880. Other reports, however, refer to an early settler named William H. Stuart as the source for the town name. Initially, the settlement called itself Stuartville, but the post office turned down that name because of possible confusion with another community.

Sundance

Rail point approximately 250 kilometers south of Churchill on the Hudson Bay line and Provincial road 290

A post office opened at Sundance in 1976, primarily to serve employees of Manitoba Hydro who were building a hydroelectric power plant on the nearby Nelson River. The name was taken from nearby Sundance Creek. It refers to a ceremonial gathering held annually by many aboriginal peoples.

Sundown

*Settlement approximately 70 kilometers southeast of Steinbach on
Provincial Road 201*

A railroad contractor named the new rail point of Sundown in 1906,
because, it is said, the crew first arrived to begin work about sundown.
Perhaps, the crew actually finished at sundown, as another explanation
for the name maintains. Either story provides a reasonable explanation.

Swan Lake

Settlement approximately 90 kilometers northwest of Winkler on Highway 23

When early settlers began coming to the area in the late 1870s, they
named the community here after the nearby lake. A post office opened
in 1881 and the railroad arrived in 1889.

The lake may have been noted as early as 1805 by American explorers Lewis and Clark as Peacock Lake. It has also been known over the
years as Buck Foot Lake and Pembina Lake. Presumably, the lake was at
one time home to a large number of swans. The name is likely a translation of an aboriginal name.

Swan River

Town approximately 170 kilometers northwest of Dauphin on Highway 10

Main Street Swan River in 1957. By permission of Manitoba Archives, Swan River 1, N4606.

The town here was established as a rail point and named after the nearby Swan River about 1900, but Europeans had already been in the area for 200 years by that point. Henry Kelsey, working for the Hudson's Bay Company, first came into the region about 1690. Peter Pond noted the river before 1800. Fur trade posts were established on the river by 1870 and the first North West Mounted Police built the first barracks in Western Canada here in 1874.

The source for the name for the stream is unclear, but it apparently comes from the black swans that once nested along the river. Some reports attribute the name to wild swans that were once regularly seen on nearby Thunder Hill.

Sylvan
Settlement approximately 65 kilometers northwest of Gimli on Provincial Road 223

When the post office opened here in 1914 it was named Sylvan—a word rooted in the Latin word for forest—because of the community's wooded surroundings. The post office closed in 1959.

Tadoule Lake
Settlement approximately 250 kilometers east of Churchill on Tadoule Lake

The community here takes its name from the nearby lake. The name is Chipewyan and means "floating ashes lake" or "charcoal lake." Speculation suggests that a forest fire that left ashes on the lake prompted the name.

Takipy
Rail point approximately 100 kilometers northeast of Flin Flon on the Hudson Bay Railway's Lynn Lake line

The rail point here was named for the nearby lake. The lake name is from the Cree for "cold water." Apparently all of the water in the area runs cold, as the Cree name for the Kississing River, which runs out of Kississing Lake and then into Takipy Lake, means a "river that is cold."

Tenby

Rail point approximately 205 kilometers northwest of Portage la Prairie on Provincial road 575

The community's first postmaster, James Griffiths, named Tenby after a town in Wales in 1895. The post office closed permanently in 1967 and the community has largely disappeared, except as a name on the map.

Teulon

Town approximately 45 kilometers north of Winnipeg on Highway 7

Charles Castle, an inspector with the Canadian Pacific Railway, helped route the railroad through this community in the early 1900s. According to local legend, grateful residents asked Castle to choose a name for the new town for them. He suggested Teulon, his wife's maiden name.

The Pas

Town approximately 140 kilometers southeast of Flin Flon on Highway 10

Walking on logs on the Saskatchewan River near The Pas about 1922. By permission of Manitoba Archives, The Pas 4, N19254.

The Pas was noted as an aboriginal settlement, called Poskoyac by La Verendrye in the 1700s. Alexander Henry noted the name as Pasquayah in 1775. Both versions are derived from the Cree for "a narrows in a river." What we know as The Pas today is situated at a long-used, narrow crossing place on the Saskatchewan River. According to one explanation, the name is simply a shortened version of the aboriginal name.

An opposing theory that perhaps has more force is that The Pas is from the French, for "gap," "passage" or "crossing." The first Europeans here were the French-speaking fur traders and the site was on *le pas* of the Saskatchewan. The French also established the fur post Fort du Pas here in the mid 1700s.

The argument for the French origins of the name is bolstered by the fact that the local post office, when it opened in 1895, was called "Le Pas." Only later, when the town was incorporated in 1912, did the official name become The Pas.

Thicket Portage
Rail point approximately 50 kilometers south of Thompson on the Hudson Bay line

Thicket Portage lies on the traditional portage between Wintering Lake and Landing Lake, and is a direct translation of the aboriginal name, Sagaskwaskow Uniga. The community is considered one of the oldest inhabited spots in Manitoba and the railroad used the traditional name when it established a rail point here in 1920.

Thompson
City approximately 400 kilometers northeast of The Pas on Highway 6

Thompson was established in 1957 after the discovery of rich nickel deposits in the area. John Fairfield Thompson was the chairman of the board and chief executive officer of the International Nickel Company at the time. The company still owns a smelter and mining operations here.

Thompson in 1957. By permission of Manitoba Archives, Thompson 17.

Thornhill

Settlement approximately 25 kilometers west of Winkler on Highway 3

Thornhill was named in the 1870s by an early settler, after a country residence in Quebec. Unlike many communities whose names the post office or a railroad later changed, Thornhill kept its name when a post office opened here in 1879. When the Canadian Pacific Railway arrived in 1882, it also stuck with it.

Apparently, the only time there was a challenge to the name was in the 1870s, when a local pioneer named Bradshaw tried to register the community's name with the land agent in Emerson. According to the local legend, the land agent wanted Bradshaw to change the town's name to Thornton, after a British diplomat. Bradshaw refused and Thornhill has remained Thornhill ever since.

Tidal

Rail Point approximately 15 kilometers south of Churchill on the Hudson Bay line

Tides from Hudson Bay extend up the Churchill River approximately this far, and hence the name of this rail point.

Tilston

Settlement approximately 145 kilometers southwest of Brandon on Provincial Road 345

A post office named Eagleton opened here in 1904. When the railroad arrived in 1907 it announced that residents could submit a list of possible names for the new station. Harold Bateman submitted Tilston, because he was from Tilston, England, and railroad officials accepted the name.

Tolstoi

Settlement approximately 85 kilometers south of Winnipeg on Highway 59

A few of the original settlers around here were former serfs on Count Leo Tolstoi's estate in Russia. But none of the former serfs had a hand in naming the new community. Railroad officials chose the name in 1911.

The Oleskiw post office operated earlier in the vicinity. That name was thought to honor Oleskiw Woychenko, who had encouraged Ukrainian immigration to Canada in the late nineteenth and early twentieth centuries.

Toutes Aides

Settlement approximately 100 kilometers northeast of Dauphin on Provincial Road 276

When the parish was established at Toutes Aides in the early years of the twentieth century, a large donation was made by a resident of Nantes, France. The donor lived near the Catholic shrine of Notre Dame de Toutes Aides and as a tribute the new parish in Manitoba became Notre

Dame de Toutes Aides. The post office took the same name when it opened in 1909, but the following year the community's name was shortened to, simply, Toutes Aide.

Traverse Bay

Settlement approximately 100 kilometers northeast of Winnipeg off Highway 59

This resort community on Lake Winnipeg takes its name from the nearby bay. The bay probably got the name in fur trade days because voyageurs traveling up the Winnipeg River would have to cross it before getting out into Lake Winnipeg, either to turn south to the mouth of the Red River, or to go on to other routes at other points on the lake. Conversely, the bay would have to be crossed in order to get to the mouth of the Winnipeg River, where the long trip to the East began.

Treesbank

Settlement approximately 65 kilometers southeast of Brandon on Provincial Road 530

The Canadian Pacific Railway established a rail point here in 1891 and residents chose the name as a tribute to the maple, ash and cottonwood trees growing along the banks of the nearby Souris River.

Treherne

Town approximately 60 kilometers southwest of Portage la Prairie on Highway 2

Pioneers traveling the Yellow Quill Trail first settled in this area in the 1870s. A post office opened in 1880 and took the name Treherne, after early settler George Treherne. Mr. Treherne may have had the postal contract and named the settlement. Six years after the post office opened, when the Canadian Pacific Railway built a line to Souris, the community of Treherne, including the post office, moved across the river to be on the new rail line.

Tremaudan

Rail point just north of The Pas on the Hudson Bay line

Tremaudan is the first rail point on the Manitoba map north of The Pas. Initially it was named Cheman, the Cree word for Canoe. In 1928 the Canadian National Railways changed the name to Tremaudan after Auguste Henri de Trémaudan, the publisher of a local newspaper.

Trémaudan had published a book about the Hudson Bay Railway more than a decade earlier. Born in Quebec, he came to Manitoba after attending school in France. He ran several French language newspapers and, in 1911, founded *The Herald* at The Pas. He also wrote extensively about Louis Riel and the Red River Rebellion and published *Histoire de la Nation Métisse*. His book *The Hudson Bay Road* was published in 1915.

Tummel

Settlement approximately 100 kilometers west of Dauphin near Highway 83

The post office here had a little trouble getting the name Tummel right. The first postmaster, Peter McDougall, wanted to name the new community after the Tummel River in Scotland, near which he had once lived. McDougall spoke with a Scottish accent, however, and the postal inspector misunderstood the name. Because of the misunderstanding the new post office officially opened as Tumbell in 1886. It took until 1922 to correct the mistake and change the name back to Tummel.

As things turned out, it didn't make that much difference. Tummel failed to thrive and the post office closed in 1938.

Turnberry

Rail point near the Saskatchewan border approximately 120 kilometers southwest of The Pas

First noted on the Canadian Northern Railway line in 1911, Turnberry is one of a series of stops south of The Pas named for towns in Scotland and the British Isles. Other rail points along the line with names of similar origin include Freshford, Whithorn, Westray and Cantyre.

Turnbull

Rail point approximately 135 kilometers northeast of The Pas on the Hudson Bay line

Thomas Turnbull was a Canadian National Railways maintenance engineer, and one-time assistant engineer on the Hudson Bay Railway. CNR officials named the rail stop here after him in 1928.

Tyndall-Garson

Side-by-side towns approximately 30 kilometers northeast of Winnipeg on Highway 44

Neighboring communities of Tyndall and Garson incorporated as a single Local Urban District in the Municipality of Brokenhead in 2003. Both communities grew up near nearby limestone quarries.

Garson was incorporated as a village in 1915, but took the name Garson in 1927. William Garson established a quarry here in the early part of the twentieth century. The early community's post office had been named Garson Station, so in a sense changing the official name in 1927 was a reversion to the original name.

Tyndall is the older of the two communities. The Canadian Pacific Railway established a rail point here during the building of the transcontinental railroad in 1877. The first post office opened in 1892. The town was named after John Tyndall, an Irish physicist. The name then became attached to Tyndall Stone, the locally quarried rock that has been used for decorative purposes throughout Canada and the United States.

Tyrrell

Rail point approximately 150 kilometers northeast of The Pas on the Hudson Bay line

Canadian National Railways officials named Tyrrell in 1928 after James and Joseph Tyrrell. The two brothers led multiple careers. Among other occupations, James was a surveyor, engineer and explorer; among other careers, Joseph worked as a geologist, historian and explorer.

Both men traveled extensively in northern and western Canada and Joseph is responsible for naming several physical features in Manitoba.

He also discovered some of the first dinosaur fossils found in western Canada near Drumheller, Alberta, where the Royal Tyrrell Museum is also named after him. Joseph helped survey possible railroad routes from Saskatchewan to Hudson Bay. The two brothers were also involved in mining operations from Ontario to the Yukon.

Ukraina

Settlement approximately 55 kilometers northwest of Dauphin on Provincial Road 273

Ukraina got its name one evening in May of 1897 around a campfire in the woods where settlers in the area camped after looking for new places to settle in the area. The pioneers fell to talking about what they would call the district that was to be their new home and they decided on the name Ukraina, after their old home in the Ukraine.

At some point after that a petition to use the name was sent to government officials and when the railroad arrived in 1898 the rail point was so named.

Underhill

Settlement approximately 80 kilometers southwest of Brandon on Highway 23

The rail point at Underhill was established in 1897 on land owned by a local farmer named John Underhill. The railroad gave their new station his name. A post office using the name opened in 1900, but closed in 1966.

Valley River

Settlement approximately 15 kilometers north of Dauphin on Provincial Road 362

Established as a rail point in 1898, Valley River took its name from the nearby river, which rises in the Duck Mountains and flows through a wide valley between the Duck and Riding mountains to Dauphin Lake. The aboriginal name was *Tewatenow Sibi,* meaning "the river that divides the hills."

Vassar

Settlement approximately 95 kilometers southeast of Steinbach off Highway 12

Vassar was established as a rail point in 1899. According to Robert Douglas in *Place-Names of Manitoba,* the railroad named it either after Ida Vassar of Kirkfield, Ontario or, according to others, Jack Vassar, who was involved in the construction of the rail line.

An alternate story relates that the name comes from Vassar Carpenter, who may have been the first infant born in the district after settlers began to arrive in 1896.

Venlaw

Settlement approximately 50 kilometers northwest of Dauphin on Provincial Road 274

An Ontarian, Alfred Mitchell, is responsible for naming Venlaw. Mitchell happened to be in the new settlement at the time the post office was established. A settler named Frank Dowkes had the postal contract and Mitchell asked Dowkes if he could name the new mail stop after Venlaw, his hometown in Scotland. Dowkes agreed to the request.

Victoria Beach

Settlement approximately 105 kilometers northeast of Winnipeg on Highway 59

Some say that Victoria Beach was named after Queen Victoria because summer residents traditionally opened their cottages here on the Victoria Day long weekend, but the tidy theory has a couple of flaws.

The railroad didn't arrive at Victoria Beach to spur cottage development until 1916, but the name Victoria Beach had already been in use for the shoreline here for at least a decade. When the railroad named the station Victoria Beach it took an existing name for this strip of waterfront.

Not only were there few cottages to open on the Victoria Day long weekend at that time, the name, for the most part, predates what is now known as Victoria Day. While Canada began celebrating Queen Victoria's birthday during her reign, and continued to celebrate it after her death, an official act establishing a "Victoria Day" holiday wasn't passed until 1952. Until at least that time, the holiday was popularly known as "the Queen's Birthday."

Virden

Town approximately 90 kilometers west of Brandon on Highway 1

When the Canadian Pacific Railway arrived at today's Virden in early 1883 the district was already known as Gopher Creek, a translation of the aboriginal name for a nearby stream and a designation long used by traders and hunters on the plains. The first post office had opened a few months before, and it, too, took the name Gopher Creek.

But with the coming of the Canadian Pacific Railway to the area the post office moved closer to the tracks on the new townsite. When it made the move, it took the name Virden. Even the railroad, which had initially called the station Gopher Creek, had second thoughts. But railroad officials changed the new station's name to Manchester, after the Duke of Manchester, rather than Virden. Only when they discovered that another district had already registered the name Manchester did the CPR decide that, like the post office, it would call the new town Virden.

The origin of the name, however, is unclear. The likeliest tale is that it is a misspelling of Verden, a city in Germany favored by the Duchess of Manchester.

Vista

Settlement approximately 125 kilometers northwest of Brandon on Highway 14

Established as a rail point in 1905, Vista at first went by the name Ita. Within the first year or two, the name was changed from Ita to Vista. By adding two letters, the name came to descrice the long prairie view here.

Vita

Settlement approximately 100 kilometers southeast of Winnipeg on Provincial Road 201

The first settlers in this area opted to call their town Szewczenko, and the first postmaster submitted that name to postal officials. The new post office only operated under the name for a few months, however, because the postal department, claiming the spelling was too complicated, changed the name to Vita, the Latin word for Life.

Taras Szewczenko, or Shevchenko, was a well-known Ukrainian poet. Support for that name continued within the town, but even local settlers were unsuccessful in their attempts to get the name restored. The town has remained Vita for the last century.

The school division here, however, took the name Schevchenko until the local division was absorbed into a larger district. The name of the local high school has kept the town's original name and is still known as Schevchenko.

Vivian
Settlement approximately 35 kilometers east of Winnipeg on Highway 15

Vivian Station was established as a rail point on the Grand Trunk Railway's main line in 1911. The post office opened in 1913 using the same name. "Station" was dropped from the name at the request of local residents in 1954.

While there's no direct evidence to support the theory, the name likely shares its origins with other stations that received female names along the railroad in this area at the time of construction. There's circumstantial evidence indicating that one of the men working with construction contracts here named all four of the stops after his four daughters: Elma, Vivian, Hazel and Anola.

Vogar
Settlement approximately 165 kilometers northwest of Winnipeg on Highway 68

The post office here in 1905 was known at first as Dog Creek, a name commonly used for the nearby Lake Manitoba Indian Reserve, as well as a creek that flows from Dog Lake into Lake Manitoba.

Both Dog Creek and Dog Lake picked up their names after a band of Sioux chased a white man up the eastern shore of Lake Manitoba. The Sioux apparently chased the "white dog" up the creek and across the lake. According to the legend they didn't catch the man until he reached Watchhorn Bay north of Dog Lake back on the Lake Manitoba shore. As a result of the man's capture the aboriginal name for Watchorn Bay was Dog Hung Bay.

The name for the community here changed from Dog Creek to Vogar about 1920. Taken from the Icelandic language, *Vogar* refers to small bays. Presumably, the bays in question are on the nearby lakes. While Vogar is not situated on the water, both a bay on Lake Manitoba and another on Dog Lake are only a short distance away.

Waasagomach

Settlement approximately 275 kilometers southeast of Thompson on Island Lake

Waasagomach (locally, the preferred spelling is Wasagomack) is named after nearby Waasagomach Bay. The bay's name is taken from Cree words that mean "round bay."

Wabowden

Settlement approximately 100 kilometers southeast of Thompson off Highway 6

Wabowden sounds like a fine aboriginal name, probably taken from the Cree language, but it's not.

Railroad officials made up the name. First known as Setting Lake, the community changed its name to Wabowden to conform to the name of the rail point established on the Hudson Bay line in 1928. Canadian National Railways officials named the station after W. A. Bowden, the chief engineer of railways in Ottawa. The name uses the initials of his given names and all of the letters of his last name. The railroad had used the same system to name Ashern, on another Manitoba rail line, for another railroad employee, A. S. Hern.

Wakopa

Settlement approximately 75 kilometers south of Brandon on Provincial Road 341

The settlement of Wakopa seems to have led an Old West-style existence for the past 150 years or so. It sprang to life on the edge of the

A Boundary Commission depot near Wakopa in 1870s. By permission of Manitoba Archives, Boundary Commission (1872 – 1874) III, N11953.

Turtle Mountains near the American border where two prominent trails, the Missouri and Boundary Commission, crossed in the 1870s.

The first independent merchant and resident in the district was fur trader Bernard Lariviere. He was so highly regarded by the Sioux that a chief named Lariviere *Wakopa*, or "white father." Accused of being a whiskey trader, Lariviere was a wanted man south of the border where American authorities thought somewhat less highly of him than the Sioux.

According to some stories, a Hudson's Bay Company outpost was on the site when Lariviere arrived, but the new merchant and several friends drove the bigger company's employees away in what became known as the "Battle of the Broken Wheel." Allegedly a Red River Cart overturned and broke a wheel, during the skirmish.

In 1876, after the Battle of the Little Big Horn in Montana, a band of Sioux escaping the American cavalry came through Wakopa with Custer's horse in tow, showing off the general's saddle, along with several white scalps. During the 1885 North-West Rebellion, a group of aboriginals pretending to take a body for burial in the Turtle Mountains were captured near Wakopa by the Border Patrol while smuggling a Gatling gun into the country. Reports suggest the gun was destined for Riel's men.

In the 1880s Lariviere and the settlement at Wakopa prospered. Initially, the town went by the name Lariviere, and the community's founding merchant was also the local justice of the peace. As the years went on the town boomed along with other new towns in the area, but when regional railroads passed the community by in favor of routes through other towns a slow decline began. Businesses prospered more readily in nearby villages instead of Wakopa. The town hung on, though, and in the 1920s North America's most prolific murderer of the time, known as the Gorilla Strangler, was captured here.

Still, Wakopa eventually turned into a ghost town, following once more its Old West destiny. In the 1970s a single family bought the few buildings remaining here.

Waldersee

Settlement approximately 140 kilometers northwest of Portage la Prairie on Provincial Road 260

Waldersee was named after a German count in 1908. Count Waldersee commanded an alliance of troops from western nations in China to put down the Boxer Rebellion of 1900.

Wampum

Settlement approximately 95 kilometers southeast of Steinbach off Highway 12

The word *wampum* has an aboriginal origin, but when the rail point was established here the name didn't have anything to do with the aboriginal people of the area or anywhere else for that matter. The rail point and post office were named after Wampum Baking Powder, the brand used by the cook for the construction crew building the branch line here.

Wanless

Settlement 45 kilometers north of The Pas on Highway 10

The Canadian Northern Railway established Wanless and named it after Jack Wanless, an early homesteader in the region and prominent resident of The Pas. Wanless provided the financial backing for a number of northern Manitoba prospectors, only some of whom were successful.

Warren

Settlement approximately 30 kilometers northwest of Winnipeg on Highway 6

The post office opened in this Interlake community in 1882. At that time it was named Hanlan, after Ned Hanlan, then considered the champion oarsman of the world. When the railroad arrived in 1905 they renamed the stop here after the chief clerk of the railroad's western vice-president, A. E. Warren.

Warren Landing

Settlement south of Norway House on Big Mossy Point on the north shore of Lake Winnipeg

Warren Landing is named for John Warren, an employee of the Hudson's Bay Company. Warren spent several months here with Selkirk Settlers who had fled the conflict between the fur companies at Red River. He helped the settlers return to their homesteads and the conflict eventually subsided.

Peace between the companies, however, did not come fast enough for Warren, who was killed in a later clash with the North West Company in 1815.

Wasagaming

Settlement approximately 100 kilometers north of Brandon on Highway 10

The post office for this resort community inside Riding Mountain National Park was first named Clark Beach, after the first cottage owner on nearby Clear Lake. In the early 1930s, however, the federal

Department of Interior held a contest to rename the community. Edna Medd of Winnipegosis, Manitoba won the contest. Her choice of a name, Wasagaming, is a word of Ojibwa origin that means "clear water."

Waskada

Village approximately 140 kilometers southwest of Brandon on Provincial Road 251

After settlers in this region petitioned for a post office in 1883 the government granted the request and assigned the present name. Officials said that name was aboriginal in origin and meant "the best of everything."

Some have suggested the name is an approximation of the aboriginal *wa-sta-daow*, a phrase allegedly heard often by homesteaders when they would ask aboriginal people about the quality of land in a region. "Wa-sta-daow," people would be told, or in English: "It's better farther on."

The aboriginal people, of course, just wanted the homesteaders to keep going, to leave them alone instead of stopping anywhere near where they were.

Waterhen

Settlement approximately 145 kilometers northeast of Dauphin on Provincial Road 276

Waterhen is named after nearby Waterhen Lake. The lake is a translation from the aboriginal name for the waterfowl commonly called mud hen.

Waugh

Rail point at the eastern end of the Greater Winnipeg Water District Railway on Shoal Lake

Richard D. Waugh was the mayor of Winnipeg when work began on the service railroad and aqueduct that still supplies the city with water today. Waugh was born in Scotland, but came to Winnipeg in 1881 as a teenager with his parents. Founder of the Winnipeg Real Estate Exchange, Waugh was first elected mayor in 1911. He served, with a one term break, until 1916.

Work on an aqueduct to provide a new source of drinking water for Winnipeg began while Waugh was mayor in 1914. The railroad was an integral part of the construction of the aqueduct, and for many years it also provided revenue to counteract the expense of carrying Lake of the Woods water to the city. In addition to transporting workers and material for the construction and upkeep of the aqueduct, the railroad provided services for goods and passengers along its 150-kilometer route. The station at Waugh, where water began flowing toward the city from a bay on Shoal Lake, was named to honor the mayor.

Today, the City of Winnipeg still operates railroad and aqueduct, but the railroad ended private business along the line in the 1990s. It functions today as a means for carrying workers and materials to maintain the aqueduct, and to provide security for the city's water system along the route.

Wawanesa

Village approximately 50 kilometers southeast of Brandon on Provincial Road 344

Established as a rail point in 1890, Wawanesa originally had the name *Sipewiske*, an aboriginal word that meant "crooked river." The name referred to the new community's location on the Souris River.

Wawanesa in 1897. BY PERMISSION OF MANITOBA ARCHIVES, WAWANESA 1, N827.

Some of the settlers in the region disliked the name, however, because they said it sounded like "sip of whiskey," which put the town in a bad light. So the name was changed to Wawanesa.

This name, too, is also of aboriginal origin, but a controversy exists over its meaning. One claim is that the word means "beautiful vista." Another says it is "wild goose nest." Both versions could be derived from aboriginal words very close to Wawanesa.

In Ojibwa, *wawi* and *nika* name a wild goose or a kind of wild goose. Some reports say the name Wawanesa comes from an aboriginal word for the whippoorwill and another source says it is from the Sioux language and means "no snow." There is no certain explanation.

Waywayseecappo

Settlement approximately 155 kilometers northwest of Brandon on Highway 45

The community here, on the Waywayseecappo First Nation, is named after Chief Waywayseecappo who led his people in Treaty 4 discussions with the federal government. That treaty ceded land to Canada in exchange for reserve lands in western Manitoba and Saskatchewan.

Translated to English from the Ojibwa, the chief's name meant "Standing Proud" and is derived from the way male grouse and prairie chickens display their feathers during the mating ritual.

Weir River

Rail point approximately 225 kilometers south of Churchill on the Hudson Bay Railway

The rail stop here was named in 1928 after the nearby river. Aboriginal people traditionally built weirs to catch fish at the river's mouth on the Nelson. Before it was known as the Weir River early cartographers used aboriginal names that generally meant "fishing river," or "fish-dam river."

When early surveyors first explored this region about 1912 looking for a route for the railroad, an incident of some sort sparked them to note the stream as "Asshole River," but for some reason the name never caught on.

Wekusco

Settlement 200 kilometers northeast of The Pas on Provincial Road 526

Established as a rail point on the Hudson Bay Railway, Wekusco took its name from Wekusco Lake, which lies approximately 20 kilometers north of the settlement. In the Cree language, the name means "sweet grass" or "herb." (see Herb Lake entry)

Wellwood

Settlement approximately 80 kilometers northwest of Portage la Prairie just off Highway 5

Established while the new Canadian Pacific Railway line was being built in 1882, Wellwood was named after James Wellwood, a minister in the area at the time who had homesteaded near Minnedosa.

Reverend Wellwood arrived in Manitoba from Ontario in 1880 and was probably the second resident Presbyterian minister in the area. Later, he also worked for the province as a school inspector.

Wellwood also sent regular records of weather conditions in Manitoba to Ottawa. He and his family initially homesteaded three kilometers southeast of Minnesoda, but when the telegraph wires preceded the railroad to the area early in 1883, a private wire was run out to the Wellwood home so his weather conditions could be reported faster.

When the railroad arrived in Minnedosa the Wellwoods moved to town and the box of recording instruments was set on the hill behind their house. After Wellwood's death, members of the family continued to provide official weather reports from the area until the middle of the twentieth century.

Westbourne

Settlement approximately 35 kilometers northwest of Portage la Prairie on Highway 16

The first post office here operated under the name White Mud River, after the nearby river. Before that the place was First Crossing, because it was at the first crossing of the White Mud on the Edmonton, or Saskatchewan, Trail.

In 1873, the name changed to Westbourne at the suggestion of the missionary Reverend Henry George, who operated a mission station here. George had once lived on Westbourne Street in London, England. In addition to being named after his former address, George allegedly made the suggestion to commemorate pioneer missionary John West, who like George came to Canada under the auspices of the Church Missionary Society.

West had been appointed chaplain to the Hudson's Bay Company in 1819 and came to the Red River settlement in 1820. Once here he turned his attention to the aboriginal community instead of devoting himself to the needs of the settlers and the fur company. He traveled widely across Rupert's Land, but was generally unpopular with both the settlers and fur traders.

One of the reasons for his unpopularity with fur traders was that he opposed marriages that were deemed "according to the custom of the country." These, of course, accounted to the majority of unions in the territory. West also refused to baptize children he considered illegitimate because of the nature of their parents' marriage. Company officials also worried the fur trade might be harmed by West's constant evangelism in the aboriginal population.

In 1823, West returned to England on what was supposed to have been a temporary leave of absence. He never returned to the North West. Later, he published a journal of his work with the fur company, but he remained in England until his death in 1845.

Posing for a photograph at the farm of Donald Stewart near Westborne in 1872. By permission of Manitoba Archives, Westborne – farms 1, N20607.

Westgate

Settlement approximately 200 kilometers south of The Pas on Highway 77

Westgate was established as the last rail point in Manitoba, just before the rail line crossed the border into Saskatchewan. As such, the stop became the "west gate" for the railroad in the province.

West Hawk Lake

Settlement approximately 135 kilometers east of Winnipeg on Highway 1

The community here is named for the nearby lake. The post office was called "Whiteshell" until 1976 when the name changed to correspond to general usage. The resort community was commonly referred to by the name of the lake, so the post office followed suit.

The name of the lake, which sounds as if it could have been long in use by fur traders and aboriginal residents, is actually relatively new. It was named after a surveyor named Hawk. Evidently Mr. Hawk already had one lake named after him in Ontario, so the Manitoba Lake with his name became West Hawk Lake. In Ontario the name of his lake was changed to East Hawk Lake.

Westray

Settlement approximately 35 kilometers south of The Pas on Highway 12

First noted on the Canadian Northern Railway line in 1911, Westray is one of a series of stops south of The Pas named for towns in the British Isles. Other similarly named rail points on the line include Freshford, Whithorn, Turnberry and Cantyre.

Wheatland

Settlement approximately 45 kilometers northwest of Brandon on Highway 25

As early as 1882 the name Wheatland was in use to refer to a spot west of the current location. When the railroad arrived in the area the community name remained alive, moving to the rail line in 1906. The name describes the bountiful wheat lands of western Manitoba.

Whitemouth

Settlement approximately 90 kilometers east of Winnipeg on Highway 44

This community on the Whitemouth River came into existence as a rail point on the Canadian Pacific Railway. A post office opened in 1880, named after the nearby river. The river's name describes the white water at its mouth a few kilometers to the north.

White Mud Falls

Settlement approximately 125 kilometers northeast of Winnipeg on Highway 11

The community here takes its name from nearby White Mud Falls, one of nine original waterfalls on the Winnipeg River between Lac du Bonnet and Pine Falls before hydro-electric dams were built. The falls here were known descriptively as *terre blanche* by early voyageurs and the current name is a translation.

Today, White Mud Falls is one of the best-known rapids on the river, partly because the power dams haven't completely obscured the spot and partly because Canadian artist Paul Kane painted a well-known image of the falls. Kane visited here in the 1840s on a journey that took him across the Canadian and American West.

Whitewater

Settlement approximately 100 kilometers southeast of Brandon off Highway 3

The Southwestern Colonization Railway established Whitewater as a rail point 1886, naming it after Whitewater Lake. The lake lies north of the settlement and the name is descriptive. Because the lake is shallow, its white-mud bottom gives the appearance of white water.

At one time a community was planned for the shores of Whitewater Lake. George Morton was the owner of a cheese factory in Kingston, Ontario, but he came to Manitoba in 1878 and explored the countryside around the lake. In the rich hay lands bordering its waters Morton saw potential for dairy farms and cheese production.

A friend of Canada's first Prime Minister, John A. Macdonald, Morton persuaded a number of wealthy friends to invest in what became the Morton Dairy Farm Company. The company then purchased a huge tract of land at a bargain price on the lake in 1881 and began bringing in farmers under the colonization regulations of that time. Officials at the Canadian Pacific Railway told Morton a rail line would be built to his new community within about a year.

Morton's cheese company brought over a thousand head of cattle to the area in 1882, but instead of wintering animals on the land the cattle were kept in corrals walled with swamp hay. Restricted in movement, hundreds of them died over the winter and the Morton Dairy Farm Company folded.

It was probably just as well since the railroad didn't arrive the next year as promised, or the year after that. The CPR didn't arrive in the area until 1886, and even then it passed south of Morton's settlement on the lake. Instead, the railroad established the new settlement of Whitewater. By that time Morton had moved on to new ventures nearby in the new rail town of Boissevain.

Whithorn
Rail point 45 kilometers southwest of The Pas on the Canadian Northern Railway

Like Westray, and other points on the railroad south of The Pas, Whithorn was named after a community in Scotland. (see entries for Westray, Turnberry and Freshford)

Whytewold
Settlement approximately 35 kilometers north of Selkirk on Provincial Road 232

Naming it after a CPR vice-president, the Canadian Pacific Railway established Whytewold Beach as a rail point in the early years of the twentieth century. The post office dropped "beach" from the name when it opened in 1904. Today, Whytewold is part of the amalgamated village of Dunnottar, along with the surrounding communities of Matlock and Ponemah.

Wilde

Rail point approximately 65 kilometers east of Thompson on the Hudson Bay line

The rail point here was named after Sergeant W. B. Wilde of the North West Mounted Police. Wilde was shot and killed by a Blood Indian named Charcoal in 1896.

The trouble started after Charcoal caught another member of the Blood band with one of his two wives. After killing the other man Charcoal fled with both of his wives, his two young sons, a grown daughter and one of his mothers-in-law. En route, he shot and wounded a North West Mounted policeman named McNeil for no apparent reason.

Charcoal and his band left no trace for some time afterwards, but then a camp was found near Chief Mountain on the Alberta and Montana border. Charcoal's daughter and mother-in-law, along with one son, were captured. Once more, however, Charcoal escaped, but this time with only one of his sons and his two wives. In the Porcupine Hills north of Pincher Creek, the wives and son ran away from the fugitive and Charcoal moved on alone.

When members of the nearby Peigan Reserve found out Charcoal was in the area they formed a posse to go after him, and sent word to Sergeant Wilde at the police detachment in Pincher Creek. Wilde caught up with the Peigan posse just as they were closing in on Charcoal.

As Wilde yelled for him to stop, Charcoal whirled and fired. The bullet knocked Wilde from his horse. Charcoal shot again, killing the Mounted Policeman where he had fallen. Then Charcoal grabbed Wilde's horse and escaped again.

The Peigans took Wilde's body to Pincher Creek. Charcoal, in the meantime, turned up back on the Blood Reserve where he was captured and held by a woman who was reported to have weighed more than 300 pounds. Charcoal was taken to Fort Macleod where he was tried and executed for the two murders.

Willbeach

Rail point approximately 180 kilometers northeast of Thompson on the Hudson Bay line

Willbeach was named in 1928 after northern pioneer William Beech, even though the spelling of the name of the man and the rail point are slightly different. Beech was a prominent promoter of northern development. He once homesteaded near the mouth of the Nelson River. He is also credited with locating and suggesting the Churchill townsite as a terminus for the railroad.

Windygates

Settlement approximately 55 kilometers south of Winkler on Highway 31 near the international border

There was once a post office at Windygates, and a rail point on a Canadian Pacific Railway spur line here. Today, the name survives as a border crossing point between Manitoba and North Dakota. The name may be descriptive of the prevalent winds at this border gate. Or perhaps there were simply a lot of farm gates blowing in the breeze when folks had to come up with a name. A school district in the Windygates area was known as Chicken Hill, so local people seem to have had a way with catchy names.

The more likely explanation for the name, however, is that the rail point and post office here were named for the village in Scotland with that name. The Scottish village is best known for its distillery, the makers of Cameron Brig Scotch whisky.

Canadian Customs check point at Windygates. PHOTO BY TED STONE.

Winkler

City approximately 120 kilometers southwest of Winnipeg on Highway 14

Valentine Winkler erected the first buildings here in 1892 and the town adopted the name Winkler the following year. Winkler was born in Ontario, but moved to Manitoba in 1879 to open a grain and lumber business in nearby Morden. He was also elected to the Manitoba Provincial Legislature the same year the community of Winkler was named after him.

Between 1915 and his death in 1920 Winkler served as the province's minister of agriculture and immigration. A plan he developed to provide one cow on credit to every Interlake settler became known as the "Winkler Cow Scheme."

Winnipeg

City on Highway 1 at the junction of the Red and Assiniboine rivers

Winnipeg grew up around the old fur trading post of Fort Garry. The Selkirk settlers began arriving here in 1812. Initially, retired fur trade employees also settled here. The first Canadian post office opened in 1870 and was called Fort Garry. In 1876, however, the post office's name changed to Winnipeg, as the new city outstripped the old fur post in importance.

Fort Garry on north side of Assiniboine River in 1873. BY PERMISSION OF MANITOBA ARCHIVES, BOUNDARY COMMISSION (1872 – 1874) 42, MAY 1873. N140117.

The new name was taken from the large lake north of the city, whose name was traditionally thought to have come from aboriginal words for "bad water." One school of thought holds that the earliest traders in the area the misapplied the name "bad water." The aboriginal name was meant for Hudson Bay. Aboriginal people of the area called Lake Winnipeg, "the big lake."

The name was applied to the settlement around Fort Garry as early as the 1860s. Several other names for the new settlement were also suggested before the Manitoba Legislature incorporated the new City of Winnipeg in 1873.

Winnipeg Beach
Town approximately 15 kilometers south of Gimli on Highway 9

The resort community of Winnipeg Beach, chosen by Canadian Pacific Railway officials, takes its name from the nearby beach on Lake Winnipeg.

Winnipegosis
Village approximately 60 kilometers north of Dauphin on Highway 20

Winnipegosis is named for the nearby lake, which apparently derives from aboriginal words meaning "little muddy water." Evidently the name refers to the murky waters of the Mossy River that empty into the lake. The name may have sometimes been misapplied to both Lake Manitoba and Lake Winnipegosis since the earliest traders coming into the area seldom knew of the narrow strip of land separating the two bodies of water.

Wivenhoe
Rail point approximately 165 kilometers northeast of Thompson on the Hudson Bay line

Wivenhoe was established as a rail point in 1928 and named after one of the two ships the Company of Adventurers sailed into Hudson Bay in 1670. The other craft, the *Prince Rupert,* arrived first and traveled to the bottom of the bay to re-establish fur trade begun on a trial voyage made by the Nonsuch in 1668.

The *Wivenhoe* struck out in the late summer of 1670 for the estuary where the Nelson and Hayes rivers empty into Hudson Bay. It reached the mouth of the Nelson on August 31, intent on turning this strategic location (with a water route extending into the heart of the continent) into a fur-trading center in North America that would rival Montreal.

But winter comes early on the bay and the *Wivenhoe* had been delayed getting to the Nelson. The men decided that, rather than build a post so late in the season, they too would continue south to spend the winter at the new post built by the crew of the *Prince Rupert*. They could have established a summer trade the following year on the Nelson or Hayes. As matters turned out, however, a summer trade was impractical and the company took another dozen years to establish a permanent post at what would become York Factory.

Wivenhoe was also a shipbuilding center in Britain where a number of early ships to explore the arctic were built.

Woodlands

Settlement approximately 25 kilometers northwest of Winnipeg on Highway 6

A post office opened at Woodlands in 1874. The name, attributed to the first postmaster, describes the area. The community of Woodlands is in the southern Interlake and the generally treed countryside here, especially to the north, contrasts sharply with the open prairie to the south.

Woodside

Settlement approximately 50 kilometers northwest of Portage la Prairie on Highway 16

The name describes trees on one side of the community or the other, and perhaps both. Noted on a Department of Interior map in 1874, the little settlement on the Whitemud River was first known as Stoney Ford. Later, it became Second Crossing, because it was the second place on the trail between Fort Garry and Edmonton that crossed the Whitemud.

York Factory

Settlement on Hudson Bay at the mouth of the Hayes River

The Hudson's Bay Company first came to the estuary at the mouths of the Nelson and Hayes rivers in 1670, but a dozen years passed before the company established anything like a permanent post in the area. For a short time after it was established in 1682 the post here was known as Hayes Fort, but it was renamed York Factory almost immediately.

The factory part of the name had nothing to do with the manufacture of goods. The word also denotes an establishment for traders carrying on business in a foreign country or a merchant company's trading station. The new fur post called York was where the chief factor lived. The site was named after James, Duke of York, later King James II. Before becoming king, the Duke of York served a short-term as perhaps the most ineffective governor in the long history of the Hudson's Bay Company.

For the three decades after 1670 every post in the general area, on several sites, would be won and lost and sometimes won again by the company in a seesaw battle with the French. The French captured York Factory and then the British recaptured it, destroying and rebuilding it over and over again. Control of the site changed hands six times as the two countries vied for power on Hudson Bay and for access to the inland fur trade it afforded.

In the 1690s the French controlled every fur post on the bay, except York Factory. Then the Hudson's Bay Company foe captured that post too. It wasn't until after the Treaty of Utrecht in 1713 that the region was finally acknowledged as British territory. And even then occasional incursions by the French continued for most of the rest of the eighteenth century.

For the most part Hudson Bay and York Factory remained English from 1713 on, and for almost two hundred fifty years the Hudson's Bay Company maintained a permanent post here. And for a good share of that time it was more than a mere fur post. It was the company's headquarters in North America. Everything the company traded was brought in through York Factory. Every fur bought by the company passed through the post before being exported to England. For a time, after the amalgamation of the Hudson's Bay Company with the North West Company almost all of the trade goods in the Canadian North and West were brought in through York Factory.

By the mid 1800s the York Factory included more than thirty buildings, plus a nearby aboriginal settlement. Not only was York Factory the starting point for trade and most of the exploration of the Canadian West, it was one of the largest trading centers in all of western North America. The chief factor's residence, in sub-arctic isolation, contained a large library and a piano.

In the last half of the nineteenth century, though, York Factory's predominance in the fur trade ended. Trade goods mostly came overland on steamboats, and then railroads. York Factory became, simply, another trading post, like all of the others. By the 1930s all traffic from Europe through the bay had stopped. Most of the company's buildings at York Factory were torn down or deteriorated in the sub-arctic environment.

In 1957 company officials closed operations and abandoned the fur post completely. Even most of the aboriginal people moved away. Much of the local Cree community moved to a spot two hundred fifty kilometers upstream on the Nelson River at Split Lake, establishing a community at York Landing that eventually became an aboriginal reserve. Others moved to Shamattawa.

Today, only the great, white depot building remains on Hudson Bay, but York Factory has been officially named a National Historic Site.

Children playing near cannons at York Factory in 1916. By permission of Manitoba Archives/ R.D. Campbell Collection 143.

York Landing

*Settlement approximately 115 kilometers northeast of Thompson on
Split Lake*

The Cree community here, known as York Factory First Nation, used
to call the shore of Hudson Bay, at York Factory, home. When the old
fur post closed, after nearly two hundred fifty years at the site in 1957,
many members of the community decided to move upstream on the
Nelson River to Split Lake, at the mouth of the Aiken River a few kilometers north of the Hudson Bay Railway tracks. The community's
name, of course, comes about because the site is where people from
York Factory landed when they came here.

Zbaraz

*Settlement approximately 75 kilometers northwest of Gimli on Provincial
Road 329*

Zbaraz was named for a village in the Ukraine when the post office
opened here in 1913. The post office closed in the 1950s, but the settlement has kept the name.

Zhoda

*Settlement approximately 30 kilometers southeast of Steinbach on
Highway 12*

Zhoda is apparently a Ukrainian word, perhaps a neologism that means
harmony or agreement. A post office opened using the name in 1911.

Names by Category

Names commemorating specific People:

Alexander
Alonsa
Amery
Angusville
Arnaud
Arnot
Ashern
Austin
Back
Baden
Bagot
Bakers Narrows
Barrows
Belcher
Belmont
Berens River
Binscarth
Birnie
Bissett
Boissevain
Boyd
Brandon
Bridgar
Budd
Button
Bylot
Decker
Isabella
Lavinia
McConnell
Moore Park
Camper
Camperville
Camp Morton
Cardale
Carman
Carrick
Carroll
Cartwright
Cayer
Chater
Churchill
Clanwilliam
Clarkleigh

Coulter
Crandall
Chesnaye
Cromer
Dand
Darlingford
Deleau
Denbeigh Point
Dering
Douglas
Drybrough
Dufrost
Dugald
Dunlop
Dunrae
Easterville
Elie
Elma
Elphinstone
Elma
Emerson
Erickson
Eriksdale
Ethelbert
Fannystelle
Faulkner
Finger
Forrest
Fortier
Franklin
Garland
Garson
Gillam
Giroux
Gladstone
Glenella
Goodlands
Grahamdale
Graysville
Greenway
Griswold
Gunton
Hadashville
Halcrow

Hallboro
Hartney
Harwill
Haskett
Hazel
Heaman
Herchmer
Hone
Hockin
Hodgson
Holland
Inglis
Jacam
Jetait
Jenpeg
Kenton
Kenville
La Broquerie
Ladywood
Langruth
La Salle
Lauder
Laurier
Letellier
Lyleton
Luke
Macdonald
MacGregor
Makaroff
Manson
Marchand
Margaret
Mather
Matheson Island
McAuley
McConnell
McCreary
McMunn
McTavish
McVeigh
Medard
Medora
Minto
Molson

Morden
Morris
Munk
Myrtle
Narcisse
Neelin
Newton
Ninette
Niverville
O'Day
Odhill
Olha
Olgilvie
Olha
Orok
Osborne
Ostenfeld
Otterburne
Paterson
Pierson
Ponton
Powell
Purves
Rackam
Randolph
Rathwell

Rawebb
Rennie
Rivers
Roland
Rossburn
Rossville
Rounthwaite
St-Georges
St. Malo
St. Pierre-Jolys
Scarth
Schanzenfeld
Sclater
Sidney
Sprague
Seddons Corner
Selkirk
Seymourville
Sherridon
Sherritt Junction
Shilo
Sidney
Sifton
Silver
Sinclair
Spearhill

Stonewall
Stuartburn
Teulon
Thibaudeau
Thompson
Tolstoi
Treherne
Tremaudan
Turnbull
Tyndall-Garson
Tyrrell
Underhill
Vassar
Wabowden
Wanless
Warren
Warren Landing
Waugh
Wellwood
West Hawk Lake
Whytewold
Wilde
Willbeach
Winkler
York Factory
Zbaraz

Names from Other Places:

Arizona
Altona
Amaranth
Arden
Balmoral
Bruxelles
Carberry
Chortitz
Clandeboye
Culross
Dalny
Deloraine
Dunnottar
East Braintree
Ebor
Eddystone
Edrans
Fairford
Foxwarren

Freshford
Glenlea
Gretna
Hecla
Headingly
Horndean
Holmfield
Katrime
Kelloe
Kleefeld
Kola
Libau
Lorette
Mafeking
Matlock
Medika
Middlebro
New Bothwell
Notre Dame de Lourdes

Oakville
Onanole
Oxford House
Petersfield
Plumas
Reykjavik
Rosenort
Ross
Rossendale
Ste. Agathe
St. Claude
St. Malo
Solsgirth
Somerset
Steinbach
Tenby
Thornhill
Toutes Aides
Tummel

Turnberry
Ukraina
Venlaw

Virden
Westbourne
Westray

Whithorn
York Landing

Descriptive Names:

Boggy Creek
Broomhill
Clearwater
Delta Beach
East Selkirk
Fishing River
Gardenton
Grand Beach
Grand Rapids
Grandview
Green Ridge
Garden Hill
Haywood
Hazelglen
Hazelridge
High Bluff
Hillside Beach
Inwood
Milner Ridge

Mountain Road
Newdale
North River
Oakbank
Oak Bluff
Oakburn
Oak Point
Oak Lake
Oakner
Oak Point
Oak River
Oakville
Oatfield
Ochre River
Overflowing River
Pelican Rapids
Plum Coulee
Piney
Poplarfield

Poplar Point
Powerview
Red Rose
Ridgeville
Riverside
Riverton
Rock Ridge
Rosebank
Roseisle
Rosetown
Sandy Hook
Shellmouth
Southport
Steep Rock
Tidal
Vista
Wheatland
Woodlands
Woodside

Names of Aboriginal Origin:

Arrow River
Athapap
Atikameg Lake
Big Black River
Birdtail
Cormorant
Cranberry Portage
Makinak
Crane River
Cross Lake
Duck Bay
Duck River
Fisher River
Herb Lake
Herb Lake Landing
Highrock
Kinosota

Manitou
Matago
Menisino
Miami
Miniota
Minnedosa
Moose Lake
Napinka
Neepawa
Ninga
North Knife River
Pawistik
Payuk
Pikwitonei
Pukatawagan
Pipestone
Pipun

Pukatawagan
Red Sucker Lake
Skownan
South Knife River
Thicket Portage
Wakopa
Wasagaming
Waskada
Waterhen
Wawanesa

Names from other languages:

Altamont
Arborg
Arnot
Beausejour
Bield
Blumenort
Brochet
Caliento
Dauphin
Erinview
Glenboro
Grande-Clairiere

Grande Pointe
Gross Isle
Grunthal
Halbstadt
Hnausa
Ile des Chenes
Komarno
Lundar
Mariapolis
Neubergthal
Neuhorst
Osterwick

Plumas
Point du Bois
Polonia
Portage La Prairie
Prawda
Rosa
Rosenfeld
Schoenwiese
Sommerfeld
Strathclair
Vita
Zhoda

Names Commemorating a Concept, Incident or Event:

Bacon Ridge
Bowsman
Dropmore
Moore Park
Elkhorn

Fraserwood
Justice
Lenswood
Moosehorn
Norway House

Starbuck
Sundown
Snowflake
Wampum

Literary, Mythological or Religious Names:

Baldur
Benito
Beulah
Brunkild
Clandeboye
Eden

Flin Flon
Gimli
Melita
Ninette
Ponemah
St. Anne

St. Rose du Lac
St. Francois Xavier
St. Pierre-Jolys
San Clara
Sylvan

Promotional, Manufactured or Hybrid Names:

Beaconia
Belair
Dominion City
Dunrae
Hamiota
Meleb
Norgate
Novra
Renwer

Shortdale
Westgate

Names from nearby Natural Features, Animals, Landmarks, Ships, Businesses or Institutions:

Arrow River
Badger
Basswood
Bellsite
Birdtail
Boggy Creek
Bowsman
Brochet
Brookdale
Mallard
Millwood
Calders Dock
Cooks Creek
Cormorant
Cottonwoods
Crane River
Cross Lake
Crystal City
Cypress River
Dauphin River
Deepdale
Deerwood
Denbeigh Point
Duck Bay
Duck River
Elm Creek
Falcon Lake
Firdale
Fisher Branch
Fishing River
Fork River
Fox Mine
Gilbert Plains
Gods Lake

Gods Lake Narrows
Gods River
Granville Lake
Great Falls
Gull Harbour
Gypsumville
Heming Lake
Herb Lake
Herb Lake Landing
Highrock
Homewood
Island Lake
Jackhead
Kettle Rapids
Lac Brochet
Lake Francis
Lakeland
Laurie River
Lena
Little Grand Rapids
Lockport
Lowe Farm
Lynn Lake
Manigotagan
McArthur Falls
Meadow Portage
Minitonas
National Mills
Nelson House
Netley
Nonsuch
Pine Falls
Pine River
Pit Siding

Rapid City
Red Deer Lake
Root Lake
Roseau River
Schist Lake
Seven Sisters Falls
Shoal Lake
Simonhouse
Sipiwesk
Snowflake
Snow Lake
Souris
South Indian Lake
Spence Lake
Sperling
Split Lake
Sprucewoods
Stony Mountain
Sundance
Swan River
Swan Lake
Tadoule Lake
Takipy
Traverse Bay
Victoria Beach
Waasagomach
Weir River
Wekusko
Whitemouth
White Mud Falls
Whitewater
Winnipeg
Winnipeg Beach
Winnipegosis

Miscellaneous Names and Names of Unknown Origin:

Birtle
Domain
Fairfax
Harding
Kelwood
Kinosota

Landmark
Princess Harbour
Regent

Bibliography

Amaranth Historical Society. *Seasons of our Lives: A History of Amaranth and District*. Ameranth: 1985.

Arborg Historical Society. *A Century Unfolds: History of Arborg and District 1889–1987*. Arborg: 1987.

Arnaud Historical Committee. *Arnaud Through the Years*. Arnaud: 1974.

Arnes History Book Committee. *The Point and Beyond: Arnes and District 1876–1900*. Arnes.

Arrow River and Miniota Women's Institute. *Bridging the Years, 1879–1967*. 1967.

Basswood and District Historical Society. *Basswood: a century of living, 1878–1978*. Basswood: 1979.

Beulah Women's Institute. *Minnewashta Memories, 1879–1970*. Beulah: 1971.

Binscarth History Committee, *Binscarth Memories*. Binscarth: 1984.

Boissivain History Committee. *Beckoning Hills Revisited: Ours is a Goodly Heritage, Morton-Boissivain, 1881–1981*. Boissivain: 1981.

Brown, O.E.A. *Settlers of the Plains*. Gilbert Plains: Maple Leaf Press, 1953.

Cardale Reunion Book Committee. *Foot Prints & Chalk Dust*. Cardale.

Chatfield Old-Timers Club. *Wilderness to Wildlife: Chatfield and District History*. Selkirk: 1981.

Collier, Anne. *Portage La Prairie 1870–1970: a history of Portage La Prairie and surrounding district*. Portage La Prairie: City of Portage La Prairie, 1970.

Collier, Anne M. *A Rearview Mirror: a history of Austin and surrounding districts*. 1967.

Committees representing J. A. Victor David Museum and New Horizons. *Reflections: Turtle Mountain Municipality and Killarney, 1882–1982*. 1982.

Domain History Book Committee. *Further Down Memory Lane*. Domain: 2001.

Domain Women's Institute. *Down Memory Lane*. Domain: 1971.

Douglas, Robert. *Place-Names of Manitoba*. Ottawa: Geographic Board of Canada, Department of Interior, 1933.

Dyck, Betty. *Hugging the Meridian: Macdonald, a Manitoba Municipal History, 1881–1981*. Sanford: Macdonald Municipality, 1981.

Edward History Book Committee. *Harvests of Time*. Pierson: 1983.

Enns, F. G. *Gretna*. Gretna: Village of Gretna History Committee, 1987.

Epp-Tiesson, Esther. *Altona: the story of a prairie town*. Altona: D.W. Frieson & Sons, 1982.

Eriksdale Municipal Heritage Advisory Committee. *Beyond Beginnings*. Eriksdale: 1996.

Fisher Branch Historical Society. *A Place of Our Own*. Fisher Branch: 1982.

Ham, Penny. *Place Names of Manitoba*. Saskatoon: Western Producer Prairie Books, 1980.

Hambley, George H. *The Golden Thread: The Last of the Pioneers, the story of the districts of Basswood and Minnedosa, 1874–1970*. 1971.

Hamiota Women's Institute. *A History of Hamiota Village and Municipality, 1879–1956*. Hamiota: 1956.

Hilbre Homecoming Committee. *Passport to the Past*. Hilbre: 1991.

Interlake Pioneers. *Hardships and Happiness*. Steep Rock: 1974.

Lac du Bonnet Pioneer Club. *Logs and Lines From the Winnipeg River: A history of the Lac du Bonnet Area*. 1980.

Lindell, Lucy. *Memory Opens the Door*. Eriksdale: 1970.

Lundar Historical Society. *Wagons To Wings*. Lundar: 1980.

Manitoba Conservation, *Geographical Names of Manitoba*. Winnipeg, 2000.

Manitoba Village History Committee. *Many Trails To Manitou-Wapah*. Alonsa: 1993.

McCreary History Book Committee, *McCreary Milestones & Memories*. McCreary: Rural Municipality of McCreary, 1987.

McPherson, Murray. *The Brandon Hills Story.* Brandon Hills Historical Committee, 1979.

Minto and District Historical Society. *Minto Memoirs: History of Minto and District.* Minto: 1979.

Minto and District Historical Society. *Minto: People of Pride.* Minto: 1998.

Morton, W.L. *Manitoba: A History.* Toronto: University of Toronto Press, 1957.

Mulligan, Helen and Wanda Ryder. *Ghost Towns of Manitoba.* Heritage House Publishing, 1985.

Mummery, Robert M. *Tanner's Crossing: The Early History of Minnedosa, the Struggle to Build a Frontier Town on the Little Saskatchewan River.* Minnedosa: Minnedosa Tribune, 1998.

Newman, Peter C. *Casears of the Wilderness.* Penguin Books Canada, Toronto, 1988.

Newman, Peter C. *Company of Adventurers.* Toronto: Penguin Books Canada, 1985.

Newman, Peter C. *Merchant Princes.* Toronto: Penguin Books Canada, 1992.

Niverville and District Historical Society. *Niverville: A History, 1878–1986.* Niverville: 1986.

Norsundal Cultural Group. *Yesterday's Dreams Today's Memories.* Dallas: 1985.

Rainbow's End: Kinosota / Alonsa 1923–1983. Alonsa: 1985.

Reekie, Isabel M. *Along the Old Melita Trail.* Saskatoon: Modern Press, 1965.

Ruidnyc'kyi, J.B., ed. *Manitoba Mosaic of Place Names.* Winnipeg: Canadian Institute of Onomastic Sciences, 1970.

Rural Municipality of Louise. *Echoes of the Past: A history of the Rural Municipality of Louise and its People.* 1968.

Rural Municipality of Mossey River. *Memoirs From the Past: Mossey River History Book Committee.* Fork River: 1999.

Russell, Francis. *Mistehay Sakahegan, The Great Lake: the beauty and treachery of Lake Winnipeg.* Winnipeg: Heartland Publications, 2000.

St. Clements Historical Committee. *East Side of the Red: the Rural Municipality of St. Clements.* East Selkirk: 1984.

Sigurgeirsson-McKillop, Ingibjorg. *Mikley, the Magnificent Island: treasure of memories, Hecla Island 1876–1976.* 1979.

Vodden, Diana and Haraldine. *In Rhythm With Our Roots: A History of Manitou and Area.* Manitou: Manitou Centennial Book Committee, 1997.

Ward, Wilda. *The Men from El Dorado: a blast from Bissett's past.* 2002.

Welsted, John, John Everitt and Christopher Stadel, eds. *Manitoba Geography: Its Land and Its People.* Winnipeg: University of Manitoba Press, 1996.

About the Author

Ted Stone, author of the highly successful *It's Hardly Worth Talking If You're Going To Tell The Truth*, has been collecting stories on the Canadian prairies for 25 years. His numerous titles include *100 Years of Cowboy Stories, A Roundup of Cowboy Humor, Alberta History Along The Highway, British Columbia History Along the Highways and Waterways* and *It's So Cold On The Prairies: Wit and Wisdom About Winter.*